Open Hand, Closed Fist

Open Hand, Closed Fist

*Practices of Undocumented Organizing
in a Hostile State*

Kathryn Abrams

UNIVERSITY OF CALIFORNIA PRESS

University of California Press
Oakland, California

© 2022 by Kathryn Abrams

Library of Congress Cataloging-in-Publication Data

Names: Abrams, Kathryn, author.
Title: Open hand, closed fist : practices of undocumented organizing
    in a hostile state / Kathryn Abrams.
Description: Oakland, California : University of California Press,
    [2022] | Includes bibliographical references and index.
Identifiers: LCCN 2022006341 (print) | LCCN 2022006342 (ebook) |
    ISBN 9780520384415 (cloth) | ISBN 9780520384422 (paperback) |
    ISBN 9780520384439 (epub)
Subjects: LCSH: Emigration and immigration—Political aspects—
    History—21st century. | Political activists—Arizona—History—
    21st century. | Immigrants—Arizona—History—21st century. |
    Emigration and immigration law—History—21st century. |
    BISAC: SOCIAL SCIENCE / Emigration & Immigration |
    POLITICAL SCIENCE / Public Policy / Immigration
Classification: LCC JV6271 .A27 2022 (print) | LCC JV6271 (ebook)
    | DDC 325/.1—dc23/eng/20220413
LC record available at https://lccn.loc.gov/2022006341
LC ebook record available at https://lccn.loc.gov/2022006342

31 30 29 28 27 26 25 24 23 22
10 9 8 7 6 5 4 3 2 1

*For my parents, who would have loved
to have seen this book*

*And for Bill, Eli, and Maya, who made it—
and so much else—possible*

Contents

Acknowledgments

Writing, like agency, is most often the product of a collective effort. It is a joy to be able to thank the members of the "collective" that motivated, challenged, and sustained me as I worked on this book.

No empirical project—particularly one that spans years and requires travel—can succeed without financial support. I was lucky to have the support of my law school and university at every stage of the process. Dean Chris Edley and Interim Dean Gillian Lester believed in the project from its inception and supported it with a generous seed grant that funded much of the initial research. I was also fortunate to receive a Bridge Grant, a program of the University Committee on Research that supports mid-career scholars undertaking a change in methodology or substantive focus. I am finally grateful to the law school's current dean, Erwin Chemerinsky, an energetic supporter of this project, who has been eager to accommodate my need for time and space to complete it.

The Princeton Law and Public Affairs (LAPA) Fellowship gave me the extraordinary gift of a year free of teaching and service obligations to mull over the first phase of my research and create an analytic structure for the book. Special thanks to LAPA Director Paul Frymer, who insisted that the year was ours to do whatever we wanted with, and that we should feel obligations only to our own projects and plans, and Associate Director Leslie Gerwin, who organized and participated in the workshops that gave rise to many of the ideas explored here. Thanks also to my "fellow fellows," Nina Dayton, Jim Fleming, Melynda Price,

David Rabban, and Sarah Schindler, who listened carefully and offered valuable insights, as I worked out my ideas on storytelling and performative citizenship. And much gratitude to the writing group whose meetings at the Small World coffee shop were a source of fascinating ideas and unconditional support: Susan Brison, Karen Jones, and Linda McClain.

This project was also strengthened by the many exchanges and conversations that I had at conferences, lectures, and workshops. Conferences at Rutgers University School of Arts and Sciences, Princeton University, University of Michigan Law School, Harvard School of Education, Queen's University Belfast Law School, and University of Copenhagen Department of Cross-Cultural and Regional Studies, as well as multiple meetings of the Law and Society Association, The Vulnerability and Human Condition Initiative at Emory Law School, and the Refugees and Immigrants Conference at Berkeley Law School, all provided generative opportunities that tested and refined my ideas. Lectures at Dickinson College, University of Technology-Sydney Law School, and Whitman College also enabled me to discuss these ideas in a more extended format. I also benefited from fruitful exchanges with law faculties at Osgoode Hall, University of Kentucky, University of Colorado, Cardozo Law School, and University of Wollongong, as well as Berkeley's Law School, Center for the Study of Law and Society, and Law, Philosophy, and Political Theory Workshop.

I am lucky to work at a law school, and at a university, that encourage intellectual collaboration of all kinds, within and particularly across disciplines. This ethos has made it easy to draw insight and support from a wide range of colleagues. My appreciation goes first to Leti Volpp and Ian Haney Lopez, who mentioned to me more than decade ago, that a statute called SB 1070 was fueling vigorous protests by immigrants in Arizona. I also owe a huge debt of gratitude to those colleagues who mentored me as I learned empirical legal methods. Kristin Luker and Cal Morrill welcomed me into their courses on qualitative empirical methods; they answered endless questions at all stages of the research. KT Albiston was a provident source of bibliographic recommendations and advice about interviewing. Leti Volpp provided generous mentoring in the area of immigration law. I was fortunate to be part of lively working groups that helped me to develop many of the ideas in this book: the Strategic Working Group on Law and Humanities at the Townsend Center for the Humanities and the Immigration, Rights, and Framing Reading Group.

Many people, both at Berkeley and beyond, offered generous and generative commentary on chapters, papers, or panel presentations based on this research and shared generative commentary. Thanks to Roxana Altholz, Abbye Atkinson, KT Albiston, Irene Bloemraad, Ming Hsu Chen, Lis Clemens, Lauren Edelman, Kevin Escudero, Martha Fineman, Catherine Fisk, Laurel Fletcher, Shannon Gleeson, Kinch Hoekstra, Desmond Jagmohan, Michael Jones-Correa, Sonia Katyal, Hila Keren, Taeku Lee, Katerina Linos, Stu Marvel, Joy Milligan, Saira Mohamed, Cal Morrill, Melissa Murray, David Oppenheimer, Andrea Peterson, Bertrall Ross, Jeff Selbin, Jonathan Simon, Sarah Song, Rachel Stern, Veronica Terriquez, Leti Volpp, Kim Voss, and Chris Zepeda-Millan. I'm grateful to Russell Robinson, Ian Haney Lopez, and Devon Carbado for conversations about how to bring myself into the narrative of the book and to claim my relation to the questions at issue, rather than simply acknowledging my experiential distance. And members of my Write on Site group—Kristin Luker and Yvette Lindgren—have offered commentary, advice, laughter, and support over years of coffee and work.

This book has also benefited greatly from the effort and insight of many students. My law school seminars on social movements and on the immigrant rights movement offered rich ground for the development of many ideas. A particularly generative venture was the undergraduate course on the immigrant rights movement that I taught through Berkeley's American Cultures Engaged Scholarship program. This program enables faculty to involve their students in community-based scholarship and service. Through this course I learned about social movement organizations by and for immigrants in the Bay Area—a valuable basis for comparison with the Arizona context—and supervised students as they participated in the work of these organizations. Victoria Robinson and Andrea Wise, who direct this innovative program, were enthusiastic and resourceful partners in this enterprise, as was Alex Mabanta, who brought great insight into community service as the graduate student instructor for the course. My research was also enriched by the efforts of a terrific group of students from Berkeley's Undergraduate Research Apprenticeship Program (URAP), who worked with me in analyzing the interviews. Thanks to Astrid Ackerman, Jesus Aguiniga, Crystina Arreola-Nuñez, Josselyn Bonilla, Jaquelyn Caro, Genesis Garcia, Rosa Hernandez, Helen Lim, David Maldonado, Edward Rivero, Maria Rohani, and Emily Van Rheenan. Thanks also to the graduate student researchers who brought energy and insight to this project: Marco Flores, Xiaoling Qin, Vasanthi Venkatesh, and Pauline White Meeusen.

And much appreciation to Kathryn Heard, then a PhD student in the Law School's Jurisprudence and Social Policy (JSP) Program (now on the faculty of Dickinson College), who brainstormed ideas on the early phases of the research and kept my Feminist Jurisprudence class on course while I flew back and forth to Phoenix. Finally, I'd like to recognize two particular students whose exceptional efforts bookended the project. Genevieve Renard Painter, then a PhD student in the JSP program (and now on the faculty at Concordia University, Montreal), made me realize, through the rigor of her own example, how much methodological preparation I needed to undertake this study, and accompanied me on my earliest trips to Phoenix and Tucson. And Kimberly Chen found me through my URAP page at the very end of the project and asked—miraculously—if she could be of help. She did everything from the "reverse image" search that helped me to identify the photographer responsible for the wonderful cover photo, to last-minute spot-research projects, to an eleventh-hour mastery of the *Chicago Manual of Style*— with energy and good spirits.

An additional team was vital in taking this project from audiofiles and notes to published book. Susan Weiss, herself a longtime activist, transcribed the vast majority of the interviews, with precision and avid interest. Ileana Salinas provided skilled interpretation for the Spanish language–based interviews, as well as occasional transcription, and vivid, illuminating perspectives on her participation in the movement. Maura Roessner at University of California Press was the acquisitions editor that authors dream of: she grasped the aspirations of the project from the first, and her unflagging belief in it was leavened with sound judgment and pragmatic advice about negotiating the processes of manuscript submission, peer review, and revision. One of her masterstrokes was to introduce me to Chris Lura, a wonderful developmental editor, who with a keen eye, a light touch, and a spirit of collaboration helped me to angle the manuscript toward a more general reader. Five peer reviewers, at two stages, improved the manuscript immeasurably with their generous, perceptive, and deeply knowledgeable suggestions. Madison Wetzell led the production troops with resourcefulness and flexibility. Jon Dertien and Sharon Langworthy at BookComp dealt patiently with last-minute changes at the copyedit stage and scores of misaligned endnotes. And Diane Ovalle, Puente activist and photographer, provided the galvanizing cover photos, which so compellingly capture the "open hand" and "closed fist" of this movement. She also reached out to secure the permissions of the four intrepid activists, whose courage in the action portrayed in her photo ignited the Undocubus campaign discussed in chapter 4.

Many friends lived—and actively engaged—with this project over the course of almost a decade. Helen Borrello, Heidi Hintz, Miranda Johnson, Nancy Kaspar, Tracy Mitrano, and Amy Utstein discussed the movement, the research, and the writing process with inexhaustible enthusiasm on walks and runs and over coffee, meals, and phone or zoom calls. Susan Zeiger and Daniel Katz-Zeiger made the trek to hear an early panel presentation. Gina Sconza was an inspired and innovative guide to the Spanish language, happy to focus our lessons on the politics and culture of Spanish-speaking countries, even if that has meant that I still struggle at times with verb conjugations. And Hila Keren, frequent coauthor and dear friend, inhabited this project with me, sharing her own theoretical perspectives on emotions, oppression, agency, and hope.

My family lived with this project on a daily basis and endured all manner of inconvenience as I flew back and forth between Berkeley and Phoenix. My children, Eli and Maya Kell-Abrams, grew from teenagers to adults as the work proceeded. I'm grateful for the forbearance they showed when I interrupted their precious moments of down time to remind them that kids their age were staging hunger strikes, getting arrested for civil disobedience, and creating a movement. And I'm grateful for the ongoing stream of questions and observations with which they greeted my progress through the project. Bill Kell supported me in every way I could imagine, and then some, throughout the long duration of this effort. He was adamant about protecting my time—and equally adamant that I needed to return to Phoenix for another round of research after Trump was elected (a position I initially viewed with exhausted disbelief from the swamp of first-round data analysis and postelection ennui). But he also had a sixth sense for when I needed a good meal, a good laugh, or a few minutes with our dogs.

My parents fostered in me the energy and commitments that have fueled my career and animated this project. My father, Gerald Abrams, made teaching, research, and the world of academics so compelling that it seemed to me the only reasonable path to follow. And my mother, Gloria Abrams, taught me my first lessons about agency and responded to any new experience or observation with a curiosity that always made me think. As lifelong Democrats, they initially wondered why I wanted to spend so much time in a "red state," but they were soon riveted by the movement I was studying. Our conversations in the last years of their lives often revolved around Phoenix, immigrant activism, and what

I was learning. It is my greatest regret of this project that I was not able to finish it while they were still alive. My sister, Nancy Deyo, has shared their enthusiasm and has been a steady source of interest and encouragement: the progress of the book is always the first thing she asks about when we talk or meet up.

And finally a huge note of appreciation to my most important mentors and teachers, the activists with whom I worked in Phoenix, who shared with me not only their stories, but their practice, as they organized, mobilized, and strategized. Where many saw constraint or hardship, they taught me to see possibility.

PART ONE

An Unlikely Movement in an Unlikely Place

Introduction

AN UNLIKELY MOVEMENT

This book explores the emergence of an unlikely social movement, in an unlikely place. In the early 2000s, Arizona became "ground zero" for "attrition through enforcement," a legislative strategy that sought to make life so miserable for undocumented immigrants that they would self-deport to their countries of origin. Through a series of ballot initiatives, referred to state voters by the Arizona legislature, the state withdrew benefits from undocumented immigrants, from bail for many crimes to in-state tuition for college-bound youth. This progression was capped in 2010 by SB 1070, a law that criminalized unauthorized presence, penalized assistance from documented residents, and empowered police to demand papers of anyone suspected of being undocumented. Officials hoped that the combined force of these measures would bring so much suffering to undocumented people that they would leave the state and the country. The threat this legislation posed to undocumented immigrants was exacerbated by Joe Arpaio, then sheriff of Maricopa County, who in 2007 had signed a 287(g) agreement to assist the federal government with immigration enforcement. The dramatic neighborhood sweeps and workplace raids he used to implement this charge made Phoenix's undocumented population, and documented Latinos drawn in through the use of racial profiling, uniquely vulnerable.

This combination of draconian laws and oppressive enforcement produced many of the effects its architects had hoped for: fear and confusion swept through undocumented communities, immigrants left the state or tried to live farther from public view. But these threats also produced something that Arpaio and state legislators did not expect: a surprising mobilization of immigrants and their allies. Mixed status communities marched through Phoenix's streets, proclaiming "no human being is illegal"; immigrant neighborhoods met Arpaio's raids with organized cop watch operations; and undocumented women of faith protested the passage of SB 1070 with a one-hundred-day vigil outside the State House, which began with prayer and finished by registering voters. Within a few short years, these efforts had produced a robust Phoenix-based movement that would become a powerful voice in national debates over immigration reform and mobilize voters across Arizona to achieve transformative state and local victories.

Despite the eventual power of this movement, its initial emergence defied expectations in many ways. Its improbable activists organized themselves with few resources and little infrastructure. Undocumented residents struggled against the stigma of illegality and criminality imposed by state campaigns, which also touched their documented Latino allies. Perhaps most notably, many participants lacked any form of legal status; they could be subject to detention and deportation if apprehended by state officials. How did this unlikely movement emerge and flourish? What kinds of practices empowered members of a group who lacked any formal relationship to state actors to become effective claims-makers in public and institutional debates? How did these practices change over time, as activists negotiated varying forms of state response? And what kinds of resources—organizational, tactical, cognitive, emotional, strategic—did they produce for the movement, which would enable it to navigate both opportunity and adversity in the future?

Open Hand, Closed Fist aims to answer these questions by analyzing the distinctive form of social movement organization that emerged in Arizona at this time: an organization that advanced the claims, centered the perspectives, and cultivated the leadership of undocumented immigrants.

AN UNLIKELY PROJECT

The trajectory that brought me to this work was in some ways unexpected as well. When I began the research for this project in 2011, I was not a scholar of immigration, nor had my previous work drawn on interviews or ethnographic observation. But my research, as a scholar of gender and sexuality, had exposed me to the literature of social movements, and the unfolding of the movement in Arizona implicated many ideas and themes I had worked with for several decades. The most evident, in the early phases of the project, was the role of emotions in public life. I had long been fascinated by the ways that emotions infused and shaped both social movements and the law. I had also been struck by the distance between this tangible interplay and dominant ideas about emotions in the popular imagination and in legal theory: their casual and often-stigmatizing association with women and other marginalized groups, their dichotomization from reason and from the domain of legal decision-making, particularly judging.

These ideas came quickly to the fore when I learned about this movement in 2011. At this time, I was completing an article that compared the role of emotions in social movement activity and in legal advocacy. Two colleagues who were familiar with my work mentioned to me that SB 1070, a new anti-immigrant law in Arizona, had sparked a series of emotionally charged encounters between activists defending and activists resisting it. My initial efforts to understand the controversy in Arizona almost immediately drew me in.

Despite my background studying emotions in social movements, what I saw when I watched the videos of protests filling the streets in Arizona surprised me. Emotions among the people demonstrating for and against the law were heightened, to be sure; but what I saw was not a reciprocal exchange of comparable emotions. Anger—often touted as the "fire in the belly" of social movements—was being expressed predominantly by defenders of SB 1070.[1] Carrying signs reading "save our state," and shouting "illegals go home," they embodied the strong and volatile emotions I had expected to see in a contentious political encounter. Something different, however, was being projected by the immigrants and allies who marched in resistance. Those resisting the law only rarely engaged with those defending it, including those shouting insults. Whatever internal response the circumstances aroused in them, (pro)immigrant marchers projected a calm that seemed only rarely tinged with indignation, and a dignity that featured prominently in their signage: "I am human," "No human being is illegal," "I am a hard worker, not a criminal." This juxtaposition evoked the encounters of the early civil rights movement, when movement leaders purposefully created a contrast between the violent antagonism of southern law enforcement and the implacable nonviolent stance of civil rights protesters.[2] I was deeply curious about the emotion work that enabled the marchers' calm, determined stance; was it instinctive?[3] Was it a more intentional effort to avoid emotions associated with racialized stigma or to project emotions associated with good citizenship? I wondered if there might be an emotional repertoire typical of movements beginning to assert themselves from positions of radical exclusion.

My interest piqued, I dug into the background of the controversy. Arizona had implemented the strategy of "attrition through enforcement" as a result of a rapid increase in unauthorized migration[4] and widespread anxiety about the demographic transition occurring in the state.[5] The strategy was the brainchild of law professor (and later Kansas secretary of state) Kris Kobach, who framed undocumented migration as placing unsupportable fiscal and public safety costs on state and local governments.[6] He proposed a set of legal impositions through which states could press undocumented immigrants to leave the jurisdiction. Beginning slowly in the early 2000s and escalating as public pressures increased, Arizona implemented many of Kobach's expedients.

The first were enacted through ballot initiatives, which were supported by large statewide majorities.[7] In 2004, Arizona passed Proposition 200, which required citizenship to vote, required ID in order to access a ballot, and made undocumented immigrants ineligible for public benefits.[8] Proposition 103, two years later, made English the official language of the state. That same year two propositions curtailed the legal rights of undocumented immigrants, denying bail to undocumented immigrants accused of serious felonies and denying undocumented immigrants legal standing to file civil actions in federal court. The most visible and controversial initiative that year was Proposition 300, which denied in-state tuition and publicly funded scholarships to undocumented students and withheld public benefits such as childcare or adult education from undocumented adults.[9] This measure hit undocumented communities with particular force, targeting youth whose upward mobility motivated their families' migration.[10]

In Phoenix and surrounding Maricopa County, these early legal developments were exacerbated by the aggressive enforcement practices of Sheriff Joe Arpaio. In 2007 Arpaio sought and secured a 287(g) agreement with the Bush administration, authorizing him to perform many of the tasks of federal immigration enforcement. He implemented this authority through two signature tactics: neighborhood "crime suppression" sweeps and workplace raids. Arpaio's operations saturated immigrant-populated areas with county officers and gun-equipped volunteers.

Through strategic use of the media, Arpaio surrounded his raids with a "circus-like" atmosphere that was humiliating as well as terrorizing for immigrants and their communities.[11]

As Arizona's prosperity began to flag dramatically with the deepening national recession, the state legislature enacted broader measures aimed at undocumented immigrants.[12] In 2008 it passed the Legal Arizona Workers Act, which required employers to verify the immigration status of all employees through a federal database and gave the state the power to penalize firms that employed unauthorized immigrants.[13] In 2010 it capped these developments with SB 1070, at that time the harshest anti-immigrant law in the country.[14]

SB 1070 comprised a range of measures, with both tangible and symbolic import, that intensified pressure on undocumented immigrants to "self-deport." The law criminalized undocumented presence in the state and the participation of undocumented immigrants in the workforce, both stark forms of internal exile. It estranged undocumented immigrants from their documented neighbors by imposing penalties for harboring, assisting, or transporting undocumented people. Most importantly, SB 1070 authorized law enforcement officials throughout the state to demand documents, in the course of any legal stop, from anyone they "reasonably suspect[ed]" of being undocumented.[15]

The legislative debates over SB 1070 revealed the emotionally inflected stigma that undocumented immigrants faced. Senator Russell Pearce, the leading sponsor of SB 1070, described immigration as a "job-taking, wage-depressing tsunami."[16] Other supporters spoke of "gut-wrenching deficits" from the "costs to the Arizona taxpayers in hospitalization, education, and incarceration."[17] Adding to the economic dispossession supporters ascribed to migration was a more immediate danger: the threat of violence. Pearce blamed undocumented communities for a disproportionate number of felonies, a pattern belied by substantial empirical evidence.[18] Moreover, he conflated immigrants crossing the border for work or family opportunity with notorious Mexican drug cartels, which were threatening the safety and destroying the property of border ranchers. The connection was fictional; as opponents argued unsuccessfully, there was no evidence that the immigrants who sought work or attended schools in Arizona played any role in the disruption of border ranches.[19] But the conflation, based primarily on their common Mexican origins, gave Arizonans a target for their accumulating anxieties: an opportunistic, marauding foe who stood against the virtues and the way of life that defined Arizona.[20]

As I contemplated this stream of legislation and its attendant fear and stigma, I began to see in the resistance of immigrants a second feature that drew me: its surprising demonstration of agency under circumstances of overwhelming constraint. As a scholar of gender and of social movements that have struggled for gender equality, I have been preoccupied with how agency emerges and functions in settings of acute structural and interpersonal constraint: how it is likely to unfold; how it may appear as it emerges; and how it may be mistaken or misunderstood when it is assessed by legal decision makers, as in prostitution or battered women's self-defense. These questions of agency under constraint seemed to me to infuse the immigrant response in Phoenix. Faced with legislative hostility, oppressive enforcement, and corrosive, stigmatizing public discourse, immigrants in Phoenix were not only asserting themselves in public actions and campaigns but striving to represent their lives as they, rather than prevalent stereotypes, conceived them.

As I sought to learn more about the sources and functioning of this agency, I became convinced that I needed to observe it firsthand. Little had been written about the features of this resistance that interested me, and they were difficult to unpack from a law school office in Berkeley, California. Consulting with my empirically trained colleagues, I outlined what I thought would be a modest qualitative empirical project: I would observe and interview immigrant activists to explore the emotions they felt and projected and the sense of agency they developed and manifested as they responded publicly to SB 1070. I scheduled my first trip to Phoenix for April 2012, to coincide with the US Supreme Court argument in *United States v. Arizona*, the Obama administration's challenge to SB 1070.[21]

MEETING PEOPLE, LEARNING ABOUT A MOVEMENT

I landed in Phoenix as lawyers from the Justice Department were challenging SB 1070 at the Supreme Court. Traversing the short distance from the airport to the city, I was buoyed by anticipation: I was eager to witness what was happening among activists and community organizers. My first stop was Carl Hayden High School: the site of a community meeting cosponsored by two local immigrant rights organizations, Puente and Somos America, and the Arizona chapter of the American Civil Liberties Union (ACLU).

Walking from the parking lot toward the school, I met Gabriel, a local real estate agent who was active with Somos America. He had become involved with the movement when he noticed that, after the first anti-immigrant propositions began to pass, mixed status families were selling their homes and moving elsewhere. When he looked into the larger demographic trends, he discovered that at the rate people were leaving, it would take three to four years to fill the homes these families were selling. He created a PowerPoint presentation for other realtors—a pretty varied group politically, he said—and he got a lot of pushback. But he didn't care, because he believed what he was saying: this legislation was bad for Phoenix, and it was wrong. When other realtors said to him, "but they're *illegal*," Gabriel replied: "It was illegal for me to drink out of the same fountain as you when I was a kid, but sensible people thought about it, and they changed the law."[22] He clearly hoped that "sensible people" would reconsider SB 1070 as well. As we approached the school auditorium, he shared a bit about the organizations hosting the meeting. Puente, he said, had "deep roots in the Mexican community," while Somos was larger, and coordinated between immigrants and a range of other groups: churches, businesses, and advocacy groups.[23]

The meeting aimed to inform the immigrant community about the legal challenge to SB 1070. As it began, Daniel Rodriguez, the youthful president of Somos, described the key arguments the lawyers had put forward in Washington that day. Although he expressed hope that the case would be decided against the law, he also recognized that opponents of the law might not prevail. He discussed, along with his fellow organizer Carlos Garcia, the director of Puente, what various outcomes of the case might mean for enforcement patterns, for defensive strategies that undocumented immigrants would need to adopt, and for the overall vulnerability of undocumented residents to detention and deportation. The organizers also announced a series of meetings in the coming weeks that would teach immigrant communities about how best to protect themselves once the Supreme Court's decision had been made. Then, at the end of the meeting, they opened the floor to questions from the audience.

Despite being scheduled on a weekday evening, after what was for many a long day of work, the meeting was well attended. As I listened to the questions posed by the community members, I was struck not only by the large number of questions but also by their specificity. I observed the care and patience with which Garcia—an understated man in his thirties, wearing a T-shirt and long hair pulled back in a ponytail—fielded the practical or logistical aspects of audience questions, while also attending to the fear or confusion being expressed. I also noted Rodriguez and Garcia's rapport with Allesandra Meetze, the executive director of the ACLU. Despite the newness of the gathering for me, this kind of exchange appeared to be a familiar experience for many of those present.

The next day, I attended a rally at Phoenix's downtown Civic Space Park. The diversity and the level of engagement among the people gathered there was even more striking than at the meeting the night before. Surveying the large crowds of protestors, I marveled at the wide array of organizations participating. Each organization's members wore the same T-shirt, turning the milling crowd into a rainbow of color. T-shirts have often been a vehicle for expressing political symbolism in immigrant protests. In the "big marches" of 2006, when millions of people took to the streets against the US House of Representatives' anti-immigrant Sensenbrenner Act, the sea of white T-shirts against red, white, and blue flags became a lasting image in the cultural imagination. However, in Phoenix that day, these variably colored T-shirts bore the names and sometimes the distinctive messages of specific organizations. There were T-shirts identifying Movimiento Estudiantil Chicano de Aztlán (MEChA), a Chicano student organization with branches at many universities; Promise Arizona (PAZ), a youth empowerment organization; Mi Familia Vota and Living United for Change in Arizona (LUCHA), Latino voter engagement organizations; and many others. A group of white people wearing mustard-colored T-shirts with the caption "Standing on the Side of Love" were Unitarian Universalists, allies in the struggle against SB 1070. There was also a small cluster of people wearing the Red Cross of the Phoenix Urban Health Collective—politically aligned with the protesters, they helped support the movement by serving as medics at its events. These groups, moreover, were acquainted with each other; as I finished speaking with activists in one cluster, they cheerfully directed me to another that they believed would be helpful. Though the marches of 2006 had been mobilized through informal networks and Spanish-language media, this rally reflected a different level of organization, a creation and proliferation of social movement organizations specifically dedicated to the defense of immigrant communities or the vindication of immigrant rights.[24]

As I watched a well-planned array of protest tactics unfold that afternoon, I became increasingly interested in these organizations' role in the broader movement. The speeches combined powerful personal stories by immigrant activists with supportive exhortations by allies. There was also a brief drama featuring elaborately painted masks held on long poles that invited attendees to chase Arpaio and Governor Jan Brewer (the masked figures) from power. The march that then departed from Civic Park took participants past a series of emblematic locations, including Arpaio's 4th Ave jail and the local Immigration and Customs Enforcement (ICE) building. It ended in a carefully choreographed incident of civil disobedience in which several youths sat down in the middle of Central Avenue, a main thoroughfare bisected by the city's light rail line. As police directed traffic around them, a host of marchers held up cell phones to capture the action and record any possible transgressions. A police wagon arrived, and a line of police in riot gear stepped slowly toward the protesters, issuing warnings. When the protesters failed to move, the police pulled them to their feet and led them to the waiting vehicle.

The day's events persuaded me that not only undocumented activists, but their organizations, should be the focus of my inquiry. I suspected that the unlikely agency of immigrant protest had been supported and shaped, at least in part, by these organizations. Their role touched an additional question about agency that had long interested me. Scholars and other commentators often describe the "structures" against which agency is asserted as institutional or otherwise systemic, while depicting agency itself as a matter of individual self-assertion.[25] For example, from this perspective, a scholar might seek to understand how a woman (an individual) negotiated an oppressive workplace (an institution). A similar approach might look at how one partner (individual) had navigated a violent relationship enabled by policing practices (systemic) that privatized partner abuse. My growing interest in social movements, however, arose from a different intuition: that collectivity might shape and support agency in the individual, and that agency could also be experienced and exercised collectively. This dynamic would seem to be present in a range of "outsider" or "challenger" social movements, which use collectivity to empower those who feel deprived of agency in their individual lives. But group-based agency would seem to be particularly important for a movement like Arizona's, which uses collectivity to empower economically disadvantaged immigrants, many of whom lack the presumptive qualification for political engagement: citizenship or legal status. It is true that some people who have become active in the Phoenix movement manifested agency as individuals. For example, Abril Gallardo, an organizer at LUCHA, contested the seizure and impoundment of her vehicle in court, literally challenging the police officer who stopped her, before she had joined any organization.[26] Other activists were empowered by the stories of, or the examples set by, tenacious and resourceful parents.[27]

But the movement in Phoenix was fostering self-direction, tenacity, and resistance not just in occasional, well-equipped individuals, but in a heterogeneous group whose sense of power and possibility were shaped by their lack of legal status—and also torqued by a state-imposed system of surveillance and arrest. Observing and interviewing immigrant activists within these organizations offered a chance to understand how such groups fueled this kind of agency.

PHOENIX ORGANIZATIONS: EMPOWERING INDIVIDUALS THROUGH COLLECTIVE AGENCY

In the research for this book, I focused on a group of Phoenix organizations[28] that explicitly centered the perspectives and cultivated the leadership of undocumented immigrants.[29] The goal was to learn about how each one, in partnership with other organizations or among its own members, was shaping collective agency among so many vulnerable people. I attended meetings, trainings, and actions planned by these organizations; I also interviewed their organizers and activists, in most cases in English, but for some adult activists in Spanish with simultaneous interpretation.[30] From 2012 to 2016, while conducting the main phase of the research, I focused specifically on three organizations: the Arizona DREAM Act Coalition (ADAC), Puente (or Puente Movement or Puente-Arizona), and LUCHA. I had identified these organizations through their support for the voices and leadership of undocumented residents and through their influential work during the major campaigns of 2012, including organizing to implement Deferred Action for Childhood Arrivals (DACA), encouraging voter engagement, and preparing the community for the pending enforcement of the "show me your papers" provision of SB 1070. From the early years of resistance to "attrition through enforcement" in the late 2000s, through the struggle for legislative change and the push for executive relief from deportation in the final years of the Obama administration, each of these organizations had an important impact.

Though all of these groups fostered the agency of undocumented immigrants, each had a distinct focus and membership. ADAC was founded by a group of undocumented scholarship students who sought to fund their education in the wake of the state's Prop 300. When I first arrived in Phoenix, ADAC had more than half a dozen local chapters, which included a parents' group, a group of "undocuqueer" activists, and a group for local high school students. It was ubiquitous in youth-led protests in the Phoenix area, and its leaders were bold and visible figures in national DREAMer politics. ADAC was loosely affiliated with the national DREAMer organization, United We Dream, which hosted ADAC members at its national convenings and offered training and funding opportunities. Although ADAC counted among its members some citizen children of immigrants and other youth allies, it was first and foremost an organization of, and for, undocumented youth.

Puente and its longtime director, Carlos Garcia, were leaders in the fight against SB 1070 and the oppressive enforcement of Sheriff Joe Arpaio. Garcia—who had grown up undocumented in Arizona before naturalizing during his teenage years—was also a skilled tactician; he deftly navigated "immigration federalism," courting the intervention of a federal government he did not trust, to curb the excesses of a state government that posed a more immediate threat. Although Puente had youth members (whose numbers grew over the course of the research), its identity as a "community-based" organization meant that it was oriented primarily to adults and families. Its ethos was not professionalizing; rather, it was committed, as Garcia put it, to "meet[ing] participants where they're at."[31] Employing an organizing strategy it referred to as "open hand, closed fist," Puente invited undocumented residents to enjoy the solidaristic support of their community as they learned practices of outward-facing resistance and community-based self-defense.

Among the three organizations that served as primary sites of my research, LUCHA was the least established when my research began. An organization that sought power for immigrants and other working families through voter engagement, LUCHA had a skeletal staff and a small cluster of participants when I first began interviewing in 2012. But its organizers, who were keenly reflective on the challenges and opportunities of organizing immigrants, and its energetic contribution to the voter engagement efforts surrounding the Adios Arpaio campaign in summer 2012, drew my interest. Its growth and diversification over the next half decade, into a powerful force for registering voters and empowering both immigrants and low-income workers more broadly, can be viewed as one of the success stories of the Phoenix movement. Unlike many Phoenix organizations, LUCHA had a membership model in which members paid modest dues. And while it centered the perspectives and cultivated the leadership of its undocumented members, LUCHA also observed less of a demarcation between its undocumented members and its documented members who had come to LUCHA, for example, to prepare for their citizenship exams.

In addition to the these three organizations, I also observed and interviewed participants in two other organizations. The first was Promise Arizona, which coalesced in late 2010 after a group of undocumented women of faith organized a galvanizing one-hundred-day vigil at the state capitol that lasted from the passage of SB 1070 in April until the district court handed down an injunction against it in late July. Although PAZ remained identified with its strong contingent of "vigil ladies," who attended rallies and marches with a portable shrine to the Virgin of Guadalupe and took part in voter engagement, PAZ was primarily a youth empowerment organization. It taught basic political education, sponsored trips to the state capitol and to Washington, DC, and trained young people to register voters. PAZ was a cosponsor (with the political arm of the hospitality union Unite Here) of the exuberant and momentous Adios Arpaio voter engagement campaign, described in chapter 3.[32]

During the later stages of my research, I also became interested in Aliento, a relative newcomer among Phoenix organizations supporting undocumented people. Aliento was founded in 2016 by Reyna Montoya, an activist I had come to know at ADAC, where she was one of the organization's leaders. Aliento embraced a goal that was new to undocumented organizing: addressing the trauma produced by detention, deportation, and their ongoing threat, through participation in the visual and performing arts. Although the arts had played an intermittent role in undocumented organizing, utilizing the arts to address trauma in undocumented communities was new. Aliento's trauma-informed focus challenged norms in Latino and immigrant communities that tended to prioritize survival and functioning over a focus on mental health. This focus led organizers to raise challenging questions about organizing practices of the movement as well.[33]

During my time observing these organizations in Phoenix, I tried to learn as much as I could about their practices, their structures, and their aspirations.[34] I attended organizational meetings and trainings; I watched and sometimes participated in marches, rallies, and vigils; and I observed encampments, direct action protests, and numerous incidents of civil disobedience. At LUCHA, I also attended and participated in the training of canvassers, drove or accompanied canvassers, and helped in the delivery of ballots (during the period in which that was permitted by Arizona law).[35] At Puente, I also attended two conferences hosted by the organization, including a nationwide convening that helped to inaugurate the Not1More Deportation campaign.[36]

In addition, I completed close to one hundred semistructured, recorded interviews, primarily with activists from these organizations. I interviewed approximately ten individuals multiple times over the course of the primary research, and four individuals became primary informants for the final stage of the research, which took place during the first years of the Trump administration. Additional details, particularly for the period 2008–12, were gleaned from a database of media and social media sources.

As a white, Anglo, citizen by birth, who was old enough to be the parent of many of the youth activists and older than many of the adult participants, I was clearly an outsider to the organizations and communities I observed. I was also a resident of California—which some activists laughingly called the "anti-Arizona"—an immigrant-friendly environment whose laws were viewed by Phoenix activists as almost incomprehensibly solicitous of the security and well-being of undocumented communities.[37] And I had very modest Spanish proficiency (acquired entirely over the course of the research), a skill that was not generally expected of Anglo allies in the movement but that could ease relationships and signal respect for immigrant communities where it had been acquired. This experiential distance shaped whether and how quickly organizations felt that they could trust me and what activists felt comfortable saying to me, particularly in the early phases of the research. (This issue is explored at greater length in the appendix.)

Sometimes organizers vouched for me and introduced me to activists within the organizations. This was particularly true at LUCHA. More often, however, I relied on a strategy of building familiarity that could lead to trust over time. After SB 1070 passed in 2010, Arizona was the focus of heightened attention by journalists and academics from outside the state, who were interested in studying the resistance and the emerging movement. As organizers reported it, these interviewers tended to come and go quickly; one organizer refused to introduce me to participants she worked with, explaining that they had been exhausted, perhaps exploited, by researchers from distant locations who gathered their information and disappeared after an initial visit or two. My thought was that if I continued to show up regularly over time and signal through my consistent presence my deep interest in the work of their organizations, it might be easier for participants to feel comfortable speaking with me. There was also a group of activists whom I interviewed multiple (sometimes six to eight) times over the course of the research, in hopes of creating greater familiarity, ease, and candor. Although these strategies extended the period of the research, they seemed to bear fruit in the sense that interviewees, over time, seemed to reflect more openly about their experiences or to share more revealing stories. Moreover, those whom I interviewed repeatedly began to share concerns about, or even critiques of, movement activity that they had not voiced in the early stages of the research. I also adopted the strategy of embracing my difference by asking activists to explain to me assumptions or features of their activity that I might have understood more intuitively had I been more experientially proximate but found valuable to hear expressed in their own words.

I was often touched, as I returned to Phoenix over several years, by the generosity with which participants uncovered identities and experiences through which they could relate to me, even if momentarily. College-going youth, or those interested in law or graduate school, sometimes approached me as an academic mentor, confiding difficulties they faced with their coursework or asking about the college or law school admissions process. The mothers at ADAC, who became a strong contingent during the years I observed the organization, sometimes approached me as a mom, questioning me in a mix of Spanish and English about my children or inviting me to sit with them during general meetings. Even my halting Spanish could occasionally be a source of connection: after I stumbled through a comment at one Puente meeting, a middle-aged man smiled in genuine empathy and shared with me the struggles he was encountering in learning English. Some activists valued the opportunity an interview provided to reflect on work that left them too little time for introspection. In this respect, the fact that I was familiar with the movement, yet was not immersed in their experience, could be a benefit. One LUCHA organizer, whom I had interviewed several times, remarked that she found our conversations a little "like therapy: talking to somebody from the outside, but who understands."[38] There is no doubt, however, that I remained an outsider to the communities about which I was learning, and that this experiential difference shaped both my perceptions of what I was observing and my interactions with those with whom I spoke.

THREE PRACTICES, THEIR TRAJECTORY, AND THEIR EFFECTS

Each of the organizations I observed during my work in Phoenix utilized three distinct practices that fostered the self-confidence and self-assertion of participants and enabled those participants to navigate the obstacles that undocumented activists face in mobilization. These practices—which I refer to as *experiential storytelling, emotion cultures,* and *performative citizenship* and which I outline later—addressed participants' internalized doubts about their capacity or entitlement to undertake collective resistance. They also spoke to external—that is, state or public—skepticism about the legitimacy of undocumented political voice. Finally, they helped participants remain in the political field even as they faced the distinctive pressures that state actors could apply to a movement of undocumented activists. These practices, as I demonstrate throughout this book, played an important role in the way the organizations' goals, strategies, and tactics were implemented over time.

The first of these practices, experiential storytelling, was employed by all organizations, often during meetings, to counter the stigma of "illegality" by offering new images of resourcefulness and accomplishment that redefined the undocumented experience. Storytelling also introduced activists to a vehicle through which each could contribute to the emerging movement. Experiential storytelling was tightly connected to another practice, *the creation of emotion cultures.* Emotion cultures, which were sometimes implicit yet shared understandings about the feelings that should accompany participation and how best to communicate them in outward-facing actions, were integral to building solidarity and agency among activists. The sense that each activist was part of a larger community that "had their back"—whatever the circumstances they would encounter—was vital, in that it eased fear, fostered feelings of capability, and enabled activists to withstand lengthy and emotionally demanding campaigns. But if storytelling and emotion cultures instilled confidence in new activists and allowed them to turn outward and present their message in the field, the movement's legitimating function was achieved largely through tactics of performative citizenship, a third practice that was central to activists' experiences and to the organizations' larger strategies. Through tactics of performative citizenship, undocumented activists took on visible, familiar political roles that were not strictly prohibited for, but had not previously been performed by, undocumented people. Tactics of performative citizenship, which included such roles as registering voters or offering testimony before legislative bodies, used familiar political practices and shared cultural understandings to convey—both to the public and to activists themselves—that participants contributed and belonged.

In addition to outlining some of the key methods that the organizations used to help foster collective agency in the face of state hostility, this book also looks closely at the ways that organizations in Phoenix engaged with the relevant institutional actors at the federal, state, and local levels. This engagement changed over the years depending on numerous factors, including who was in the White House. Looking at how these forms of engagement evolved brings into view two additional key insights into the ways that social movements of undocumented activists develop.

The first insight concerns how these practices facilitate political change over time. As the organizations in the Phoenix movement, and the national movement more broadly, swung between hope and disappointment during the Obama administration—glimpsing the promise, the deferral, and ultimately the failure of institutional recognition for undocumented immigrants—organizations began to utilize these practices in new ways, communicating growing anger and impatience and describing the state in more critical and adversarial ways. When youth organizations like ADAC first took shape in their struggle against Prop 300 and in support of DACA, activists used more optimistic, hopeful stories in their campaigns. Even adult activists protesting SB 1070 were publicly more resolute and dignified than angry or outraged. But as they confronted successive defeats over the course of the Obama administration, and ongoing workplace raids by Joe Arpaio closer to home, undocumented activists told new and more critical stories about their lives and their relation to the state. They expressed frustration, defiance, and finally outrage. Their performance of de facto citizenship shifted from cheerful participation in institutional settings to adamant protest far from the halls of governmental power, protest that evoked the contentious membership of transformational social movements. It became clear to me that storytelling, emotion cultures, and performative citizenship were not "one and done" vehicles for getting undocumented participants into the field or legitimating them before a skeptical public. They were instruments for negotiating a changing political context. Recognizing this role raised a series of other important questions. What factors tended to initiate or enable changes in these practices? Did critical stories, defiant emotions, and oppositional forms of performative citizenship assist the movement or enhance the agency of participants? Did they enlist or disenchant the movement's audiences? How did more oppositional tactics at the federal level coexist with the more collaborative, institutionally focused practices that were gaining strength at the state and local levels? The answers to these questions are complex, and some are framed by the campaigns I observed, but what this book aims to make clear is that the emotion cultures and practices of performativity within organizations evolved in ways that sought both to respond to and to shape the political landscape activists encountered in their campaigns.

A second insight concerns the longer-term effects of these practices on participants themselves. Based on the campaigns I observed, there seems little doubt that the movement's performative strategies—the public manifestation of an emotion or role that is aimed at bringing that which is manifested into being, both internally and externally—often shaped the political consciousness of participants. Yet how and when such stances became internally resonant—as well as externally persuasive—was a difficult question that arose in many ways in my work with Phoenix organizations. Does the internalization of the belonging manifested by performative citizenship, or the courage expressed in the declaration that one is "undocumented and unafraid," occur directly or over time? Does it depend on the particular tactics that organizations utilize? On the predilections or self-understanding of the person performing the emotion or role? Does it require a level of receptivity, by state actors or their constituents, to the roles or feelings being manifested? These questions were framed—forcefully if unexpectedly—by the election of Donald Trump, and I was fascinated to see a complex set of answers emerge. Some forms of performativity did seem to be internalized; the proud and confident identification activists experienced with the political system as they registered voters and canvassed for ballot issues was a good example. But some forms of emotional performativity—the repeated, vulnerable self-revelation required by some forms of storytelling, or the ongoing public manifestation of strength and persistence in the face of fear and fatigue—began to be questioned by organizers, who wondered if they might create a more sustainable movement if they tried to better understand, rather than to guide or steer, the emotion states of activists. Performativity is an innovative and provident strategy of this movement, particularly appropriate to participants who may enter activism uncertain about their own authority as agents of change. But whether and how it produces its effects varies with the particular strategy in question, its political context, and the individuals who enact it.

STRUCTURE OF ANALYSIS AND CHAPTER OUTLINE

This book presents the larger story of this vital immigrant rights movement in Phoenix and explains how key organizational practices both enabled undocumented activism and shaped opportunities and constraints for the movement, over a period of approximately ten years. It is told chronologically, from the early years of Arizona's policy of "attrition through enforcement," in the mid-2000s through the first years following Trump's election in 2016. The chapters weave together a narration of pivotal campaigns and other initiatives by organizations and activists, with a cross-chapter examination of the key organizing practices that played a central role in shaping individual political consciousness and the movement's larger trajectory.

Chapter 1 describes the consciousness of individuals produced by "attrition through enforcement." It explains how the threat produced by that policy sparked the resistance of preorganizational, pro-immigrant groups. The practices, networks, and alliances forged by this resistance enabled the emergence of dedicated organizations, which advanced the interests and cultivated the voice of undocumented people.

Chapters 2 and 3 look directly at these emerging organizations, examining the ways in which they empower undocumented participants and prepare them for outward-facing political action. In these chapters, I introduce and explain the role of the three central organizing practices. Storytelling and emotion cultures, which prepare participants unaccustomed to visibility for their public roles as activists, are examined as they function within organizations. Performative citizenship, which functions in the political field, allows activists to learn civic responsibility and shape public awareness by occupying roles associated with formal citizenship. It is described and exemplified by the Adios Arpaio campaign: a countywide voter engagement effort that aimed to unseat Sheriff Joe Arpaio.

Chapters 4 and 5 examine the evolution of undocumented activism, as participants confronted a lack of systematic legal change, coupled with state and federal immigration enforcement that continued to target and terrorize their communities. These chapters highlight the gradual shift of undocumented organizations—in Phoenix and nationally—toward a more oppositional stance, as they engaged the ambivalent and dysfunctional response of the Obama administration. This interaction is drawn out through the analysis of three campaigns: the long youth campaign that ultimately produced DACA; the voyage of the Undocubus, which took a mixed-age group of activists from Phoenix to the Democratic National Convention in North Carolina, organizing against state complicity in immigration enforcement and challenging the Democratic presidential nominee; and the Not1More Deportation campaign, through which youth and adult activists used disruptive direct action to expose the apparatus of immigration enforcement and press President Barack Obama for a comprehensive program of deferred action. These campaigns illustrate the changes in strategy and tactics of organizations and in the narratives, emotion management, and performative citizenship that structured organizational action during this period. These chapters also reflect briefly on the efficacy of these changes, for target audiences and for participants.

Chapter 6 offers a longer-range view of how ongoing social movement activity, at both state and federal levels, shaped the political consciousness of activists. Set temporally in the first weeks of the Trump administration, this chapter looks at how the consciousness activists brought to that moment was constituted by past practices and campaigns and how it generated affective and tactical resources—including a strong sense of de facto belonging and confidence in a growing skill set—that could be mobilized to respond to the new administration.

Chapter 7, the final chapter, returns to address key issues at the organizational level. It examines the ways that three organizations, buoyed by the consciousness I describe in chapter 6, managed the challenges of the early Trump period, through an adaptation of longer-term strategies and a reassessment of organizing practices. In conclusion, it discusses the implications of these developments for understanding immigrant and other "challenger" social movements.

This book engages many questions in the literatures of immigrant activism and social movements. Its account of the movement's emergence refines our understanding of the conditions and instrumentalities that enable immigrants to mobilize and build movement infrastructure in response to a specific threat.[39] Its elaboration of the practices through which organizations empower undocumented immigrants as activists sheds light on how movements organize those without status or others whose precarity or marginality impede voice or sustained activism.[40] The book's exploration of the campaigns of the Obama years not only offers a case study in the emergence of "oppositional consciousness."[41] It also shows how the organizing practices of the movement enabled adaptability in response to failures of governmental response. Finally, the investigation of the movement in the early Trump years allows for a retrospective assessment of the performative strategies of the movement: whether and how it was possible to build a sense of de facto political membership where it did not formally exist.[42] The pragmatic self-scrutiny that emerged in this period also raises the question of whether even the most enabling and adaptive practices ultimately outlive their usefulness, and how they come to be supplemented or replaced with new practices, as a movement builds for a longer-term future.[43] But beyond any of these contributions, the book tells a story of how an array of organizational practices—adapted over time and through struggle—fostered collective agency among undocumented participants, when state action had systematically disenabled it.

This agency has not, in any straightforward sense, enabled triumph. Though undocumented communities may be better organized and equipped, the challenges flowing from their status remain unresolved. The overt antagonism of the Trump administration has given way to a resumption of Obama-era inconsistency under President Joe Biden. Moreover, a story line that traces the work of a group of distinctively empowered immigrants risks obscuring the fact that many in these communities continue to experience corrosive fear and constraint or manifest a self-assertion that is riveted on the practical details of survival, rather than mobilized to create new political vistas. Yet that agency has created voice and representation for undocumented communities in Phoenix and fed a national movement that continues to press for change. How it has been cultivated, and the directions it has taken, provide lessons from which scholars and activists may learn.

CHAPTER I

Confronting "Attrition through Enforcement"

Entering Civic Space Park for a rally against SB 1070 in April 2012, I was surprised by what I saw. I had anticipated a smaller-scale version of the 2006 Big Marches, a loosely organized stream of protestors buoyantly opposing a legal assault on immigrants, manifesting visibility and voice more than strategy and tactics. What I witnessed was something different: a host of organizations whose slogans, signage, and matching T-shirts showed planning, organization, and differentiation in personnel and purpose. There were youth organizations, college groups, and organizations focused on communities or families; there were groups whose names or signage proclaimed a legislative goal, others oriented toward the engagement of voters, some that organized immigrants, and others that mobilized allies. As their program began, I saw thoughtfully crafted genres of speech, an example of political theater, a march that marked the local sites of immigrant struggle, and an incident of civil disobedience so carefully planned that the greatest challenge seemed to be the effort of police to make their way through a maze of vigilantly raised cell phones to lead the protesters to the waiting wagon.

As this event vividly demonstrated, a robust movement was emerging in Phoenix.[1] But neither its formation nor its ability to sustain itself was a foregone conclusion. The protesters I encountered that spring confronted a political landscape of unremitting hostility, encompassing elements of immiserating policy, repressive enforcement, and pervasive, stigmatizing discourse. Moreover, as a movement of youth and lower-wage workers, they could marshal only modest material resources and could rely on little or no dedicated social movement infrastructure. Yet as this chapter explains, the state hostility sparked more than one response among immigrants, and the resources that could be mobilized by activists were more plural than at first appeared. Early organizing, fueled by the threat of "attrition through enforcement," built networks, introduced practices, and gave rise to new organizations that centered the perspectives and fostered leadership of undocumented activists.

Most social movements begin with a grievance, a perceived wrong or injustice for which the state or public may be responsible. But grievances alone are not sufficient to propel those affected toward collective action. The many steps between grievance and sustained mobilization may be thwarted by external reception, internal ambivalence, or failures of communication, organization, or outreach. Scholars who study the emergence of social movements have offered many theories aimed at identifying those factors that enable participants to transform grievance into concerted action. Although theorists vary in their focus, many theories revolve around three kinds of factors that enable social movement emergence: the openness of the political system to prospective participants' claims, the resources participants can marshal to facilitate their collective action, and the elements of political consciousness or identity that can shape their willingness to assert themselves as change agents or affect their efficacy in that role.[2]

This chapter looks at the challenges these factors created for the immigrants and allies who mobilized in response to "attrition through enforcement." It shows how they met these challenges, enabling a loose alliance of individuals and participants, engaging in discrete tactics and campaigns, to coalesce into a sustainable social movement. The chapter first discusses how the political threat against undocumented and documented residents fueled the movement's mobilization, even in the face of limited political opportunity. It then describes how the movement made use of community-based networks and leadership, as well as self-produced tactical, emotional, and other resources that were vital to its emergence. Finally, the chapter discusses the challenges that organizations confronted as they encouraged a movement of undocumented participants to see themselves as legitimate, effective agents of change, despite their lack of legal status. (How the movement addressed these challenges is explored more fully in chapter 2.) This chapter explains how early responses to state hostility empowered a nascent movement for immigrant rights in Phoenix and allowed it to seize the attention of local and national publics.

WHEN POLITICAL THREAT MATTERS MORE
THAN POLITICAL OPPORTUNITY

SB 1070 passed in 2010 with a solid majority in the state legislature and high approval among members of the Arizona public.[3] The earlier ballot issues that had deprived undocumented immigrants of state rights—from bail to in-state tuition—had also passed with substantial majorities. Few state officials had moved to criticize, let alone constrain, the anti-immigrant raids or criminalizing rhetoric of Sheriff Joe Arpaio. Moreover, there was very little prospect for near-term change, as Arizona was at that time a reliably Republican state. Consequently, those most affected by "attrition through enforcement" faced a hostile political landscape, wholly lacking in the "political opportunity," or receptivity within governmental structures, that often catalyzes social movements. But state hostility did more than foreclose political opportunity: it also posed a broad-based, immediate threat to both documented and undocumented people. This threat was so galvanizing to so many that early coalitions that would form the basis of a social movement began to mobilize despite the complete absence of a political opening.

Among scholars, there has long been a debate about what constitutes political opportunity and how vital it is for the emergence of social movements, like the one in Arizona. Early proponents of "political opportunity" theories, from Charles Tilly to Doug McAdam and David Meyer, have argued that the emergence of social movements is shaped by the institutional features of political systems, and by the policy receptivity and alliances of decision makers.[4] More recent accounts have added to enduring features of political structure, such as (de)centralization of institutional centers of power or the stability of governing coalitions, a focus on features more likely to vary, such as shifting policy preferences, changes in party strength or alignment, and external factors such as wars or economic crises.[5] Where these elements reflect openness or receptivity to the claims advanced by an aggrieved group, such political opportunity may encourage group members to mobilize and to demand action by the state. Yet institutional dynamics may also shape incipient social movements in a very different way: concerted state hostility may ignite collective action by dramatically increasing the costs of passivity.

Social movement theorists have long recognized a possible role for threat in fueling social movement emergence.[6] But contemporary scholars, highlighting how excluded groups help drive social change from below, have made fresh calls for a closer analysis of the role of threat in mobilization.[7] Paul Almeida, for example, has argued that threat may be at least as powerful a factor as positive political opportunity, and that four categories of threat—deprivation of suffrage, election fraud, policy threats, and state repression—have been particularly powerful influences on the emergence of social movements.[8] Moreover, combinations of threat and opportunity, Almeida suggests, may provide a distinctively potent impetus to collective action. Scholars such as Chris Zepeda-Millan have applied these insights to the study of immigrant social movements. During the Big Marches of 2006, Zepeda-Millan has argued, immigrants responded to a threat posed by the Sensenbrenner bill, which stimulated both individual and collective elements of their identities.[9]

In Arizona the extent of mobilization and resistance to "attrition through enforcement" was in one sense surprising. There was no political institution—save perhaps the belated, qualified response of the US Department of Justice (DOJ) or the federal courts—that was receptive to the claims of undocumented immigrants.[10] State legislative and enforcement responses were starkly adverse, and the public attitudes they reinforced were sharply stigmatizing. Yet the threat that these responses created was explicit and intentional: state authorities were denying vital opportunities and imposing suffocating surveillance, specifically to incite departures among undocumented immigrants. And it was a threat that immigrants and allies, particularly in Phoenix, understood well. For undocumented youth, Prop 300's denial of in-state tuition and scholarships created a "policy" threat to the higher education to which they and their families had aspired. As Matías, a youth activist, put it, "All this work you did and all the dreams, and your parents being excited, your siblings being really excited, you're going to go to college, the first one in the family . . . and then it's not going to happen."[11] But for most the clearest threat was the "repressive" threat of state enforcement, embodied in the aggressive tactics of Sheriff Joe Arpaio. Vehicular stops, neighborhood saturation patrols, and workplace raids created an omnipresent sense of surveillance and risk. This was true even for Latino citizens. Alfredo Gutierrez, a former state senator who became active against SB 1070, explained:

> That kind of atmosphere [was] created, where . . . people like me, you know, I was absolutely afraid of being stopped by the police . . . [because the laws] provided license for the worst kinds of behavior. So the cops got into it. And of course, Arpaio encouraged it. And then you had throughout this period a governor who refused to speak out and condemn any of this.[12]

But the threat felt particularly acute for members of undocumented and mixed status families. They faced not only the potential humiliation of police questioning and abuse but a very real chance of deportation if they were stopped. "The entire family is always on edge," Carlos Garcia of Puente acknowledged. "I've had six cousins detained or deported in the last four years."[13] For some immigrants the escalating risk led them to leave the state or go further into hiding. But for others it provided a powerful impetus to reject passivity and resist. Daniel Ortega, a Phoenix lawyer who came to identify with the nascent movement through his own role in Chicano activism, described this response:

> Once you put people in the corner, that's when they are more emboldened to fight back. [They thought,] "fighting back is the only thing I have left. I'm not leaving. I'm not going to uproot my family. I'm not going to start all over. Either I'm going to stay here and fight it or I will fail to exist."[14]

Yet an increased risk of apprehension, detention, and deportation for any individual or family was not the only threat that motivated mobilization. Immigrants, as Zepeda-Millán has argued, can also be animated by a collective threat, one that implicates a shared aspect of their identities. In the case of immigrants in Phoenix, that threat was stigma. The demeaning, criminalizing discourse used to justify both legislation and enforcement produced indignation and resolve among undocumented immigrants. For Ximena, a Puente activist and mother, the passage of SB 1070 showed that "the community sees us in a bad light. That is when I decided to show we are the opposite. That we are good people and that we want to work here legally."[15] Martín, another Puente activist in his forties, added: "My tipping point in getting involved . . . was when I got tired of politicians calling me a criminal on TV."[16] Even Latinos who were longtime citizens felt a shared susceptibility in the anti-Mexican stereotypes. Daniel Ortega described it this way:

> There used to be a distinction between them and us. Those of us who were U.S. citizens, those who were born here, and those who just arrived as immigrants, whether undocumented or not. And though we knew that we were related in some way . . . [w]e didn't talk about "us," but "them and us," even in our community. And when [the state] started beating up on them, it felt like we were being beat up too, and this wasn't right. This was our family.[17]

The scope of these threats played a key role in the eventual emergence of the Phoenix movement. As the statements of early participants attested, the sense of being attacked, both individually and collectively, threatened the immediate security and the sense of dignity of undocumented and documented people alike. Yet particularly in the case of a repressive threat whose more immediate dangers can be immobilizing as well as mobilizing, the emergence of any sustained collective action will also depend on the resources that can be marshaled by the targeted community.[18] The frustration and fear that emerged in Phoenix in response to Prop 300 or the raids of Joe Arpaio could not ultimately be translated into a social movement unless the resources necessary to initial collective action were also in place—not only financial resources but networks, tactics, and practices necessary to turn aggrieved participants into activists.

COMMUNITY-BASED RESOURCES THAT SUPPORTED MOBILIZATION

The availability of resources that enable mobilization is a key determinant in the emergence of social movements. An aggrieved community requires organizations—or at least networks—to disseminate information and coordinate action. It requires ideas for messaging and acting collectively and human beings to develop or modify those ideas and carry out those actions. It requires material resources to build organizations, train participants, and perform the outreach that amplifies their messages. And because a social movement aims to change minds—whether of decision makers or of the public—it also requires legitimacy, a nontangible resource that is nonetheless vital.

Early theories of resource mobilization prioritized access to material resources. Because prospective movements enjoyed unequal access to such resources, a key question was whether an emerging movement—particularly an underresourced "challenger" movement—could marshal the external material support that would enable it to build necessary organizational and human capital.[19] However, subsequent theorists, including Doug McAdam,[20] Bob Edwards,[21] and Marshall Ganz,[22] analyzing the emergence of such "challenger" movements, argued that insufficient attention had been directed to the "indigenous" resources for mobilization possessed by ostensibly resource-poor communities. Underresourced communities may possess strong informal networks, community-based institutions that can share organizational resources, access to independent or non-English-language media, and human capital honed in nonmovement contexts. Thus more recent resource mobilization theories have emphasized the variety of resources required for social movement emergence and functioning: organizational, human, cultural, material, and legitimacy based.[23] Moreover, they have highlighted means of acquiring or redistributing resources that go beyond straightforward external patronage, including using the networks and infrastructure of nondedicated community organizations, marshaling the human resources of a larger community, and self-producing nonmaterial resources.

These later theories of resource acquisition shed valuable light on the movement in Phoenix. The story of resource mobilization among immigrants in Phoenix is a complex, yet ultimately successful, one. It featured many forms of community-based improvisation and self-produced resources, before more conspicuous forms of external or "patronage"-based support began to flow to Phoenix.

In the early phase of resistance to "attrition through enforcement," immigrants and their allies relied on a range of resources that were not specifically dedicated to the protection of immigrants but came from preexisting organizations within immigrant or Latino communities. It may not be strictly accurate to say that emerging activists "co-opted" or "appropriated" these resources (terms that are prevalent in the scholarly literature):[24] sometimes the impetus came from embattled immigrants and sometimes it came from leaders of these organizations themselves, frequently Latinos who were citizens but came from families of immigrants. But such organizations played a vital role in the earliest efforts at protection and mobilization of immigrant communities. They included Mexican cultural organizations, such as Tonatierra, or Movimiento Estudiantil Chicano de Aztlán (MEChA) chapters at local colleges and universities; Catholic churches in the Phoenix area; organizations serving day laborers or other immigrant workers; and Spanish-language media.

These groups offered varying forms of organizational resources. Tonatierra housed the earliest incarnation of Puente and supported its nascent campaigns. Catholic churches offered space for organizing protesters or training youth participants. The Painter's Union building became the meeting site for Somos America, an umbrella organization of immigrants and immigrant-serving organizations that functioned as a vital node of communication from the early days of "attrition through enforcement" through resistance to SB 1070. Arizona State University (ASU)—a state institution that educated many Latino and immigrant students—provided the site and the impetus for the first meetings of undocumented students who became the Arizona DREAM Act Coalition.

Spanish-language media helped to disseminate information to immigrant communities, a role that was also played by the ACLU of Arizona as anti-immigrant legislation and enforcement increased.

The overlapping communications networks of these groups helped to activate the inchoate but powerful human resources of the movement: the large population of longtime Latino residents and more recent immigrants who made their homes in the Phoenix area, and local leaders who had emerged from this population. These organizations also contributed cultural resources: practices, understandings, and repertoires of action that could be utilized by emerging immigrant activists. Tonatierra instilled pride through the perpetuation of indigenous cultural practices. MEChA built solidarity through awareness of Mexican identity and shared with a new generation—which included Carlos Garcia and some of the early DREAMers—the legacy of the Chicano movement. Practices honed in religious institutions, such as the vigil, made their way into immigrant protests. Organizations shared repertoires of action from the Chicano and Farmworkers movements—from student walkouts to the "unity clap" ascribed to Cesar Chavez—with Phoenix immigrants and allies.

Buoyed by the contributions of these organizations and early leaders, immigrants and allies also began to engage in another generative practice. They "self-produced" the cultural and human resources that would be integral to the creation and mobilization of dedicated immigrant organizations. A series of actions and campaigns, responding primarily to the incursions of Sheriff Joe Arpaio into immigrant neighborhoods and workplaces, built the organizational and communications infrastructure and the nascent practices among affected groups that could ground a social movement. With the advent of SB 1070, Arizona's regime of "attrition through enforcement" and local efforts to resist it gained national visibility, bringing a flow of external resources to the emerging movement.

Self-Producing Resources, Creating Movement Structures

Immigrants and allies used several strategies to turn early mobilizations against "attrition through enforcement" into a more durable movement. One of the most important was reliance on "self-produced resources": resources created by activists themselves that enabled them to form organizational infrastructure, extend organizing networks, create tactical repertoires, and build basic skills among early activists.

A key example of this kind of self-produced resource was the Respect/ Respeto hotline. In 2007, as Arpaio began his neighborhood sweeps, he established a hotline through which citizens could report the presence or activity of undocumented immigrants. This caught the attention of Lydia Guzman, a longtime pro-immigrant advocate, who had set up a hotline herself, at the request of Republican legislators, to learn how employers were faring under the 2008 Employer Sanctions Law.[25] When Guzman found that the hotline was being utilized less by employers than by employees seeking relief from enforcement actions and help for their families, she methodically recorded their information. She became a constant presence outside Arpaio's workplace raids, supporting distraught family members and connecting them with lawyers and other community resources.

When Arpaio's hotline extended his eyes and ears into undocumented neighborhoods, Guzman saw an opportunity to activate a familiar tool. "I'll establish my own damn hotline," Guzman responded, and she did.[26] The Repect/Respeto hotline became "the 911 of the undocumented community,"[27] drawing reports not only of law enforcement tactics but of labor violations, wrongful denials of services to citizen children, and other acts of public or private subordination.[28] As with her earlier hotline, Guzman saw her task not simply as collecting information but as connecting callers with resources. She explained:

> There's always an agency, or even government agencies that help them in cases like this. Where you can't deny someone their overtime or their whatever just because they're undocumented. You can't abuse someone. And the Department of Labor is very clear about that. And so I've made lots of friends with all the different [federal] agencies . . . because these folks have rights. And a lot of people refuse to acknowledge that they do. But they do have rights.[29]

As word of the hotline spread, Guzman gathered information about a growing range of infractions. She received requests to share information from civil rights organizations concerned about enforcement in Maricopa County. The mayor of Phoenix even asked for her help in getting assistance from DOJ after one of his employees was stopped by the sheriff's department. The information Guzman provided helped to fuel legal challenges such as *Melendres v. Arpaio*, the racial profiling case brought by civil rights organizations in which Guzman also testified.[30] When the state began to enforce SB 1070 in the late summer of 2012, ACLU-Arizona brought the hotline in-house, as a means of identifying the specific violations under SB 1070's "show me your papers" provision, to which the Supreme Court had left the door open.[31] Guzman trained Dulce Juarez, a longtime DREAM activist who had been hired by the ACLU, to coordinate the hotline from within the organization.

The Respect/Respeto hotline provided an essential bridge between episodic actions and the more sustained, routinized, networked activity of a social movement. It helped organizers understand the scope of the challenges faced by undocumented immigrants in Phoenix. It cultivated a practice of reporting by those targeted that could be used to hold law enforcement and other officials accountable through political or legal action. During a period when new organizations for undocumented immigrants were still emerging across the state, the hotline provided a central structure through which community members could air grievances, ask questions, and obtain referrals to supportive resources. As new organizations took shape, the hotline fostered collaboration among different constellations of activists, such as when Lydia Guzman sent word of raid-based detentions to Puente, who reached out to the impacted families and did a video or rally to put a human face on the event.[32] The hotline also became a vehicle for sharing with civil rights organizations and federal agencies, including DOJ, patterns of enforcement in Phoenix. And it aided a strategy of enlisting the federal government to curtail the worst excesses of state enforcement—sometimes through constitutional litigation—that would provide a boon to undocumented communities in Arizona.

In addition to the Respect/Respeto hotline, other kinds of "self-produced resources" fortified the budding activists and played a central role in their transition toward a durable social movement. For example, the strategies of outreach to undocumented communities, led by the organizations Puente and Tonatierra—including the strategy of "barrio defense"—were also essential in the movement's longer-term development. As the state's efforts to force immigrants to leave the state escalated, Carlos Garcia, Puente's director, observed that most efforts to resist oppressive enforcement were still being undertaken by activists who were not among those impacted.[33] As someone who had been undocumented until his teens and had many undocumented family members, Garcia prioritized the leadership of those who had experienced state hostility directly. To organize this group, Garcia worked with Salvador Reza, the leader of Tonatierra. Tonatierra, a Phoenix-based organization that supported immigrant communities through its focus on indigenous Mexican cultures, housed Puente in its early days. Together,

Garcia and Reza sought to engage those most affected in protecting their own families and neighborhoods.

One example of these efforts and their impact was their work at a large May Day rally in 2010, organized soon after the passage of SB 1070. During the rally, facilitators from Puente and Tonatierra organized the marchers into groups based on the neighborhoods in which they lived. The facilitators then invited those most affected by immigration enforcement to speak about their greatest concerns. They also encouraged them to discuss what their neighborhoods might do—how they might act together—to address or mitigate those concerns. After meeting in individual neighborhood groups, participants returned for a "report-back" to the rally attendees as a group, after which participants were invited to a later meeting at Tonatierra's offices. At this meeting, they formed twenty-six neighborhood-based "defense committees." The goal of these committees was to create a system that community members could use to share information to alert people about the initiation of police sweeps and about sites frequented by Maricopa County Sheriff's Office vehicles, as well as to develop strategies for relying on each other when neighborhoods were targeted. By facilitating the creation of these committees, Garcia and Reza expanded their organizational networks and fostered trust and solidarity among undocumented immigrants. In July 2010 the federal district court enjoined four provisions of SB 1070, including the "show me your papers" provision, shortly before the law was to go into effect.[34] This meant that the neighborhood "defense committees" that arose from the 2010 May Day rally were never fully activated for their initial purpose. But the crucial connections among undocumented community members, and between them and anti-enforcement activists, helped to shape the future engagement of both. This strategy also enabled undocumented residents to become familiar with Tonatierra and with Puente, which became an independent organization in 2011. Both of these organizations would draw on that solidarity and trust in the years ahead.

The practice of outreach to those most affected yielded another kind of preparation: the "Know Your Rights" (KYR) training. As Puente organized neighborhoods, or Guzman publicized the hotline, or Somos America—another key immigrant-rights group within the Phoenix movement—reached out to immigrant communities, KYR instruction became a staple of local gatherings. This training focused on a question vital to undocumented immigrants, about which they often knew little: how to respond in the event of a police stop. KYR instruction, led first by ACLU lawyers and community leaders and later by immigrant activists themselves, taught immigrants about the limited but important ways they could protect themselves in encounters with law enforcement. They learned what questions they were not obliged to answer and what kinds of assistance they could request. Importantly, they learned that those detained could decline to sign any document that was not translated into their native language, and that they had a right to seek advice from an attorney before doing so. This information was crucial in preventing unknowing immigrants from signing "voluntary" departures, which would result in their immediate return to their countries of origin.[35] The one place where Know Your Rights training has had "a massive impact," Alfredo Gutierrez observed, "is . . . [that] more and more people understand what voluntary departure is."[36] Guzman saw a more global effect: "I thought it was going to be empowering for the community but more than empowering. . . . [K]nowledge is a weapon, and they were empowered to the point where they were pushing back."[37] Guzman saw this pushback materialize as neighbors began to wield cell phones during Arpaio's saturation patrols:

> People were . . . empowered with their cameras. Everyone has a camera now on their cell phone. So police officers, now they had to . . . accept the fact that they were being recorded everywhere . . . when somebody was getting pulled over in the community, you have strangers come up and record it. . . . [I]n the last few raids, we were listening to the scanners like with the sheriff, and we [could hear them say to each other], "Boss, I have a couple of activists here. They're recording me, what am I going to do? Send someone to . . ."—so the sheriffs were afraid of us.[38]

These early strategies drew on another local asset: the innovative leadership of documented Latinos with strong affinities with undocumented communities. This leadership was a resource that Arizona's long-standing Latino population—a demographic rare among immigrant-hostile jurisdictions—was distinctively able to provide. Their skills and visibility enabled them to play vital roles, and their citizenship gave them a level of insulation, at a time when the consequences of public action for undocumented people were still unknown. Some, like Alfredo Gutierrez, Roberto Reveles, and Daniel Ortega, had roots in the Chicano movement. Others, like Leticia de la Vara, had witnessed their parents' involvement in that movement as children. Still others, like Lydia Guzman, Petra Falcon, and Salvador Reza, had played long-term professional or organizational roles supporting immigrant communities. As the state-led hostility to immigrants escalated, they lent their skills and their legitimacy in varying ways to efforts to organize and protect immigrants. Reveles and dela Vara served as presidents of Somos America; Ortega, after practicing immigration law early in his career, became an active mentor and adviser to immigrant youth; Gutierrez and Reveles played vital roles in organizing early protests; and Gutierrez, a former state senator, was an early participant in acts of civil disobedience protesting SB 1070. Guzman, along with Reza and Falcon, created actions or campaigns that laid the groundwork for immigrant organizations. The leadership of these experienced, community-facing individuals was an asset that distinguished Arizona from most anti-immigrant jurisdictions. These allies and the practices that they established fostered among undocumented community members the early understandings that would enable activism: a culture of reporting on state excesses, a sense that their perspectives mattered, and a willingness to rely on each other for their mutual protection.

Resource Mobilization and Youth Activism

Adding to the important resource development work by adult activists at Puente and Tonatierra was a robust response to the denial of in-state tuition by student activists at ASU. Their work—which illustrates the opportunities and challenges of undocumented youth activism more generally—also produced key resources that enabled the growing movement to become sustainable.

The transition between early mobilizing and dedicated organizational emergence was more direct for youth organizing at ASU in response to Prop 300. These young people were more prepared than many undocumented adults to assume leadership roles or manifest agency in response to state-imposed threat. This difference was attributable partly to the distinct "political consciousness" of undocumented youth: their sense of empowerment, of their relationship to the state or nation, is often different from that of their parents. As Leisy Abrego has written, youth who arrive in the United States as children or teens are socialized within the integrative environment of the public schools, where they enjoy a constitutionally protected right to K–12 education, and become not only bilingual but bicultural as a result of ongoing contact and friendships with documented peers.[39] Their sense of being functionally "American" takes root in that environment and is enhanced by the meritocratic ideas to which American education exposes them, at least until their status begins to present concrete barriers. And as theorists of that transition, such as Roberto Gonzales, have acknowledged, the limiting effects of status can be delayed for those who excel academically and enjoy mentorship in middle and high school settings.[40] The youth who faced the cancellation of their public scholarships at ASU could draw on all these strengths. Their scholarships were the result of outstanding academic performance, participation in extracurriculars and other activities that engendered leadership, and the guidance of teachers and mentors.[41] They experienced a sense of personal agency despite the crisis produced by Prop 300 and were prepared to seek out means to complete their education.[42] This intuitive, agentic response was supported by the administration at ASU, which sought to preserve youth's opportunity by locating sources of private scholarships. These circumstances created for the students not simply a path forward for their education but an institutional setting that enabled them to organize. A private scholarship orientation sponsored by university leadership provided the first opportunity for undocumented students to meet each other; many had previously perceived themselves to be "the only undocumented student at ASU."[43] They then shared their experiences navigating their status through a "blackboard" group established by the university. When they decided to meet together informally for the first time, they used the MEChA office, in a campus building. The university also established public service requirements for all recipients of Sunburst or Arizona Dream Fund scholarships (the new private scholarships), which strengthened their organizational and leadership skills and created bonds among those who participated. "We would go as a group," a future Arizona DREAM Act Coalition (ADAC) leader recalled,

> because all of us had to meet the same requirements, and it would be more much fun to go as a group than going by yourself. So we went to St. Vincent de Paul soup kitchen. We went to the veterans' homes. . . . We also went in to clean the neighborhoods. . . . And I think those events really helped us bond as a group.[44]

As the group became more independent of university structures, shifting their online conversations to Google groups and meeting frequently outside the context of campus-led meetings, they quickly discovered an animating focus for their activities: the DREAM Act, which had been proposed in Congress. A potential boon to their lives, the DREAM Act also conferred several organizing advantages. Its path to citizenship became both a means to achieve their educational and professional aspirations and an immediate goal of their organizing. It placed them in contact with DREAMers, and DREAM Act organizations nationwide, with whom they could feel the same sense of affinity that they shared in the ASU group, and from whom they could secure guidance and advice. This informal exchange later became an affiliate relationship with the national youth organization United We Dream, which was an important source of training, funding, and project-based employment.

Finally, through their work on behalf of the DREAM Act, these undocumented students began to acclimate themselves to outward-facing activism, visibility, and self-disclosure. It began with on-campus tabling on behalf of the DREAM Act. Self-disclosure to student peers, in small conversational settings, became a means of providing information and giving a "face" to the issue.[45] The possibility of greater visibility arose when an ASU DREAMer who was also a journalism student proposed to write an article on undocumented organizing at ASU. There was immediate, passionate disagreement over this further step. Elena, who later became an ADAC leader, recalled:

> Some of us, including myself . . . were saying, "You better do the story. This is a great idea." And then there was others that said, "You're jeopardizing our scholarship; you're jeopardizing our families; do not write about this; this is going to get us in trouble." And then, that's when we started the conversation.[46]

The group agreed to a debate in which two participants would present the competing views, as others weighed the options. When the debate concluded, a majority voted in favor of publishing the article.

While some left the organization in disagreement with this decision and fear of exposure, those who remained embraced a more explicitly political stance. Although the group had organized under the label SUFFRAGE (Students Uniting for Fair Rights and Greater Equality or Greater Education), they decided to create an organization whose political orientation would be clear. Thus the Arizona DREAM Act Coalition (ADAC) came into being.

Strengthening and Extending the Local Movement

If these early efforts mobilized resources within immigrant communities, laying the groundwork for more sustained social movement activity, SB 1070 further galvanized immigrant rights activists and allies, fueling the movement's growth. The all-out war on undocumented communities declared by the statute spurred new practices that, like hotlines or KYR trainings, would become familiar within the movement and would build the capacity of both documented and undocumented activists. The sense of emergency and need for action that the law instilled in so many also created bridges from immigrant communities outward, fostering alliances within Phoenix and beyond that led to external support, including funding, training, and infrastructure. Two actions that followed the passage of SB 1070—a nationwide economic boycott of Arizona and a one-hundred-day vigil at the capitol—demonstrate how this sense of urgency drove the development of key resources. These resources, and the alliances that were formed in the initial months after the law's passage, would play a crucial role in the movement's sustainability and its longer-term influence.

Within days of the law's passage, local leaders including Carlos Garcia and Representative Raul Grijalva began to call for a nationwide boycott of Arizona.[47] The boycott sought to capitalize on growing national indignation and concern about what was then the harshest anti-immigrant state law in the nation. Organizers asked supporters across the country to avoid visiting or spending money in the state. Although some feared the strike would ultimately hurt those workers activists aimed to help, both organizers and many workers themselves viewed it as a demonstration of exigency and political will. Roberto Reveles recalled:

> [I asked a local painter about this, and] the response was very impressive to me. He said—in Spanish, he says—"Si, posiblemente, yes, we possibly will [be] hurt in the short term; but in the long term, we will be all the better for it." In other words, we're willing to sacrifice in the short run.[48]

Carlos Garcia put it more bluntly: "People say it's like punching yourself in the face. But if you're willing to punch yourself in the face, you get people's attention."[49] The boycott quickly claimed the attention of a national public. When the National Council of La Raza endorsed the strike, it was, Daniel Ortega recalled, "like yelling fire in a theater."[50] Moving a conference or rescheduling a trip was a relatively undemanding way of demonstrating solidarity in the face of what many outside the state viewed as a conspicuous wrong. Ortega explained:

> Everybody felt they could do their part just by simply not flying into Arizona, coming to Arizona and spending money here. . . . And I can't think of one thing that we did that was more effective than that, because from the little guy to the richest guy, from the smallest organization to the biggest organization, they could say, "We ain't going there," and "We're not going to support their economy."[51]

By the time the boycott concluded it had cost Arizona, by one estimate, more than $140 million in revenues.[52] Beyond inflicting economic pain on the state's tourism and related industries, the boycott conferred important organizing advantages. It brought Phoenix activists into coalition with national organizations. It strengthened the networks and expanded the tactical repertoires of emerging immigrant organizations as they fielded organizational responses to the boycott. For example, as the boycott gained strength, activists developed innovative direct action responses aimed at penalizing those who insisted on coming to the state: making surprise interventions at conferences that ignored the boycott or notifying prospective funders of offending organizations about boycott violations.[53] As the strike waned, Puente worked with Unitarian Universalists, who were planning their 2012 General Assembly in Phoenix. The Unitarians planned to use their assembly as an occasion for witness against Arpaio and SB 1070; Puente educated them on the political context and helped them to select sites for their actions.[54]

The boycott also forged new, and sometimes surprising, alliances at the local level. In May 2010, soon after the passage of SB 1070, a group of more than sixty organizations—from African American and Latino groups, to faith leadership, to the Arizona Chamber of Commerce—gathered to discuss the precarious moment for Arizona. For participants in this gathering, the boycott simply underscored the economic and reputational damage politicians such as Russell Pearce and Jan Brewer were doing to the state.[55] Calling themselves the Real Arizona Coalition, the group sought "to move the state to address the issue of immigration on a federal level and not in the State House" and also, in the words of coalition member James Garcia, "[to] recast what [they believed had] been a misrepresentation of the image of the state."[56] The Real Arizona Coalition helped to disseminate among moderate citizens, including business leaders, the view that anti-immigrant legislation enacted by the state—whatever one's view of nationwide immigration policy—posed an economic threat to the well-being of Arizonans. In 2011, when Russell Pearce unveiled an even more stringent array of anti-immigrant proposals, a letter of opposition signed by more than sixty business groups helped to defeat the proposed laws.[57]

If the boycott began with support from outside Phoenix and ended by fortifying local organizations and alliances, a one-hundred-day vigil in 2010 worked in reverse, moving from the local community toward nationwide allies. The vigil, however, like the boycott, the hotline, and the "barrio defense committees," provided crucial resource development for the movement, particularly by galvanizing adult women and by connecting SB 1070 with practices of civic engagement. When SB 1070 first passed the state legislature, a handful of middle-aged, undocumented women of faith erected a small shrine to the Virgin of Guadalupe.[58] They resolved to hold vigil until Governor Jan Brewer decided whether to sign the legislation. Initially staged at Brewer's residence, the vigil soon moved to the capitol. There it became a gathering place for DREAMers and other students who had engaged in high school walkouts and for undocumented community members seeking support and information.[59] When Brewer signed the legislation, the organizers extended the vigil, persisting until the legislation was scheduled to go into effect. Over time, the vigil became a place not simply for prayer and witness but for songs, community meals, open-air films, and shared individual testimony. It also gradually became a site for service to the immigrant community. The "vigil ladies" were watchful and observant; they learned where relevant offices were housed and which supporters were citizens who might help immigrants secure what they needed. When immigrants approached the capitol with particular requests—to obtain records for their children, so they could leave the country, for example—vigil participants could often provide the information they needed. "Without even trying," reflected Mercedes, a mother in her forties who later became active with ADAC, "we started to do community service.[60]

Before the vigil ended, however, participants had taken on yet another function: registering Latino citizens to vote. Members of the national organization Reform Immigration for America (RIFA), who worked in the immigrant community and supported the vigil, encouraged vigil participants to register the many Latino allies who visited the site. Although some were initially reluctant, their time at the heart of state government ultimately showed them the importance of civic engagement. Mercedes described how she began by assisting undocumented community members but ultimately broadened her sights to citizens:

> The organization wanted us to register voters in the [c]apitol and we did not want to because we thought, we are here to pray . . . we do not want anything to do with politics. . . . But my mind change[d] when I started to understand that power is really inside the [c]apitol and not outside, like us. . . . Th[at] was when I started to understand the importance about voting and why was it happening, what was happening to us.[61]

Civic engagement proved to be one of the lasting legacies of the vigil.[62] The duration of the vigil, and its centrality to anti SB-1070 organizing, attracted the attention of the Center for Community Change.[63] At the conclusion of the vigil, the center made a grant to Petra Falcon, an immigrant activist with strong ties to faith communities, who had been a key supporter of the "vigil ladies" and their effort. Falcon founded Promise Arizona (PAZ), an organization that would seek youth empowerment through civic engagement, particularly through the registration and turnout of Latino voters.[64]

Both the boycott and the vigil had a crucial impact on building tactical repertoires, extending networks, and creating infrastructure for the movement. Although it was not always a primary goal of the original action, the organizational resources that grew out of these actions—like the voter registration work at the vigil—helped to propel the movement forward in the months and years ahead.

THE CHALLENGES OF MOBILIZING UNDOCUMENTED PARTICIPANTS

As this chapter has shown, the danger of "attrition through enforcement" —which posed both policy and repressive threats—activated Latino identity and changed the calculus regarding collective action for immigrants and allies across the state. The prospects for change in so hostile a state might have seemed grim, but the prospects for immigrants and Latino allies—should they do nothing—seemed grimmer still. In these precarious circumstances, an array of community-based resources, mobilized by indigenous leadership and fortified by the self-production of emerging activists themselves, spurred and formed the infrastructure for resistance. But as activists began to build local organizations dedicated specifically to immigrant rights and shape more durable repertoires of response, they confronted another kind of challenge, one that arose from the status of their prospective participants. If ADAC was going to expand beyond the distinctively empowered scholarship students at ASU, if Puente was going to foster the leadership of those most affected, they would need to enlist activists who faced distinctive barriers: internal barriers to visibility and participation and external barriers created by the state's power to detain and deport.

The Political Consciousness of Undocumented Participants

While political opportunity or threat and access to mobilizing resources may be crucial to the emergence of social movements, they are not the only factors that determine when grievances can be translated into collective action. The subjectivity or "political consciousness" of prospective participants can be a vital factor as well.[65] Elaborating his "political process" theory of social movement emergence, Doug Mc-Adam argued that the possibility of sustained collective action depended not only on political opportunity and the mobilization of resources; the most important factor, in his view, was the "cognitive liberation" of participants.[66] Cognitive liberation, in McAdam's' analysis, depends on prospective participants' subjective belief that change is possible—that state actions or policies that have produced their grievances are capable of change—and that they are capable of acting as effective change agents.[67] Other theorists have also highlighted political consciousness as a factor central to social movement emergence. Jane Mansbridge and Aldon Morris, for example, have emphasized the importance of "oppositional consciousness" in animating sustained, collective political action, particularly action of a contentious character. Mansbridge argues that "oppositional consciousness" emerges when members of a marginalized group "claim their previously subordinate identity as a positive identification . . . identify injustices done to their group . . . demand changes in the polity, economy, or society to rectify those injustices . . . and see other members of their group as sharing an interest in rectifying those injustices."[68] For Mansbridge, the focus is less on a sense of political capacity than on a posture of adversarial demand, yet oppositional consciousness also requires a positive association with a marginalized identity and a sense of connection to others who share that identity. Achieving those forms of political consciousness that enable social movement activity may be a particular challenge for undocumented noncitizens.

Lack of formal citizenship may make prospective activists feel anomalous as political participants. Social movements, even political debates, are often presumed to be the province of citizens.[69] Citizenship gives prospective participants a distinctive stake in public debates: the choices made by political institutions matter to them because they are, and are likely to remain, formal members of a political community. Moreover, the most visible, paradigmatic social movements of the past century have been movements of citizens. These groups faced deprivation of their equal rights, and some, like participants in the civil rights movement, confronted state-sponsored violence when they asserted them. Yet those rights—as a formal matter—were theirs to claim. The distance between their formal status and their practical treatment at the hands of the state formed the heart of their rhetorical appeals and sometimes their strategies or tactics.[70]

Noncitizens, in contrast, lack the legal membership that provides a formal stake in the well-being of their polity and a conventional claim to the attention of public actors. Moreover, they lack the vote that could enable them to hold elected officials accountable, and their unauthorized presence may raise the question of whether public officials are in any way responsible to them. A hostile environment, like that of Arizona, exacerbates these perceptions. By denying public benefits, criminalizing presence and employment, and legitimating police surveillance, the state not only seeks to deprive and intimidate undocumented immigrants; it also aims to undermine any sense of de facto membership— one basis from which plausible claims making, in the absence of formal legal status, might arise.[71]

Both a lack of formal membership and an explicit deprivation of de facto belonging can create forms of political consciousness that impede activation or mobilization. Leisy Abrego and Cecilia Menjívar have described the effects of "legal violence"—that is, subsistence in an environment of legal precarity, material deprivation, and ongoing enforcement threat—on immigrants in temporary or undocumented statuses.[72] "Structural violence" makes them reluctant to live visibly or to engage with public institutions—from schools to public agencies to law enforcement—even when they have a legal right to do so. "Symbolic violence" leads them to internalize the stigma and the lack of recourse that hostile regimes ascribe to them. Undocumented immigrants who feel demoralized or self-critical, or who struggle to keep their families safe, may find it difficult to conceive of themselves as change agents.

Greg Prieto has documented the effects of such violence on the political engagement of undocumented adults. They develop survival strategies of "avoidance and isolation"—a set of behaviors he refers to as "the shell"—that make them reluctant to engage in social movement activity or imbue it with an instrumental character.[73] Undocumented immigrants may feel that they are not entitled to raise their voices, or that their status-based disempowerment prevents them from accessing processes through which they might improve their lives. Even those who have developed a sense of capacity or agency, as an outgrowth of schooling or mastery of language, can find it eroded, as Roberto Gonzales has emphasized, by obstacles to work or higher education.[74] These feelings may deter participation outright; they may also impede the development of political confidence or the willingness to engage the public or elected officials. As undocumented activists at ASU demonstrated when they struggled to decide whether to risk exposure, the movement in Arizona needed to address these challenges.

External Barriers and Undocumented Participants

Even undocumented immigrants who could see themselves as capable political actors confronted additional, practical challenges. Like those pushing back against SB 1070, undocumented activists may face conflicting imperatives about how to position themselves as they engage the state. Their distance from institutionalized power and their disenfranchised position may make it most plausible for them to mobilize as contentious "challengers," protesting undocumented exclusion and exerting pressure outside institutional channels.[75] Yet undocumented immigrants face a weightier burden of legitimation, specifically because they lack formal citizenship. They may be obliged to establish their bona fides as credible, mainstream political actors—the kind of actors who *deserve* formal status—even as they challenge their exclusion or subordination.

Moreover, the undocumented status of movement participants also provides the state with a wider range of countermovement strategies. States have often met social movements with strategies of co-optation—quieting insurgency by offering incremental benefits or promises of representation—and repression, using or threatening violence to quell mobilizations.[76] The state may repress undocumented resistance not only through the use or threat of violence but through the use or threat of detention or deportation, a countermeasure that can intimidate participants and vitiate the strength of the movement. Those immigrants in Arizona who perceived no choice but to leave or to hide demonstrate the potency of this effect. The state may also employ a countermovement strategy based on persistent denials of recognition. This could involve the rejection of substantive positions advanced by the movement or the failure to acknowledge the political performances mounted by activists. While the effects of such strategies remain uncertain, they may demoralize, or erode the confidence of, a movement that must rely on a de facto sense, rather than a formal grant, of membership.

Although emerging organizations in Phoenix had responded to the threat of "attrition through enforcement" by developing the resources necessary to establish a sustainable social movement, they faced new challenges as they sought to widen involvement of and encourage leadership by undocumented immigrants. The status of these vital participants could impede their political confidence and render them vulnerable as they confronted the state. These challenges required different kinds of solutions than the challenges of mobilizing early resistance. The next two chapters describe how emerging organizations with undocumented members developed these solutions.

PART TWO

Building a Movement of Noncitizens

Formative Practices

CHAPTER 2

Storytelling and Emotion Cultures in Undocumented Organizations

Despite the challenges posed by state hostility and restricted access to conventional resources, a movement for immigrant rights had begun to coalesce in Phoenix in the late 2000s. Galvanized by the threat of "attrition through enforcement," innovative leadership drew on community-based networks to build crucial resources such as infrastructure, tactical repertoires, and political voice. A flow of external support following the enactment of SB 1070 in 2010 enabled new, dedicated organizations to mobilize youth and adults to protect immigrant communities and advance immigrant rights. But as organizations like Puente, Living United for Change in Arizona (LUCHA), and Arizona DREAM Act Coalition (ADAC) sought to increase the participation, amplify the voice, and encourage the leadership of those most affected by state hostility, they faced a new set of challenges, stemming from the legal status of participants themselves.

Undocumented participants, as chapter 1 explained, faced internal obstacles: living as undocumented, particularly in an environment of state hostility, could undermine the sense of value, belonging, or efficacy that would enable them to function as political changemakers. They also faced external obstacles, from a public that questioned the legitimacy of their participation to officials who could deploy immigration-related sanctions to discourage their participation. In response, emerging organizations developed three specific practices: experiential storytelling, organizational emotion cultures, and performative citizenship. The first two practices—storytelling and emotion cultures—began their work within organizations, fortifying the self-conceptions of new participants and preparing them for activism. The third practice, performative citizenship, joined with storytelling and emotion cultures as activists engaged the public, to support the legitimacy of new participants in the eyes of lawmakers, of the public, and of activists themselves. Together these practices enabled a group of committed activists who lacked formal status to develop the internal confidence and external legitimation necessary to form a credible, effective social movement.

UNDOCUMENTED IMMIGRANTS BECOMING
SOCIAL MOVEMENT PARTICIPANTS:
THREE FORMATIVE PRACTICES

Beyond the public-facing functions of countering state hostility and orchestrating pro-immigrant resistance, emerging organizations played a second vital role in the lives of those they aimed to mobilize. They offered a protected setting in which undocumented community members could develop the views of themselves and their circumstances that would enable them to risk public visibility and engage the public as activists.[1] For those who joined Puente, LUCHA, or ADAC, the storytelling and emotion cultures that functioned within these organizations offered new understandings that expanded their self-conceptions and constituted them as a group.[2] Sharing personal stories of what it meant to be undocumented dispelled stereotypes and emphasized attributes of personal and collective agency that would support participants in their impending activism. Individual narratives were bolstered, in these organizations, by a group of "metanarratives," or stories about stories, that explained the benefits of sharing experiential narratives and defined each undocumented person as someone who holds a resource (a "story of self") that brings value to the movement. Sharing that resource— an experience that could produce fear and vulnerability—relied on a kind of learning that was supported by the emotion cultures of these organizations. Emotion cultures helped support the intense, affectively charged forms of communication that characterized the movement; they also fueled the solidarity that buttressed participation and enabled activists to manage the fear, frustration, and disappointment that can arise in their political activity.

In organizations of undocumented participants, like the ones that emerged in Arizona, these practices enabled new participants to become politically "activated" and turn outward. As they did so, they began to aim their appeals not simply at fellow community members or predictable allies but at a world of strangers whose support could strengthen their cause. Storytelling and emotion cultures, which followed activists from their organizations onto the political field, played a key role in this process. But organizations in Phoenix, as elsewhere, also relied on a third practice, which is specific to outward-facing political activity: tactics of performative citizenship. These tactics place undocumented activists in roles that are culturally associated with citizenship. They are performative in the sense of enacting—placing before state officials or dominant publics—a version of the world that activists aim to bring into being: one in which undocumented immigrants are full members and respected participants in public deliberations. That enactment is achieved through the detailed performance of paradigmatic citizens' roles, from registering voters, to marching, to engaging in civil disobedience. But these tactics are not only a matter of enactment; they also have a more persuasive role. They demonstrate the capacity of undocumented immigrants to contribute to the polity, a demonstration that may render them more legitimate in the eyes of state actors or members of the public. Moreover, by enabling activists to learn the role of citizen from the inside—to understand institutions and processes and appreciate the accountability of elected officials—performative practices serve to legitimate undocumented activists in their own eyes, helping them feel they belong as participants in their local, state, and even national political communities.

This chapter explores the way three organizations in the proimmigrant movement in Arizona—ADAC, LUCHA, and Puente—incorporated organizational storytelling and emotion cultures into their work. Looking closely at the impact on the undocumented members, it outlines how these practices helped to empower and activate new participants. Chapter 3 then explains the role of the third central practice, performative citizenship. That chapter traces the operation of performative citizenship in the Phoenix context by looking at the Adios Arpaio voter engagement campaign of 2012, led by Promise Arizona (PAZ) with the collaboration of youth organizations including ADAC and LUCHA.

THE ROLE OF EXPERIENTIAL STORYTELLING IN ORGANIZATIONS OF UNDOCUMENTED IMMIGRANTS

Storytelling is a prominent and ritualized feature of life in many undocumented organizations. Long before activists tell their stories to state actors or members of the public, they learn to craft, share, and respond to experiential stories within organizations. Although this activity is more visible in DREAMer or other youth-based organizations, even community organizations like Puente, which do not incorporate story-telling explicitly in the format of their community meetings, encourage one-on-one sharing with prospective members, share brief anecdotes to describe the courage or persistence of community members, or highlight storytelling by those most affected at public vigils or rallies.

Storytelling as a practice reflects varying influences that shape the lives of undocumented immigrants. Sharing one's story may be an instinctive response for those emerging from an environment in which they have been pressed to keep crucial details of their lives from others. The form draws on Latin American histories and traditions, in which first-person *testimonios* bore witness to state-based violence and defied the erasure of official evidence.[3] Storytelling, as I observed it in Arizona, also reflects the US context, where a "confessional" style dating back to religious re-vivalists and nineteenth-century abolitionists has enjoyed a renaissance in recent online culture.[4]

Experiential stories, as they are shared in organizations, have several features.[5] Most relate a series of events in the life of an individual, usually the speaker herself. These events are organized temporally, so as to pres-ent a beginning, middle, and end. Finally, this sequence of events gains coherence and meaning through its relation to a conceptual structure, frequently some kind of opposition or struggle. For example, the stories youth learn to tell when they train as canvassers at LUCHA, a Phoenix-based organization that builds local political power through voter en-gagement, involve "a challenge, a choice, and an outcome." Like ADAC, an undocumented youth organization that focuses on educational oppor-tunity and federal legislative change, LUCHA uses storytelling as a central practice in integrating its new participants and preparing them to com-municate its message to officials and the public. Some of the stories that are shared at LUCHA and ADAC meetings are "kernel" stories—short descriptions of an action or event in the storyteller's life that illustrates an insight or proposition—while others are longer stories with a discernible narrative arc.[6] Undocumented stories in these organizations—like most experiential narratives—are socially organized.[7] Even when they reflect individual experience, stories are shaped by the organizational contexts in which they are told. The setting of undocumented organizations shapes not only the story lines that tend to be favored but expectations about when and why stories are offered and how listeners should respond.

The circumstances under which stories are offered in organizations like LUCHA or ADAC are exceptionally broad. They may be offered by a speaker as a means of introduction: one of the cofounders of ADAC, for example, who returned to the group to talk about her work in labor rights, prefaced her remarks by saying: "Most of you know my story as a *DREAMer*, but tonight I want to share my story as a *worker*."[8] Stories may also be shared as a form of celebration. For instance, when a new president was elected at ADAC from among the group's members, this youth activist shared his story at his first meeting as president, to mark the transition to his new role.[9] Stories may also be offered in the course of brainstorming or strategizing: two adult activists from ADAC, for example, who had proposed a novel form of direct action, shared a story about how they had seen the tactic work in their country of origin.[10] One central occasion for storytelling, however, is the socialization of new members. Youth organizations have made storytelling a prominent feature of their trainings or general meetings: members learn from the outset how to compose, share, and receive a compelling experiential story and how to understand the importance of stories to the movement's goals.

The centrality of storytelling became clear at a house meeting I observed at LUCHA in June 2013, which was aimed at recruiting new voter engagement volunteers.[11] As I joined the gathering, the room was buzzing with the energy—and the animated conversation—of two dozen teenagers. The din stilled slightly as Abril Gallardo, one of the organizers, announced that they would start by learning to share their stories. This approach was not unique to this gathering—storytelling is a staple of the canvassing in which those present that night would be participating—but the new, mostly high school-age participants didn't know this yet. They only knew they might be asked to speak before a group of twenty or thirty people—many of whom were complete strangers—and to share details of their often-challenging lives. Over the next half hour, Abril guided them through a methodical exercise, based on the storytelling model of Marshall Ganz, a sociologist who organized with the Farmworkers movement.[12] For the first stage of the activity, participants broke up into small groups. They were asked to frame a "story of self": a personal, experiential narrative that is organized around "a challenge, a choice, and an outcome." Although two team leaders who were present had led off by sharing their own stories, the new participants were full of questions, and a flurry of hands shot up into the air. Someone asked if the "challenge" had to focus on their lives as undocumented or as members of mixed status families. It can if you want, Abril replied, but you should feel free to pick your own "challenge." What mattered, she explained, is that the situation was new or unfamiliar in some way, and that it presented you with a problem to be solved or a choice to be made. The youth then got to work, jotting down notes about their stories, sharing snippets with their fellow group members, laughing, and relaxing slightly as they got acquainted.

The "challenge, choice, outcome" structure LUCHA used that evening is well-known among Phoenix organizations serving undocumented immigrants. Not only does its straightforward causal structure make sense to young volunteers; but it also helps participants understand times when they have exercised agency in their own lives. Focusing on a choice that has had consequences for their lives highlights the resources that even the least experienced or shyest among them possesses. Most pick an example in which they made a sound choice in the first instance, but even those who do not can often see in retrospect what they learned from their missteps. Both are strengths that they may not have recognized and can bring to their work in the movement. That evening, when the group reconvened shortly after, Abril asked a few volunteers to share their stories with the room. Primed by their experience in small groups, participants found—with relief made audible through laughter, exclamations, and finger snapping—that sharing their experience was easier than many had expected.

Next, Abril suggested that they relate their "stories of self" to a "story of us": a narrative that emphasizes features, perspectives, or life experiences that members of the group have in common. "What defines a 'story of us'?" she asked. People called out shared experiences: being immigrants, having parents who work late or juggle two jobs, being Latino, dealing with high school (laughter here), fearing family separation at the hands of Joe Arpaio (nods and more snapping). Abril drew out some of these elements and connected them to themes in the "stories of self" that they had just heard, hurrying a little as she noticed the meeting time flying by. The new volunteers listened carefully to this account, an occasional smile or nod marking a glimpse of shared purpose.

Abril then moved to the final phase of the discussion: how the "story of self" and the "story of us" fuse with the "story of now," an urgent demand of the present moment, for the communities of which participants are part. As immigrants, as Latino youth, as members of vulnerable families, they need a greater voice—greater power, she says—to resist the hardships that state officials are imposing on them. Increasing the voice of Latino allies in elections, Abril explained, is one powerful vehicle for doing this. From this final "story," she introduced the upcoming civic engagement campaign and explained the role of volunteers. The kickoff event was a voter registration table at a local grocery store: Who can be there to help? She asked. Phones came out and heads went down as participants considered their schedules and weighed their commitments. Tentatively at first, but with a snowballing enthusiasm, young volunteers agreed to staff the table at the grocery store, attend the first canvass in a Latino neighborhood, and more.

Those who joined this campaign had received a valuable introduction to the organization's work: sharing a pivotal moment in their own lives, talking about the needs of the community, and connecting both to the electoral participation of Latino citizens. A serious few could now see the vote as a vehicle for change—a view that would become more prevalent as they canvassed their neighbors. But many more glimpsed a sense of camaraderie and possibility: they could be decision makers in their own lives, and they could talk to strangers on behalf of a community they were beginning better to understand.

At ADAC, where new participants tend to join the organization before embarking on particular campaigns, storytelling is woven into the fabric of the general meetings. At many meetings I attended between 2012 and 2015, after a small-group icebreaker and before the business of the day, the group would pause for a "DREAMer's story": a member of the organization would share their path to the present moment. These stories helped create a sense of community, familiarity, and possibility among the participants.

On one spring evening, as I arrived at the ADAC meeting site, the DREAMer's story was being offered by Luis, a college student known to his fellow ADAC members as a championship runner. The story that Luis told that evening narrated a familiar struggle to afford a college education after Prop 300, but it was refracted through the lens of which university would offer him a scholarship, whether he could afford his running shoes, how he could make it to 5:00 a.m. practices when he was living at home, 30 miles from campus, and didn't have a car. It was was a story of laser-sharp focus and unflagging persistence. But as Luis went on to explain, he was not alone in his efforts: he had a mentor in his coach at ASU, who recognized his commitment and helped him find a dorm room on campus. It was there, he said, where he met another DREAMer named Matías and other DREAMers who had founded ADAC. Over time, they became a second community for him, a home apart from the track team. Their support was crucial, he said, when he endured his next challenge: the deportation of his older brother. As his ADAC colleagues helped him to speak out about his brother and against Obama's deportations, he found a new kind of voice and turned toward a new form of leadership.

The careful, supportive attention that greeted Luis's story that evening sent new members a surprising yet affirming message: you can share your most difficult moments, and you will be met with recognition and acceptance. Participants also learned from these stories the many things of which DREAMers may be capable, lessons that challenge not only state-supported stereotypes but the helplessness they may themselves be feeling. Verónica, recalling her first days at ADAC, described her wonder at the things she had heard: that undocumented youth could not only be student leaders—which some of them knew—but championship athletes or small business owners. She remarked, "I never thought I could do that. But then they opened my eyes."[13] These examples of resourcefulness, tenacity, or achievement may reactivate in youth participants the sense of capacity they experienced during their early years in school, before they began to confront the constraints of undocumented adulthood. But stories like Luis's are not simply narratives of individual triumph; they also emphasize the forms of mutual support and collective action—including that of an organization like ADAC itself—that enable undocumented youth to thrive.

After the opening DREAMer's story, ADAC meetings would often turn to the introduction of new members. Sometimes, emboldened by this organizational ritual, new members would share a bit of their own story: a "kernel" about their lives or a short description of what has brought them to the meeting. When a new member shares a story, the focus and support of those present quietly intensifies. Members respond with affirmations, nods, or enthusiastic finger snapping; if the new participant is struggling, members may take the speaker's hand or offer other supportive touch. This kind of storytelling and reception may help new members feel a part of the group. As Marisol, an ADAC youth member, described her first meeting:

> It was amazing to me to just be sitting there and having all these people stare at me, [as] I am exposing myself and being very vulnerable. . . . They held my hand, and they told me and my sister that it would be okay. And that's when I knew that I wanted to create that kind of safe space for other people as well. That was my first moment where I knew that that's where I wanted to be and that's what I wanted to do.[14]

As Marisol's comment underscores, activists at organizations like ADAC don't simply learn to share their story when they enter organizations. They also learn how to tell stories and how to think about the value of the stories they tell. This larger process is supported by organizational "stories about stories," which I refer to as "metanarratives."[15] These metanarratives are integral in motivating activists to tell stories and in helping them to share stories in ways that are effective for the movement.

Metanarratives: Organizational Stories about Stories

I first identified these organizational "stories about stories" serendipitously in the course of my research. During my first months in Arizona in 2012, I was struck by the ubiquity of storytelling in undocumented activism; I began to question activists about why stories were so prevalent and what benefits they offered the movement. I assumed, perhaps unreflectively, that their answers would help me to craft a first-order, descriptive account of how storytelling functioned in the movement. But what I heard in the answers I received was something different. I heard activists speak with conviction about effects of storytelling that they couldn't predictably discern from their position as storytellers. For example, they shared ideas about how, precisely, storytelling functioned to persuade listeners, though this was something it would have been hard for them to know, as they were offering rather than receiving stories. I heard them venture confident views on questions whose answers struck me as indeterminate or as a matter of perspective—for example, what kind of knowledge is most important in making immigration policy. I also noticed more overlap than I had expected in the answers I was hearing. Finally, I sensed in some of the statements about storytelling a kind of affective intensity that gave them more the character of a credo than of a simple description.

It gradually occurred to me that I was hearing not so much an empirical account of how narrative worked or what caused narrative to be an effective tool in various contexts as a form of received wisdom or *a shared organizational view about how narrative functioned.* I found support for some of these understandings in the training materials used, for example, in civic engagement campaigns.[16] But unlike storytelling itself, which tends to be learned by explicit example, metanarratives often seem to be disseminated informally: articulated, in kernel form, by lead organizers; modeled less explicitly by more experienced activists;

and circulated among newer participants until they became a kind of received organizational wisdom. A common feature of these metanarratives is that they construct storytelling as a source of strength and contribution for activists; viewing storytelling in this way helps to foster their outward-facing participation. Three metanarratives that are prominent in the Phoenix organizations I observed help to illustrate this point. I discuss them in turn.

Metanarrative 1: *Stories are a unique vehicle for persuasion because of their detail, immediacy, and the emotional connection they create between teller and listener.* This metanarrative was widely present among youth-focused organizations like LUCHA and ADAC. It speaks to a common question among new activists: Why do we tell stories when we advocate for ourselves with elected officials or with the public? Stories offered by undocumented activists present the primary "frames" of the movement: the paradigmatic figure(s) of the undocumented immigrant around whom organizing takes place, the injury or wrongs suffered by those figures, and the institutional or public response that may ameliorate these wrongs.[17] These messages may be delivered in other ways: as abstract claims or as arguments buttressed by various forms of data or empirical evidence. The benefits of storytelling within organizations may become rapidly apparent to activists, as they experience the sense of connection and the broadened vistas of possibility they create. But the advantages of stories in the public sphere may remain elusive. The first metanarrative speaks to this question. It roots the claim of stories in two features: their concreteness and immediacy and the emotional bonds they forge between storyteller and listener.[18] These advantages, often illustrated by activists with examples from their own experience, shape the ways that stories are formulated and narrated in the movement.

Storytelling gains purchase, first, from its concreteness: the description of lived experience lends detail and immediacy that would not be present in a more abstract account. Marisol, of ADAC, explained this advantage through a specific example:

> A lot of people just assume that . . . crossing the border is hard. But unless you walk through the desert yourself, unless you felt that kind of thirst, or unless you saw all the little graves out there in the desert from the people that just didn't make it, [you] don't really know what it means to cross the desert.[19]

A story from one who has made this crossing can provide the small yet revealing details—the searing thirst, the crosses marking the barren landscape of the desert—that those lacking experience cannot summon.

Such stories engage the imagination of audiences by helping them to see, hear, or feel the details of a situation they have never witnessed. This last insight points to the second major claim for storytelling: its affective charge creates a bond between storyteller and listener.

A story is not simply an array of factual details; it represents an important life experience that produces an emotional response in its narrator. It may be a powerful response, an echo of the joy or terror evoked by the initial experience, or it may be a subtler response, a moment of wistfulness or pride produced by the process of recollection, a current of impatience or urgency. Whatever their magnitude or coloration, these responses reveal the familiar human being in what might otherwise be an unfamiliar story. They invite listeners to engage the story affectively as well as cognitively, to empathize with the person before them. This empathetic connection, in turn, creates receptivity to the narrator's message. Some activists convey this insight by referencing the heart as the metaphorical seat of affective connection. "You can motivate and mobilize an entire community based on stories," Marisol declared. "Of course, you need facts to back up those stories and to reinforce it to the people that are more business-minded, *but everyone has a heart, and you can reach out to them through those stories.*"[20] Other activists describe a more specific process of empathetic identification. With storytelling, Luis explained:

> [You] pretty much force your shoes [onto somebody] and tell them to walk a mile. Because a lot of people, they're not open to that, and they try to disassociate ... any type of human connection.... [But with a story,] you tell them, "No, we're both humans here. Put on these shoes. They fit you too." That's when they start saying, "You know what? I think, in your shoes, I would have done the same thing."[21]

By helping listeners to see the storyteller as a human being like themselves, experiential narratives can enlist not just the imagination but the empathy of audiences who may be experientially distant from the events that stories relate.

At one level, this metanarrative may seem neutral in its effects on the empowerment of activists. Its nominal focus is not on activists but on what makes stories an effective way to communicate the frames of the movement. These strengths become desiderata that help activists shape the raw material of their lives into compelling stories. At another level, however, this metanarrative embodies a strong claim about who can wield the power of storytelling. The qualities that distinguish stories in the minds of activists are not the skills of the artist or expert. While narrative theorists might highlight the unexpected reversal or the abrupt shift in narrative perspective, undocumented activists cite the more straightforward virtues of concrete detail and emotional valence.[22] If these are indeed the advantages of storytelling, then virtually any undocumented activist can achieve them. This view of narrative persuasion is democratizing and authorizing; it makes clear that a range of activists can confidently contribute to the movement. This theme is captured explicitly in the second metanarrative.

Metanarrative 2: *Everyone has a story, and you can use it to change people's minds.* Undocumented activists view stories not simply as exemplary tales that capture the circumstances of their community in particularly compelling ways but as resources that every affected person possesses, which enable them to engage the outside world. This metanarrative is communicated explicitly in the course of many organization-based trainings.[23] But it is also expressed and reinforced through casual conversations among activists. The following story, from Patricia, a canvasser at PAZ, is typical:

> I was talking to a volunteer, and we were waiting for the bus or the light rail. . . . I was like, "So what's your story? Why are you here?" And she's like, "I don't have a story." And throughout my . . . trainings, they taught me that *everybody has a story.* So I started asking her questions, and she told me why she got involved. Her family's undocumented. One of her brothers went to jail. And she just started telling me basically everything that I didn't know about her. After that, I told her that that was her story, that she could use that when she went out to talk to her friends and to strangers. Then a few days ago, she was out registering people to vote, and I remember they came back in the van, and [she said], "We were going to register this guy, and he didn't want to, but I told him my story and totally changed his mind, and he registered to vote." So it's just like giving that voice to people that they don't know they have.[24]

Several elements in this story tend to recur in narratives communicating this shared insight. The first is the context of an unscripted conversation between fellow activists. The second is the doubt expressed by the newer activist: despite the reassurance of group leaders, the new recruit—like many new activists—remains unsure that she has a personal story distinctive or compelling enough to do the work of the movement. The third is a moment in which the more experienced activist elicits and affirms her colleague's story by asking a few simple questions about her life. What is striking about this aspect of the story is its nonspecificity.

The senior activist elicits a few details about her colleague's life and declares them sufficient to constitute her "story." These details are closer to annals or chronicles than to a full-fledged story; as described by the senior activist, her colleague's "story" reflects no temporal organization, no narrative structure.[25] Hearing this brief account, we are not certain exactly what in this "story" would persuade a listener. But persuade it does: the final element of this type of narrative is often the report that the novice's story has been offered and has produced a change of mind. In some stories like the Patricia's, the dynamic that produced the change remains obscure. In other variants, activists report that the story permitted them to reach an unlikely listener through an unexpected connection. In stories that convey this metanarrative, the opacity at the heart of the account may, paradoxically, be its strength.[26] Neither the vector of change nor the specific character of the story is crucial, because this metanarrative is not a story about how stories persuade. It is, rather, a story about how the life circumstances of virtually any undocumented activist can yield the desired effect: in other words, how virtually any undocumented immigrant can contribute to the work of the movement. This message is particularly powerful for participants who are young, or shy, or believe that their experience has given them no obvious resources—such as a story of detention or deportation might provide—for contributing to the movement. This lesson, about the resources that inhere in apparently undramatic lives and the surprising results they can produce, has helped many reticent organizational members emerge as robust public participants.

Metanarrative 3: *Manifesting vulnerability through storytelling incites action in listeners.* The first two metanarratives answer two questions: Who can tell a story? and What attributes make storytelling more compelling than other modes of political communication? But they say little about what makes one story better than another—that is, about the content of stories or the specific ways in which they should be told. This third metanarrative combines a view of the kind of substantive messages prospective audiences need to hear with a view of how those messages should be conveyed.

One purpose of public storytelling is to introduce undocumented immigrants to those who believe, whether accurately or not, that they have had no direct contact with undocumented lives. When you have looked a person in the eye, as activists sometimes say, and experienced that person as a fellow human being, it may be harder to accept demonizing narratives, such as those popularized by "attrition through enforcement."

But simple visibility is not enough. If undocumented activists want listeners to take action, they must describe an injury arising from their lack of status that demands a remedy, and that a listener may help them to obtain. DREAMers are thwarted in their efforts to secure an education or work in their chosen fields; they require the naturalization offered by the DREAM Act, or the work permits provided by DACA, to achieve their goals. Families confronting immigration enforcement face the loss of a loved one; they require executive relief from deportation to be reunited or to stay together. Listeners can help by contacting their representatives or pressing the president to issue an executive order; when elected officials are up for reelection, this too is a chance for audiences to make their views known. In one sense this metanarrative concerns the *content or structure of effective stories*: to motivate listeners to take action, you must tell a story that shows a harm imposed by the state and holds out the possibility of a state-created remedy.

But this metanarrative also conveys a view about *how stories should be told*. Because stories work by creating affective bonds between storytellers and listeners, storytellers must not only convey (factual) vulnerability at the hands of the state; they must also manifest (emotional) vulnerability before their audiences. This means making present to the listener experiences of fear, anguish, or hopelessness in order to elicit some kind of response. As one youth activist put it, expressing pain "cause[s] pity, that causes a feeling of empathy or anger . . . and that can lead to action."[27] To initiate this dynamic, emotions that might otherwise be considered private must be allowed to surface in public settings. Marisol cited her experience at a large voter registration meeting: "So I found myself tearing up in front of 300 people. And then I look out to the audience, and then these 300 people are crying. They're hugging each other. *And then I knew that that's when my message would come across the strongest.*"[28]

While this metanarrative may be authorizing in its inclusiveness—any participant, at least in theory, can communicate difficult emotions—it evokes ambivalence in some participants. These activists feel a tension between sharing those feelings that will communicate their plight and avoiding the projection of "weakness." Weakness, whether signaled by tears, or despair, or evidence of inadequate resistance, is a felt taboo for many activists, which they describe in varying ways.[29] For some, revealing weakness violates cultural norms. Among Latino immigrants, Reyna Montoya, an ADAC leader, explained, "it's [l]ike 'let's move on'—like 'we're strong . . . we got it. We have to keep going.'"[30] For others, showing vulnerability may conflict with an ingrained habit of "staying strong" for their families, or with their emerging sense of themselves as "fighters" for their communities.[31] Consequently, some activists struggle to reconcile the demands of this organizational metanarrative with their personal, cultural, familial, or even activist norms about manifesting vulnerability.

Some activists achieve a kind of reconciliation by crafting stories that underscore their agency, even as they describe injury and manifest suffering. Marisol, who saw a moment of power in the tears she shared with her audience, quickly reminded them: "I know we're here crying, and we're thinking we're the victims, but don't think like that. We're warriors too. We can get our message across, and you have rights. Don't let people mistreat you." In this brief message, Marisol signaled competence ("We can get our message across"), capacity for resistance ("We're warriors too"), and moral and political agency ("you have rights . . . don't let people mistreat you").

Yet for other activists, a sustainable compromise between sharing vulnerability and feeling agency is more elusive. For these individuals, manifesting vulnerability may erode their sense of personal agency, even as it helps their community. Ileana Salinas is a longtime youth participant who became active after a two-day detention when the car in which she was riding was stopped by law enforcement. She has found satisfaction in being part of the movement, but telling her story, particularly to older, white audiences, has given her an uncomfortable feeling: "It's like I need to be able to show my pain so that you can feel something for me, so that you can take action from this."[32] I was initially surprised by Ileana's sense that she had been collaborating in her own victimization, not simply because I have heard her tell versions of her story, with grit and composure, on many occasions, but because what I have always heard in this story is her uncanny, resourceful self-assertion. When I mentioned this to her, however, she demurred: "I just recently went to give like a sermon [at a largely white church] and I talked about the story," she said. "The feeling that I got afterwards, even though it wasn't the feeling that I wanted to bring, was more like the victimization. I felt more like the pity instead of like, 'oh, we can do something.'"[33] Ileana remains committed to the movement, but when she conveys her pain to those outside her community, she feels not the possibility of shared agency ("oh, we can do something") but a compromising sense that she is presenting herself to be seen as an object of pity.[34]

Thus for some activists, the effect of storytelling on their personal, if not political, agency remains an open question. But a more common feeling—particularly among new participants—is a need for guidance and support. After years of suppressing, neglecting, or redirecting painful emotions as a means of "moving forward" under challenging circumstances, new participants may need direction and reassurance in attempting greater emotional transparency. Natalia, a canvasser for PAZ, voiced this view:

> I can [now] connect to others the way I could never do it before, because . . . [I allow] myself to be a little vulnerable, in a way. [I]t's something that you have to work on a lot. You don't develop being genuine all by yourself. . . . It takes a village to raise a child, they said, so it takes a village to become who you are in [a public campaign].[35]

Offering this and other guidance that equips undocumented activists to function in an unfamiliar and challenging public sphere is the goal of a second practice: the creation of organizational "emotion cultures."

THE ROLE OF EMOTION CULTURES IN ORGANIZATIONS OF UNDOCUMENTED IMMIGRANTS

The storytelling by undocumented immigrants and the metanarratives that support it rely directly on emotional expression and perception of the people in the storytelling exchange. Yet the emotional dimensions of storytelling—which help participants engage in outward-facing persuasion and help that persuasion do its work—are but one example of the pivotal, yet complex, role that emotions play in undocumented activism. Emotion pervades the public life of this movement; marches are buoyed by solidarity, by turns dignified, hopeful, and defiant. The words of speakers are flooded with feeling, whether pride or resolve, grief or outrage. Within organizations, emotions also run close to the surface. Participants tear up in the course of meetings; they share their commitment to each other in words and through touches, hugs, and enthusiastic finger snapping. These emotions are vivid and spontaneous, reflecting and enhancing the meaning of activism to participants. Yet within organizations, emotions may also be visibly supported, cultivated, and even managed. Organizers remind participants regularly that "DREAMers never quit" or that "the community has [their] back." These practices are part of an "emotion culture" that has emerged, in varying forms, in Phoenix's undocumented organizations.[36] Through this culture, organizations introduce and normalize a set of emotional dispositions toward activism, other activists, and state actors. They also offer a more explicit emotional pedagogy that suggests the kinds of feelings activists should be experiencing, and when. Organizational practices thus shape the emotional dimension of activism, both for new and for more experienced participants.

The recognition that organizational "emotion cultures" may be crucial for activists—particularly those mobilizing from the political margins—is not new, either for organizers or for scholars of social movements. These practices, for example, pervaded the civil rights movement, in which mass meetings, replete with storytelling, song, and emotional exchange, helped persuade activists of their "first class citizenship"[37] and counter their fears of repressive, state-supported violence.[38] This work, however, is particularly vital in undocumented organizations. Lack of status, and targeting through immigration enforcement, can undermine the sense of confidence, capacity, or authorization necessary to engage in public claims making. And if mobilizing emotions are difficult to foster, demobilizing emotions of fear and frustration may arise all too easily in a movement that runs risks with almost any form of public visibility and has often been thwarted in its larger policy aspirations.

To shine a light on the ways that emotion cultures function in organizations of undocumented immigrants, this section explores how they shape the socialization of activists in two kinds of groups: community-based organizations (focused on adults and families, including youth) and youth-based organizations (focused specifically on youth participants). Through their emotion cultures, both types of organizations perform two general functions. First, they create an environment that mitigates the effects of "legal violence" and fosters those emotions that enable immigrants to mobilize. In particular, through the sharing of stories, meals, cultural events, or other activities that bring out common experiences, struggles, or values, organizations nurture the sense of solidarity among activists that brings meaning and greater security to outward-facing activism. They also cultivate feelings of worthiness and confidence in new participants. Second, through their emotion cultures, organizations manage emotions that might impede or discourage ongoing movement activity. Drawing on language, role modeling, and emotionally infused practices, organizations ease the fears of enforcement that arise with public visibility; counter the stress or fatigue that can arise from a steep learning curve; and allay the frustrations produced by governmental delays, hypocrisy, or failures of recognition. Because each type of organization works with prospective activists with different kinds of experiences, vulnerabilities, and strengths, their emotion cultures often have distinct features and achieve these goals in different ways. The following sections describe emotion cultures first in community-based organizations and then in youth organizations, and highlight similarities and differences between them.[39]

Emotion Cultures in Community-Based Organizations

As with storytelling, the operation of emotion cultures function visibly in the meetings through which organizations engage their members and welcome new participants. On a Monday in November 2014, I attended a weekly "community meeting" at Puente. This meeting, which brought together some forty or fifty people, particularly families, showed how emotion cultures infuse the activities of this organization and help to direct and motivate its participants. On that day, as evening approached, we filtered into Puente's "community center," a large, refurbished house in a residential neighborhood north of the capitol. As usual, the meeting began with shared food and conversation. People clustered in groups, sharing greetings and news, while toddlers careened between friendly adults and children chased each other around the crowded hall. Folding tables were spread with *cafecito* and plates of *pan*, *frijoles*, or whatever members had brought to share. The only sign that this was a purposive political gathering was a member seated near the door, greeting those who were new and taking contact information. Though most conversations were in Spanish, reflecting a predominance of Latino members, Anglo participants like myself were welcomed in English by the official greeter and by various members. These members approached warmly—one smiling woman placed a cup of hot chocolate in my hands—and encouraged us to make a plate and meet others who had gathered. The eating and greeting continued for half an hour or more, with no sense of pressure to proceed to official business. As people wound up their conversations, and school-age children moved their play outside the building, the room was configured into a large, multilayered semicircle, and the meeting began.

At this meeting, as is typical at Puente, the proceedings were casual: parents fed or comforted babies; people ducked in and out of the room with cell phones as the need arose. The meeting also reflected no apparent hierarchy: this meeting was facilitated by one of a small number of youth leaders, other meetings have been led by adult members. Meanwhile, Carlos Garcia, Puente's longtime director and lead organizer, strolled around the perimeter of the room, greeting a late arrival or transacting a bit of business with a community member. As is customary at Puente, the meeting opened with a question, posed to the group as a whole. The questions that are used to open these meetings vary in nature; they may be about organizational direction or an invitation to share a more personal reflection. At this meeting, immediately following Dia de los Muertos, the question was a personal prompt: "Describe a departed relative who was particularly important to you." At another meeting, the first after the new year, the question was organizational and forward looking: "What are your aspirations for Puente this year?"

On this evening, once the initial question was posed, the discussion quickly moved from the facilitator to those assembled. People responded, beginning at one side of the semicircle and winding around the room to the other. Some offered a few hesitant words; others spoke emphatically, humorously, or at length. On nights when there is a large turnout, this sharing can take a long time; more than half of this particular meeting was devoted to answering the opening question. Yet every person was given time to speak, and those gathered listened patiently, nodding, murmuring, and sometimes laughing or clapping warmly, in response to the answers.

Only after each person had spoken, and the discussion leader had offered a few concluding words, did the "business" portion of the meeting begin. Organizers that evening discussed individual cases, in which Puente was fighting the detention or deportation of a community member. They described internet petitions or direct action events used to target a member of Congress, an ICE official, or the public. These announcements were led from the front of the room but punctuated by additions from those seated in the semicircle. Throughout, organizers and members voiced appreciation for the contributions of participants, who had played roles ranging from planning to public action. At the community meetings I have witnessed, there tends to be particular enthusiasm for those who have undertaken risky tactics—direct action, civil disobedience, frank public critiques of state action—or those who have persisted in speaking out about detained loved ones. They are lauded for their courage (sometimes described as "heroes") and celebrated for their commitment to the community. The facilitator at this meeting then described efforts to support families affected by detention and deportation, with members sharing what they knew about those most severely impacted or making specific requests for assistance. This portion of the meeting was the most sober, as many know—and all fear—this kind of suffering. When there are developments in pending legal actions—against Sheriff Joe Arpaio, for example—there may be a brief talk by a lawyer who has been invited to explain the details. On that evening, the meeting concluded with a discussion of upcoming actions. Planning began on the spot, with those responsible energetically enlisting volunteers. Once business was complete, a Cesar Chavez–inspired unity clap, familiar in many Phoenix organizations, ended the meeting. There was no rush to depart when business was complete; more greetings and conversation followed, as community members gradually dispersed.

Though a weekly meeting at Puente can feel more like a neighborhood potluck than a meeting of a grassroots resistance organization, its environment offers a window on Puente's emotion culture. Although it welcomes youth, Puente is a "community" organization, focusing on adults and families.[40] Organizing undocumented adults can present distinctive challenges. As immigration sociologists have observed, adults do not undergo the empowering, integrative socialization that undocumented youth may experience in the public schools. They are precariously employed in low-wage, often exploitative jobs, which remind them constantly of their vulnerability to enforcement; they are, in fact, most frequently targeted for detention or deportation. Many have developed self-isolating routines—Greg Prieto calls them "shells"—designed to protect themselves and their families from official encounters and minimize chances of immigration enforcement.[41] Their ongoing responsibilities for supporting their families leave them less time and less mental or emotional bandwidth for activism. And their fierce stigmatization in anti-immigrant localities like Phoenix may persuade them that they have less to offer. Though some organizers view these tendencies as barriers, noting that adults are "more hammered" by the circumstances of "attrition through enforcement"[42] or have less time or energy to commit to activism,[43] Carlos Garcia approaches the question less categorically. He notes that "some people have it within them" to turn outward and resist, whether or not anything specific has happened to them: it is "in them that they want[] to get involved, and then fight and in one point get arrested and risk their whole livelihood on it."[44] Others are pressed to take action they might never have contemplated because "their [] family member or someone they know has been caught."[45] Still others follow a more gradual path, moving from small acts of planning or logistical support to more ambitious or risky tactics. For organizers, Garcia explains, what is important is "meeting people where they're at and then developing them as they go."[46] Although this credo may mean providing specific, graduated options for participation, "meeting people where they're at" has an emotional component as well. It means enabling participants to become members of a social movement organization by first becoming members of a community and fostering the solidarity with others that eases fear and fuels confidence. In this way, even the most tentative or fearful may be encouraged to participate.

This effort can be glimpsed in many features of the weekly meeting. As people enter the meeting, there is no clear sense of joining an organization or a campaign, no abrupt transition that signals to newcomers that they are leaving their familiar, daily lives behind. People arrive with their spouses, their children, maybe an offering of food. They may see neighbors or those they recognize from their larger community. They spend a good chunk of the evening in friendly conversation. Participants may be reassured, even bolstered, by the warmth of the welcome and the appreciation of everyone present. This is one message of the opening question and the patient attention to answers from everyone present: *Here you are respected and valued, whether you are a tentative visitor or a veteran activist, whether you are sharing your personal experience, or proposing a direction for the organization.* In addition, as speakers voice aspirations or offer glimpses of personal experience, listeners realize that they are among people who share important dimensions of their own experience—as migrants, as Latinos, as members of families or neighborhoods. In that sense, the opening question plays a role that is similar to storytelling in youth organizations.

In addition, newcomers witness the unmistakable commitment of community members to each other. This may be demonstrated through physical touch—hugs abound as entering families greet each other—or through verbal expression. Most importantly, however, it is expressed through acts of solidaristic support. Families undergoing enforcement-related trouble receive the immediate and resourceful support of the entire community, whether it is help with expenses, a ride to the detention center, or a community-wide vigil held on behalf of a loved one. It is also clear, as discussion leaders pay tribute to successful actions, that members of this community are capable of unexpected things. Whether in energetic and resourceful planning or extraordinary forms of resistance, members of the community routinely surprise themselves and their neighbors with their capacity to act. Amid such demonstrations of capacity, solidarity becomes not simply reassuring but a source of aspiration. These surprising acts by the people sitting beside you suggest that you may have untapped reservoirs of capacity as well.

These powerful emotional messages are part of a larger organizing approach that Garcia refers to as "the open hand and the closed fist."

The "closed fist," Garcia explains, "is the one we use to fight back" against the state's incursions.[47] This might mean forming defense committees or protesting to demonstrate resolve and raise community consciousness, at visible sites such as the capitol, the ICE building, or Joe Arpaio's Fourth Avenue jail. In these actions undocumented community members could have their first taste of public action, perhaps under "cover" of their documented counterparts, and experience its satisfactions. Over time, with growing confidence and with the demands of varied campaigns, the "closed fist" might encompass coming out as undocumented or forms of direct action, from boycotts to hunger strikes to civil disobedience.

But this kind of resistance effort can be sustained in the face of tangible risks only if those becoming active feel supported by a larger community and their connections with each other. This logic was crucial at a time when state action was aimed at putting undocumented residents under siege. Garcia observes:

> The intent [of attrition through enforcement] was to make our lives so miserable that we self deport. So our goal is to find ways, in which people can find community or kind of reverse that feeling that they'll self deport. That they'll be supported by their community, they'll have events, and they'll learn their rights. Where they'll have those sorts of things and won't feel like they have to self deport.[48]

As "attrition through enforcement" first unfolded, the "open hand" strategy that Garcia introduced at Puente sought primarily to deny Pearce and Arpaio their victory. Now, however, it fortifies immigrants for the mobilizations that lie ahead. The "open hand" nurtures the emotional resilience of the community: a quality that makes everyone more secure. It is fostered not only in weekly meetings in the shared tasks of artistic creation: the colorful banners, masks, or T-shirts whose creation forms the energizing prelude to major actions. It is also nurtured through the group's frequent fiestas, dances, and cultural events, featuring singers, musicians, and spoken-word artists. These events strengthen emotional bonds and cultural pride and fight despair and ongoing hardship with moments of creativity and pleasure. There is no blinking hardship in this group. Members lose loved ones to deportation, struggle through detention, face neighborhood saturation patrols, and watch work evaporate in the face of a threatened raid. But they also hold fiercely to family and friends, support those most affected, and come together for moments of joy. Watching others around them, they learn to push themselves—in ways both old and new—to keep their communities safe.

Emotion Cultures in Youth Organizations

Puente, as a community-based organization, has developed emotion cultures that respond to the mixed-age membership and the prevalence of families in that context. But other organizations that focus more directly on youth participants, such as ADAC, develop different emotion cultures. Despite the differences, these emotion cultures also play an integral role in preparing new members for the organization's work and in helping undocumented participants initiate and persist in outward-facing activism.

In youth organizations, emotion cultures engage new participants in a different way. Rather than fortifying people through their familiar identities, they inaugurate new identities that draw on strengths youths already possess but place them in demanding, exhilarating new roles. Young participants embrace these roles with the support of others, whose fears and aspirations resemble their own, and who are undergoing a similar transition alongside them. The emotion culture of youth organizations doesn't so much meet new participants where they are—in the manner of community-based organizations—as invite them to take the leap to a new place. This can be an exciting place; youth organizations in Phoenix are hives of activity, with confident, skilled youth leaders informing their community and executing bold and highly visible actions. But it can also be a daunting place; youth quickly recognize that they have joined a high-risk, high-frustration movement. They must manage an ongoing fear that their public action will bring them to the attention of law enforcement and expose them to apprehension, detention, and deportation. There is also a steep learning curve for people with little public experience or exposure; activists often feel overwhelmed by the tasks they are required to take on. The Phoenix movement, like the movement nationwide, has also faced a steady stream of disappointments, particularly in their efforts at the federal level; participants must often confront these challenges even as they are managing the emotional and logistical fallout from a friend or family member's detention or deportation.[49] Consequently, participants moving toward a role of with new visibility and responsibility may, particularly at the outset, feel fearful, frustrated, disappointed, or generally overwhelmed or exhausted.

But navigating this emotional transition is essential for the participants to be able to engage in their work at the organization. And it is through stories that this emotional transition begins. Stories, as we have seen, draw out empowering elements of identity that can be submerged in the hostility of the immediate environment.[50] Stories also ease feelings of demoralization or stigma that can impede activism; they foster kinship and connection among youth who have experienced similar challenges.[51] The bond they feel with others can be a motivating force in their outward-facing activism; as one teenage participant put it, "the fact that they're your friends, you're pretty much doing it . . . not [so] much for yourself but for them as well, in honor of the friendship."[52]

But if stories initiate the transition to a demanding role, that transition is also fostered by a multilayered emotional pedagogy. As at Puente, modeling is key. Youth develop confidence that they can take on the difficult roles of activists because they have seen others like them do so.[53] In youth organizations—in which storytelling is a central part of activism—this means learning not only to project resolve but to display vulnerability, revealing emotions that are complicated or painful. Organizers walk a fine line in this regard, projecting a businesslike, can-do attitude toward the challenges of the work but not hesitating to share powerful emotional responses. At one meeting, I watched an ADAC organizer describe a highly publicized border fence reunion she had organized among a group of DREAMers and their relatives who remained in Mexico. Although she was confident and matter-of-fact in describing the logistical obstacles she had surmounted to bring this event to fruition, she teared up when describing the encounter between the youth and their loved ones.[54]

Organizers may address feelings of inadequacy or exhaustion by offering participants new frames for understanding what they are feeling. One vehicle for this reframing is aphorisms—memorable expressions that circulate among activists—that help participants to reinterpret uncomfortable feelings associated with activism. Leaders in youth organizations often tell new participants, for example, that "working outside your comfort zone is the way you grow."[55] An organizer's version of "pain is weakness leaving the body," this aphorism encourages new participants to interpret their frequent sense of being out of their depth as a sign that they are acquiring new skills and growing as activists. Organizers also use "emotives," descriptive statements about what people are feeling that function as normative directives, to encourage in listeners the feelings they purport to describe.[56] Emotives may be used in youth organizations to counter frustration: "DREAMers never quit" or "we thrive on adversity" were expressions I often heard.[57] The normative force of the description arises not only from its (repeated) assertion but also from its connection to a new and valued identity: of DREAMer, of empowered immigrant or activist.[58]

Emotives have also been vital in the management of fear; they supplement the first line of defense, which is usually solidarity. Deep ties to similarly situated others do not simply persuade activists that they have value and that their capacity will be extended through collectivity. They persuade participants that when they act, the community "has their back." Organizers remind activists of those occasions when community response has mobilized the public or moved the government to exercise its discretion when members are detained.[59] This mutual assistance helps participants to feel safer.[60] They report that they feel more willing to march, to protest, to come out as undocumented, or to engage in acts of civil disobedience, because they know that if they are harassed by law enforcement or detained in the course of public risk-taking, they are part of a community that will be with them; will defend them; and, if they are taken by enforcement officials, will work assiduously for their release.[61]

Yet sometimes more is needed to propel activists into the fray, at times when they cannot anticipate its outcome or implications. Here they have been buoyed by the best-known emotive in this movement: "We are undocumented and unafraid."[62] This phrase is not a straightforward description of what people are feeling; in fact, some activists describe using it at times when they have felt very much afraid.[63] In part, "undocumented and unafraid" articulates an aspiration: it is the bold and unapologetic stance from which organizers hope to engage state actors. For activists, expressing this aspiration—with the thread of defiance it connotes—can help to resolve emotional ambivalence in the direction of pride and self-assertion. Marisol, the ADAC activist, explained: "Speaking publicly is very scary. Sharing your story is very scary. Having a one-on-one civil debate with an anti-immigrant person is very scary."[64] But declaring herself to be "undocumented and unafraid" draws out a stronger response, a feeling that "I refuse to be a victim of my circumstances. I refuse to be turned into this little person because of a situation I'm in."[65]

This emotive may also achieve its effect through reassertion over time. As activists repeat it, and officials or members of the public respond to it, feeling "undocumented and unafraid" can become a self-fulfilling prophesy, often reinforced by the fearless actions participants take as they claim it, whether "coming out" at a public rally or engaging in civil disobedience. Alejandra, another youth activist, explained:

[In the beginning] it was . . . I guess, like an empowerment phrase . . . even if [people] were still afraid, they didn't have to show they were afraid to the public . . . even if they were dying inside . . . you had to put that face on where it was—"you know what? I'm not afraid." As people started telling their stories and started coming out, they started noticing that it really wasn't something to be afraid of; that it was something you could live with, that you were ok with. [And] when you sa[id] so, certainly people believe[d] you . . . so even if it started as . . . an empowerment phrase, it became true over the years.[66]

In the sense that it produces, over time, the feeling it claims to describe, being "undocumented and unafraid" is a performative strategy—a way of bringing into being, by asserting or enacting—that works in the domain of the emotions.[67]

A final strategy for mitigating fear and frustration is the purposeful fostering of counteremotions: the present-focused emotion of joy, the future-focused emotion of hope, as well as the broadly fortifying emotion of solidarity with others. This strategy has an important legacy in high-risk movements; the role of song, for example, in the civil rights movement has been hailed as bringing solidaristic joy and release to fearful participants.[68] All of the organizations I worked with in Phoenix—whether youth focused or community based—cultivate a sense of hope or possibility by celebrating small victories, particularly in a campaign whose larger outcomes may be disappointing or uncertain.[69] A week after the 2012 elections, the Adios Arpaio campaign staged a picket and rally, with the announced goal of urging the secretary of state to complete the counting of provisional ballots.[70] A rally that might have been dimmed by the disappointing victory of Arpaio at the polls became instead a celebration of the fifty thousand new voters who had been registered. Participants chanted, cheered, and lifted their candles to the possibility of "turning Arizona Blue."[71] This exuberant expression of hope in the future buoyed exhausted campaigners for the continuation of their efforts.

The injection of moments of joy into protest activity itself may also ease the weight of fear, fatigue, or uncertainty in long and difficult campaigns. During the Not1More Deportation campaign, for example, protesters led by Puente activists marched to the Phoenix ICE building for a mass civil disobedience action.[72] When they found the office closed (in what they viewed as probable anticipation of their action),[73] they staged a fiesta on the grounds of the Phoenix ICE building, dancing under garlands of paper flowers.[74] The fiesta was an act of defiance in the face of the ICE office's defensive strike, but it was also an occasion for release, cohesion, and joy among tense protesters with a long campaign ahead of them.

In both youth-focused collectives like ADAC and communitybased organizations like Puente, organizers enlarge the self-conceptions and fortify the emotions of new participants in ways that are adapted to their distinctive circumstances and needs. These vital transitions equip participants to move toward outward-facing activism. The practice of storytelling, as discussed earlier in this chapter, helps redefine undocumented status to encompass resourcefulness and possibility; emotion cultures buttress activists for mobilization and foster adaptability and tenacity. Both practices cultivate the solidaristic bonds among activists that not only nurture individual agency but create collective force for self-determination and resistance.

Yet as some examples in this chapter demonstrate, the practices of undocumented organizations also have an aspirational, performative flavor. The emotion cultures of these organizations, for example, incite participants to assume emotional stances that assist activism, which they project first and assimilate more thoroughly as they gain experience and confidence. Such practices may be particularly suited to undocumented activists—inexperienced with or daunted by visibility and public action—who must learn and grow as they go. The most striking example of this aspirational enactment in the movement is its strategy of performative citizenship—a third key practice—in which undocumented activists, in the course of their campaigns, enact roles evocative of the political membership that they hope to have formally recognized. This practice, which joins with storytelling and emotion cultures to empower undocumented participants as they enter the political field, is the focus of the next chapter.

CHAPTER 3

Performative Citizenship
and the Adios Arpaio Campaign

After appreciating what a citizen is, I make an effort to be what
some people say I am not . . . a citizen is a person that cares
about their community, that stays on top of what's happening
and that doesn't just only worry about [themselves] but also
looks out for others. And that's the kind of thinking that I try
to keep in my mind . . . not only [to] convince people that I can
be a citizen, but prove to them that I am fully capable of being
what a citizen stands for.

—Roberto, team lead from 2012 civic engagement campaigns

The concept of citizenship. We try to follow that. Because it's
what we want, ultimately. Right? . . . You have to be it, to
become it.

—Alejandra, canvasser from 2012 civic engagement campaigns

Roberto is an undocumented immigrant from Mexico. He migrated with
his family as a preteen and had lived in Phoenix for roughly a decade
when I met him in 2013. He had watched as his older sister, an excellent
student, struggled to attend ASU after the passage of Prop. 300, which
barred in-state tuition to undocumented students. She became a founding
member of Arizona DREAM Act Coalition (ADAC), and in 2011 Roberto
became involved as well, when he drove a group of ADAC members to
a United We Dream Congress. By then he had "[fallen] from the cloud
of being just a typical person" and begun to realize, as he approached
the end of high school and began to consider college, that his struggle
would be the same as his sister's.[1] He was increasingly drawn to ADAC's
meetings, where he admired the hopeful energy of the young people and
heard stories that resonated with his own experience. In summer 2012

he joined ADAC's DREAM Voter campaign, realizing how important it was for people to vote.[2] "No matter how many people hear your story," he explained. "If they don't get into action, nothing is going to change." In his mind, voting was a vehicle for transforming empathy into action.

Although he described himself as "quieter than other people," Roberto quickly became one of ADAC's most successful canvassers. He listened carefully to the stories of prospective voters; he explained the urgent stakes of the vote. Soon he was canvassing every day, first, he said, "for passion. And then, it became a responsibility to me. I felt like if I didn't do it, who was going to do it?" As his comment makes clear, Roberto began to draw from the campaign an appreciation of the meaning of citizenship. It was not simply a question of "the card . . . or the papers," nor was it a question of how American citizens behaved, because many failed to exercise the privilege of voting that their status gave them. Instead, through his experience canvassing, Roberto developed an ideal sense of a citizen as "someone who cares about their community, that stays on top of what's happening and that doesn't just only worry about [themselves] but also looks out for others." His campaign work not only instilled this view of civic commitment, it became a way to manifest it: "to prove that [he was] fully capable of being what a citizen stands for."

Roberto's intention to be "what a citizen stands for" illustrates the kind of "performative citizenship" that undocumented activists in Phoenix regularly utilized in their efforts. Like the selfproduced resources that initiated the movement (see chapter 1) or the storytelling and emotion cultures that prepared undocumented participants for activism (see chapter 2), "performative citizenship" has become one of the central practices through which Phoenix activists conduct their work and through which their political consciousness has taken shape.

This chapter outlines the pivotal role that performative citizenship played in forming activists as political participants as they pursued their work in the political field. It highlights how taking on visible roles associated in the public mind with full political membership produced not only political knowledge but a sense of legitimacy and belonging among those fighting the hostility of Arizona officials. For activists like Roberto and Alejandra, citizenship was not simply a status to which activists aspired: it was a socially meaningful, politically transformative role that they claimed, through intention and through practice.

Performative citizenship, as a practice conducted over time, produced two kinds of legitimation, both of which brought activists closer to the formal membership they sought. First, these tactics challenged, and in some cases revised, perceptions of undocumented immigrants among officials and members of the public.[3] Second, these tactics transformed the subjectivity of many undocumented activists themselves, providing the knowledge, experience, and expectations that enabled them to internalize the political belonging they publicly performed. This chapter looks at strategies of performative citizenship used by Phoenix activists in their struggle against "attrition through enforcement" by focusing on the Adios Arpaio campaign, a voter registration effort aimed at unseating the sheriff of Maricopa County. By shining a light on activists' work in this campaign, this chapter makes clear how performative citizenship helped to create in fact the kind of political membership activists hoped to have recognized in law.

PERFORMING POLITICAL BELONGING

Undocumented activists in Phoenix are not the first migrants without legal status to take on political roles traditionally performed by citizens. In the United States and other immigrant-receiving nations, activists without status have participated in a variety of public campaigns. They have demonstrated and advocated, displaying the knowledge, commitment, and authority conventionally associated with citizenship. These campaigns may seek rights or benefits paradigmatically associated with formal membership, such as the right to vote in school board or local elections[4] or access to in-state tuition at educational institutions.[5] They may seek legislation that makes the lives of undocumented residents less precarious, such as protection from retaliation or wage theft in the workplace.[6] Some scholars have characterized these efforts as reflecting an alternate form of citizenship, often though not always focused on local institutions, which contrasts with the weak engagement that is often typical of formal citizens.[7] Others have described them as challenging dominant views of citizenship as a static, binary status, and of sovereign nation-states as controlling their boundaries and their membership.[8]

As these analyses suggest, political engagement by noncitizens can alter the political landscape in polities where it occurs and transform participants themselves. It is for this reason that some scholars have described it as "performative citizenship,"[9] because, like J. L. Austin's performative utterances,[10] it can enact the change—the transformation of the polity and the political "subjectification" of new participants—that it asserts.[11] Or, as Judith Butler described the performance of gender, it can recursively reconstruct a binary—the distinction between citizens and noncitizens—that was presumed to be given.[12] Performative citizenship can produce change by creating a rupture in political conventions or expectations; it can also produce a longer-term effect that reconstitutes shared expectations about who may participate in politics and how. My primary focus, here and in the chapters that follow, is less on rupture than on ongoing reconstitution.

Rupture is created by new forms of action or appearance that depart dramatically from "established practices, status[es], and order[s]."[13] When undocumented immigrants marched against the Sensenbrenner bill in 2006, they unexpectedly claimed a space of political demand and action that had previously been associated with citizenship. Their protest challenged citizens' expectations and inaugurated a new political reality in which noncitizens—even those lacking any formal status— could be engaged participants.[14] Immigrants' public self-identification as undocumented, as Peter Nyers has observed, produced a similar moment of abrupt departure. Because, as a matter of history and convention, "citizenship has been the identity through which claims to be political are enacted,"[15] undocumented activists who break their expected silence and "assert themselves as [] visible and speaking being[s]"[16] break with that order and reconstitute themselves as political participants.

Though moments of rupture may upend expectations and offer a new vision of the political domain—one in which immigrants without legal status are visible, claims-making actors—the recuperative power of conventional assumptions and practices is great. The legacy of the 2006 marches against the Sensenbrenner bill, for example, suggests the limits of even powerful disruption. Though the marches rolled out across the country, the vote—and other attributes of formal membership—proved elusive.[17] Whether practices that create a rupture can do more than seize the momentary attention of the public and suggest novel yet distant possibilities depends on a more durable kind of civic performance.

This form of civic performance, which voter engagement activism in Phoenix illustrates, aims not to rupture but to reconstitute the public domain, as well as citizenship itself. It allows activists to bring closer "the reality they speak of," whether that reality be their substantive demands or their own transformation into political subjects.[18] These efforts rely on two forms of legitimacy. One is the legitimacy of new participants in the eyes of the public. Those who witness an undocumented activist engaged in public debate may glimpse a startling new image of political belonging, something they haven't previously considered. But before they can respond to her demands, they need to accept and integrate into their vision of politics this new image of the public participant. The second form of legitimacy concerns the political consciousness of activists themselves. A participant's sense of herself as a political subject may be glimpsed in a moment, but it becomes a more durable, familiar identity—the kind necessary to sustain ongoing participation in a social movement—only through action and reflection over time. The mode of performative citizenship that addresses these internal and external needs for legitimacy, like the mode that produces more dramatic departures from political expectations, involves taking on roles paradigmatically associated with citizenship. However, these are not brief, striking roles such as appearance or self-identification. They are more sustained activities that model and teach attitudes and responsibilities conventionally associated with citizenship.

Often these activities reflect roles that are widely accepted as features of political membership, from lobbying Congress, to asserting constitutionally protected rights, to registering voters. The reconstitution implicit in such engagement comes not from the innovative character of the acts, which are familiar to the point of being prosaic, but from the novel demands they may be used to convey and from their performance by those without legal status. Speaking to elected officials, or registering neighbors to vote are not proscribed for undocumented people, yet political convention associates them so strongly with state-validated forms of political membership that it may be surprising, even disorienting, to see them performed by those who lack legal status.[19] But while the performance may create a moment of incongruity or rupture, what allows it to transform the public sphere in more durable ways are the changes in perspective that ongoing activity of this kind can produce, in observers and participants themselves.

In this chapter and in chapters 4–6, I explore three modes of performative citizenship that have emerged among activists in Phoenix. The most paradigmatic, and least controversial, concerns participation within formal institutions and processes, such as the electoral process. This mode of performative citizenship is illuminated by the Adios Arpaio campaign of 2012. This effort, which sought to register and turn out Latino voters to defeat the anti-immigrant sheriff of Maricopa County, featured visible, broad-based neighborhood canvassing, performed by undocumented immigrants. As noted earlier, it proved to be transformative for those involved and legitimating for important segments of the public. Toward the end of the chapter, I introduce two modes of performative citizenship that have been more uncertain in their effects.

One is an "oppositional" form of performative citizenship that operates outside of institutional settings and sometimes outside of the law itself. These highly visible acts, undertaken when institutional processes have stalled or failed, are exemplified by direct action and civil disobedience. They bolster the self-conceptions of participants and their communities, yet they spark varied responses in observers. A final category of performative citizenship, which I describe as rights claiming, is more modulated in its opposition, because is it mediated by law. It involves rights-based challenges to public officials that occur in the context of law enforcement encounters or federal lawsuits. These actions fuel the political confidence of some participants, particularly in the vital context of law enforcement encounters, but their role in external legitimation is limited by their lesser visibility.

Like the emotion cultures explored in chapter 2, tactics of performative citizenship reflect varying combinations of intentionality and intuition.[20] While I occasionally heard organizers speak of modeling a certain kind of civic commitment, such as when Living United for Change in Arizona (LUCHA) planned a cleanup of the neighborhood immediately around the capitol, more often there was simply an unspoken—yet symbolically powerful—connection between the roles taken on by undocumented activists and culturally familiar performances of citizenship.[21] Activists sometimes articulated this connection, even when organizers did not. For example, ADAC activists Roberto and Alejandra, whose words opened this chapter, saw the performative potential of civic engagement in canvassing, particularly in relation to its prospective audiences. Performative citizenship that encompassed conventional, institutional forms of citizenship seemed more likely to be cultivated for its external impression, because of the close fit between the acts undertaken and cultural images of civic commitment. Oppositional tactics and rights assertion were more likely to be focused on securing particular outcomes, although they could also produce performative effects.[22]

ADIOS ARPAIO AND THE CIVIC ENGAGEMENT CAMPAIGNS OF 2012

In the summer and fall of 2012, a small army of youthful volunteers—some as young as middle school, and many undocumented—walked neighborhoods door to door to persuade Latino citizens to exercise their right to vote. A key "hook" for their campaign was Joe Arpaio, the anti-immigrant sheriff of Maricopa County, whose saturation patrols of immigrant neighborhoods and raids on low-wage employers had sown fear in undocumented communities. The announced goal was to replace Arpaio, and other anti-immigrant officials, with more responsive political actors. The means—and the longer-term object—was to change the demographics of the Arizona electorate by turning a group of low-propensity voters into robust participants. The Adios Arpaio campaign, run by the immigrant organization Promise Arizona (PAZ) and the hospitality union Unite Here, registered roughly 35,000 new voters, most Latino. Similar efforts by allied organizations, including LUCHA and ADAC, added another 13,000. An equally profound transformation occurred in the young volunteers themselves. By participating in "civic engagement" campaigns, youth who had not previously participated in politics, and whose families were often beset by immigration enforcement, developed the skills that equipped them to organize, the understanding of electoral processes that allowed them to instruct and galvanize others, and the political voice and accountability that enabled them to emerge as claims makers.

National organizations like Voto Latino or Mi Familia Vota, which see growth in Latino voting as benefiting immigrants, have long focused their efforts on "civic engagement." In Arizona, however, the connection between Latino participation and immigrant rights is tighter, and the narrative more cautionary: disparities in electoral participation enabled the passage of legislation that not only targeted undocumented immigrants but surveilled and stigmatized their documented coethnics. The first campaigns to enlist undocumented activists as canvassers sought to harness the political fallout of SB 1070: undocumented canvassers stressed the urgency of Latino political voice by sharing their experiences under "attrition through enforcement." Successive campaigns targeted additional races with high stakes for Latinos or immigrants. Voter registration campaigns illustrated one model of immigration federalism utilized by undocumented organizations in Phoenix. Local elections, in which Latino voters might perceive a more urgent stake, were used to incite participation that could move national institutions toward more comprehensive solutions.

PAZ, which arose from a one-hundred-day vigil led by undocumented mothers against SB 1070 and then turned its focus to youth empowerment, became an early leader in registering voters. The first campaign organized by PAZ sought to deny a full term to Jan Brewer, the interim governor who had signed SB 1070 into law. This campaign, staffed by out-of-state fellows and organizers from ADAC and Reform Immigration for America (RIFA), recruited local high schoolers, mostly

Latino and many undocumented, to volunteer as canvassers. Students had more available time than adults; they were bilingual; their age, and often their status, meant that few could find paid employment.[23] Some youth were energized by the prospect of fighting back against a statute that had threatened their families and communities; others enjoyed the sociality of working with high school classmates and friends. Although some of these newcomers to electoral politics were discouraged when Brewer prevailed, two successful campaigns that followed helped to solidify the appeal of civic engagement work for undocumented youth.

The most visible, and widely resonant, was the campaign to recall state senator Russell Pearce, the primary sponsor of SB 1070 and the legislative leader of "attrition through enforcement." Randy Parraz and Citizens for a Better Arizona (CBA) mobilized an unlikely coalition of Latinos, Mormons, and moderate probusiness Republicans to replace Pearce with a more moderate candidate, Jerry Lewis. CBA enlisted youth activists from PAZ and ADAC to assist with the canvassing. This role appealed to those who had experienced firsthand the effects of Prop 300 and SB 1070. "I lived in Russell Pierce's district, so it was extremely important for me," an ADAC canvasser explained. "He's the creator of Prop 300, which is out-of-state tuition. He's the creator of SB 1070 and many other anti-immigrant laws. So it was fundamental for us to participate in that."[24] The unexpected success of the Pearce recall, in turn, magnified the hope of young participants. It was not only a sweet victory over a powerful foe but a portent for the future. "We would get a lot of people who would tell us that we couldn't do it, [that] 'he's one of the most powerful senators in office,'" one participant noted. "The night that we found out that he was recalled, [it was] the best feeling ever. Like we can actually do it. Like if we did it once, why can't we do it again?"[25]

Promisingly, pro-immigrant organizations "did it again," with the 2011 campaign to elect firefighter Daniel Valenzuela to the Phoenix City Council. Valenzuela ran for election in District 5, a district that comprised central and west Phoenix. District 5, a geographically large district, was 55 percent Latino and largely working class and had one of the lowest voter turnout rates in the city. Valenzuela was convinced that his path to election lay not in securing the support and endorsements of the political establishment but in making face-to-face contact with district residents and explaining the value of the vote. A strong supporter of immigration reform, Valenzuela reached out to a group of students who had organized for the DREAM Act, promising that if they would "walk for him," he would "walk for them." Valenzuela explained:

If you are popular, if people like you, and if you say, "I want you to walk for me," you might get three or you might get five. If you say, "I want you to walk *with* me"—the key word is *with*—"and if you can organize"—which I consider myself an organizer—then you might get 10 or 12. But when people believe that you are walking for them as much as they are walking for you, that is when something special will happen.[26]

This combination of commitment and unflagging effort ("If you're going to beat me, you are going to out-play me; you will not out-work me")[27] that Valenzuela offered was met and equaled by the growing group of students, who dubbed themselves "Team Awesome." Team Awesome reminded reluctant voters that disengagement allowed representatives to neglect them and their interests. "People were so disenfranchised from the process that they didn't care," noted a Team Awesome organizer. "But one of the pushes we gave was: You not caring about [candidates] is them not caring about you."[28] Notably, they also illustrated the consequences of representatives' indifference by sharing their own experiences as undocumented immigrants. Moreover, rejecting conventional wisdom that they focus on higher-propensity voters, Team Awesome set out to reach voters throughout the geographically sprawling district. In the end, they knocked on seventy-two thousand doors, reaching some voters so many times that as one volunteer put it, "They [would be] like, 'Oh my God, stop calling, I get it.'"[29] Moreover, because the group grew large and gained momentum, they were able to campaign in several other districts, promoting Democratic mayoral candidate Greg Stanton. Valenzuela won the city council seat handily, in an election that saw the Latino turnout in District 5 increase by close to 500 percent and the Latino turnout throughout the city increase by 300 percent.

By 2012, many immigrant organizations in Phoenix had begun to see mobilizing the Latino vote as a means of electing more responsive officials. This approach made 2012 a distinctively important year: voters faced not only Obama's reelection bid, a prelude to comprehensive immigration reform, but a Senate race featuring former surgeon general Richard Carmona, and a bid for reelection by anti-immigrant sheriff Joe Arpaio. LUCHA prepared for a major get-out-the-vote initiative, and ADAC rolled out the "I am a DREAM Voter" campaign, an effort to secure the pledges of registered voters to support issues that would benefit DREAMers.[30] A new umbrella organization called the One Arizona Table coordinated the work of these varied organizations, preventing duplication of labor and setting registration goals.[31]

The 2012 civic engagement efforts received a national boost, as funders saw in the Arpaio race an opportunity for large-scale mobilization. Arizona was in the sights of Tom Snyder, the national political director of Unite Here, a hospitality workers' union that prioritized legislation to support working families. The ability to move such legislation required a durable coalition of the emerging majority electorate: Latinos, African Americans, youth, and single women. Arizona's changing demographics made it fertile ground for such a coalition, and Snyder sought to discover whether an infusion of funding for voter registration could help. He was impressed by PAZ, which had propelled civic engagement efforts with a largely volunteer force, and with NOI (New Organizing Institute), the nonprofit that had trained Promise's volunteers.[32] And he saw the defeat of Joe Arpaio—admittedly challenging but uniquely motivating for Latino voters—as the "tasty hook" that could drive the campaign.[33] Snyder raised $1.5 million to fund an experiment. With PAZ and Central Arizonans for a Sustainable Economy (CASE) (a 501(c)(3) organization that works closely with Unite Here) at the helm, the Adios Arpaio campaign was born.

The 2012 campaign registered tens of thousands of new Latino voters, a surge that Arizona had not previously seen despite its steady demographic transition. But the campaign also created a force of several thousand volunteers, many undocumented, who were experiencing activism for the first time. The undocumented youth who entered activism through canvassing were a new and larger group of participants; many were younger and less educationally accomplished than the early DREAMers. Recruited at local public schools, most knew little about politics, and some were too young even to glimpse the impending age-related restriction of their opportunities.[34] Yet many of these youths had lost relatives or friends to deportation or had known the fear produced by Arpaio's raids or the threat of SB 1070. Moreover, empowering experiences of training together and of engaging prospective voters proved transformative for many participants. They created the motivation for a grueling, improbable campaign that yielded important consequences. For a number of participants, they created more durable new attitudes toward activism and the state.

LEARNING FROM ADIOS ARPAIO

Integral to the Adios Arpaio campaign and other examples of civic engagement was neighborhood canvassing. Although ADAC and LUCHA also engaged voters at "high-volume" sites such as shopping centers or schools, virtually all organizations saw the neighborhood canvass as a central vehicle for enlisting Latino voters. Teams of volunteers, working in small groups of two or three, fanned out over a "territory": a designated plot of a neighborhood that had high concentrations of targeted residents.[35] Armed with a map and a list of names and addresses, canvassers' job was to "door knock" at each home and speak to the listed resident or anyone else there who might be eligible to vote.

Canvassers provided prospective voters with information about the offices and issues on the ballot. They described the registration process, how to sign up for the Permanent Early Voting List (PEVL), or where to vote on election day. The most critical task, however, was to explain the urgency, and the potential, of registering and casting their ballots. Canvassers might ask prospective voters about issues that were important to them: state or national issues, such as immigration enforcement, or local issues, concerning schools, violence, vandalism, or access to public parks. Any of these issues could be used to demonstrate that, without electing responsive officials, voters could not expect the matters they cared about to be resolved. But canvassers often used their own stories of struggle to highlight the importance of defeating anti-immigrant candidates or electing those who were responsive to Latino and immigrant communities. These narratives often focused on hardships created by Arpaio or by "attrition through enforcement" and showed how challenges could be met through collective effort. This narrative offered by Elías, a LUCHA canvasser, provides an example:

> [Being undocumented] didn't actually affect me until I graduated. . . . [W]hen I graduated, my parents told me that, ". . . I don't think we can afford your education. It's a lot of money, and I don't know if you can go to college this semester." That kind of just broke me inside. . . . But the worst part was having to see my mom and my dad. I would actually see them cry because they couldn't provide for us what we needed, and they couldn't find a solution. . . .
>
> I'm so glad that I [found this organization] because [otherwise], I would have never been here. . . . I would not have been able to go out there and share my experience and motivate people. . . .
>
> I want [you] to vote . . . because I've been through this and I don't want to see your [family], I don't want to see your friends, I don't want to see anyone else having to go through what I went through. . . . Vote, because I know what I'm telling you when I tell you this, [] a lot of people are suffering. And it's really through your vote that you're going to be able to help these hardworking families stay together.[36]

The empowering collectivity of their organizations, which canvassers sometimes referenced, prefigured the collaboration between documented and undocumented immigrants that could usher in more responsive officials.

Arpaio's race offered a particularly compelling case for such a coalition. The racial profiling that occurred in neighborhood sweeps and under the "show me your papers" regime of SB 1070 extended to documented Latinos; many prospective Latino voters lived in mixed status families or had friends or neighbors who were undocumented. As PAZ director Petra Falcon explained, "People took it personal that any person of color was going to be asked for their papers. And . . . you no longer have . . . people of color, Latino families, in Arizona—who are not connected to somebody who has been abused by Arpaio or has suffered [] deportation."[37] The terrorization of the undocumented communities and the harassment and humiliation of their documented counterparts would continue so long as Arpaio remained in office. Removing him from office, through an expanded Latino vote, was thus a vital imperative for both groups.

Canvassing, and the powerful political education this "door knocking" provided, often proved to be transformative for young participants. Participation in large-scale campaigns like Adios Arpaio is demanding work: logistically, interpersonally, emotionally. It requires a range of organizing skills that new volunteers may not have acquired or used before. They learn to read a map; to collaborate closely with new acquaintances; to instruct, debrief, and critique peers and supervisees; and to meet numerical targets. Canvassing is also done at high volume, in the enervating summer and fall heat of Phoenix, over long days, for weeks on end. Participants are effectively separated from their regular routines, from their families, and from any friends who are not also in the campaign, for weeks at a time. The immersive character of the experience and the challenges it presents can engender new priorities and a new maturity. As Patricia, an Adios Arpaio volunteer, put it: "It's a tough job. It's very stressful. We all make sacrifices. Family especially. The sacrifice of us not eating at home every day. The sacrifice of not seeing our sisters or moms or dads, not playing with our dogs, not hanging out with our friends. I don't remember when was the last time I saw one of my friends outside of work."[38] The physical rigors of canvassing and the sacrifices it requires of volunteers, many of whom are barely beyond adolescence, focus participants' attention on the important task before them. Abril Gallardo, a LUCHA organizer, explained: "Okay. I'm here.

It's hot. I could be on my bed or drinking some fresh lemonade. But I'm here. I have this voter in front of me. I've got to make sure, when I leave this door, that person has a clear understanding of what's happening in the community and how his vote is going to impact [that]."[39] These nascent attitudes enable persistence over a long campaign and fortify returning participants for the varied challenges of future activism.

The responsibility of even recent volunteers for supervising newer canvassers sets a premium on emotional maturity and self-regulation. Francisco, a canvasser for LUCHA, recalled how he worked to maintain his composure when a neighborhood resident called him a "wetback" because he was training a new volunteer.[40] Organizers also modeled this emotional self-management following the election results in 2012. After learning of Arpaio's electoral victory, they set aside their own frustration to remind volunteers that despite this outcome, they had achieved a record-breaking number of registrants, who would ultimately change the politics of Arizona.[41] In developing these resources, volunteers drew on a youthful, friendship-based form of solidarity that was purposefully fueled by organizations such as PAZ. Civic engagement groups encouraged young canvassers to invite school friends and family to join them. Lunch breaks and evening debriefs that served tactical purposes also nurtured bonds between volunteers. The environment at PAZ at lunchtime often resembled a high school cafeteria: laughter and animated exchange filling the small space, as clusters of youth chatted or put their heads together over shared videos. As one Adios Arpaio volunteer said of her fellow team members: "We have become like sisters and we do everything together; even on our days off we're together. We hang out every day."[42] This sense of intimate familiarity buoys volunteers in their difficult work and propels the ongoing effort.

Beyond these organizing skills, participants develop capacities that are more specific to the movement and its hallmark tactics. The exchange of stories that can occur on the doorstep is often vital to the success of canvassing, so canvassers, who may never have told their stories publicly, learn to share with strangers the difficult parts of their lives. This means, first, being willing to speak to strangers: a challenge for some younger volunteers that the imperatives of the campaign help them to overcome. "I've always been a shy person," Patricia, a PAZ volunteer, admitted, "[but] I learned that my voice counts, that I had to lose [my] shyness so that I can inform my community . . . [and get] other youth involved."[43] It also means becoming emotionally transparent enough to share personal pain with unfamiliar voters. This was a challenging part of the experience for Natalia, an older Adios Arpaio campaigner who was also a mom: "When you tell your story of self, it [can] be emotionally hard . . . to just stand there and say it," she explained. "And then, in our field of work, we have to say it over and over and over again, because [we] meet different people."[44] In responding to this challenge, participants lean hard on the emotional pedagogy of their organizations. As Natalia observed in chapter 2, "It takes a village to become who you are in the campaign world."[45]

For canvassers, however, listening carefully and empathetically to the experiences of prospective voters is as crucial as sharing their own. Reyna Montoya related the story of a woman who was so alienated from politics that she cried as she described her frustrations with President Obama. But by listening attentively to the woman's frustrations, she gained the woman's trust and ultimately persuaded her to give electoral voice another try.[46] Natalia described how careful listening enabled her to appeal to a reluctant voter:

> I actually met someone that never wanted to vote. She said . . ."I just don't believe. My vote doesn't count. It's just one vote. . . ." [She was also] an Arpaio supporter. So I was like, "Okay, I'm going to walk away." So I'm walking away, and then I said, "No, wait a minute. You have children, don't you?" And she said, "Yeah, they're my kids." "Do you know that there's over 432 uninvestigated sex crimes [in Maricopa County]?" Her face dropped. She's like, "What?". . . She registered. I went back and collected her ballot. So she voted. . . . We just used [the] story that she already had . . . and integrate[d] the politics side to it so that she could see.[47]

These skills—from attentive listening, to emotional self-regulation, to the ability to speak confidently with strangers—are the skills of community organizers. But they are also the skills of active citizens: those who appeal solidaristically to their fellows and to state actors, as they advance a vision of a shared future. The visible honing of these skills highlights a distinguishing feature of the Adios Arpaio campaign: its role as a platform for "performative citizenship." Voter registration campaigns enable undocumented activists to perform publicly roles that are culturally associated with citizenship, and which communicate, from the "inside," central lessons of political membership. Facilitating voter engagement is a distinctively powerful instance of this strategy because the electoral process is so strongly associated in the public mind with citizenship, and because the lessons it teaches canvassers enable them to understand and to invest themselves in that process. In registering and turning out Latino voters, undocumented volunteers not only appear as visible actors on the political landscape, a change that is striking in and of itself. They take part as deeply engaged participants, even as experts,[48] in a process from which their status is often presumed to exclude them.[49]

The spectacle of undocumented immigrants enabling the signal act of American political participation was not lost upon observers of the 2012 campaign. Many of those canvassed lauded the participation of undocumented activists. The trust that many citizens placed in canvassers, to do everything from informing their participation to delivering their ballots, showed a respect for these efforts that likely shaped their broader perceptions. Prospective voters saw the act of registering others, when canvassers could not vote themselves, as a sign of their commitment, particularly in the hot Arizona sun.[50] Some also viewed it as a sign of their integration. Eduardo, an ADAC canvasser, explained: "[People] were supportive. You see a kid, you see someone, a young person, come to you to tell you their story. And . . . they understood the fact that you're a Dreamer, you were brought here and you bec[a]me so American, American enough to go out there and register people to vote. People saw that."[51]

Some public officials echoed this view, emphasizing the impact that the canvassers' stories and their commitment produced on their constituents. Daniel Valenzuela recalled:

> I was standing there on election day and . . . older gentleman—comes over, and [] says . . . "Daniél, I'm voting for you. There was a young lady who came to my door, and it was 117 degrees outside, and I was concerned for her, and I gave her a bottle of water. I'm voting for you because that young lady believes in you." And . . . that moment told me something. People were walking into that [polling place]. . . . But they were voting for Vanya Gabara. They were voting for Tony Valdevinos, for Lydia Hernandez, for one Dream Act student after another. That's who they were voting for.[52]

Not all citizens embraced the political reorientation the canvassers' efforts portended. In early 2016, the Arizona legislature passed a law that made ballot collection a felony, punishable by a year in jail and $150,000 fine.[53] Ballot collection, for those voters on the PEVL, had been a key activity for canvassers engaged in registration and get out the vote efforts. The legislative sponsor of the bill cited the possibility of voter fraud, although there had been no allegations of such fraud in preceding campaigns.[54] The primary goal of the law may have been preventing the registration of new voters, rather than disabling canvassers specifically. "These voters are giving us their ballots gratefully," argued One Arizona chair Ian Danley, "the only people criticizing this are people fundamentally afraid of Latinos voting."[55] But the obvious concern about the results of their efforts and the association of undocumented canvassers with the possibility of voter fraud suggests that, for some officials, stigmatizing views of immigrants and Latinos may have survived even the committed efforts of canvassers.[56]

A more decisive shift in consciousness arising from the performance of this role, however, occurred among canvassers themselves. Many canvassers had no previous knowledge of politics; they signed up because it was something they could do with their high school friends, or because they felt helpless in the face of family deportations or their inability to access higher education and saw the campaign as a way to respond.[57] Canvassing transformed many of these self-conceptions.

Canvassing offers an immediate civics lesson to undocumented participants. They learn about the structure of local government and the responsibilities of particular officials. Perhaps more importantly, this knowledge becomes a basis for understanding electoral control. Phoenix canvassers came to see how citizens can shape or yield control over policy through their choices about the vote. These understandings were affirmed for canvassers as they saw them resonate with voters. Mercedes, one of the original "vigil ladies" who later became a voter engagement canvasser, related:

> One time I got a man who right away wanted to close the door on me. He said, "I don't want to vote! They always do whatever they want anyway." He was very angry: "I don't even know anyone and I don't know anything about politics!" I told him, "Pardon, but you don't need to know about *politics*, you only need to know a little about *justice*. Or do you like what's going on?" "No, what Arpaio is doing makes me really angry!" "*That's why Arpaio is there, because the people who want him vote and the people who don't want him don't vote, like yourself.*" "Ok then, give me the ballot!" And that was it.[58]

Canvassers also begin to conceive a relationship between themselves and the political process. Adios Arpaio participants learned that they could be sources of information and motivation in a process that many never previously thought of entering. Some were also surprised to discover that they saw more potential for influence in the ballot than many of the citizens they approached. "They are the hopeless, and we are the hope," one canvasser declared, with a mixture of affirmation and wonder.[59] The desire to communicate this sense of possibility to prospective voters fueled long days of canvassing.

If canvassers bring knowledge and hope to the voters they meet at the doorstep, they draw from these encounters a powerful sense of connection to the electoral process. At the most basic level, undocumented canvassers come to understand that they will be virtually represented by the voters that they enlist. Julieta, an ADAC canvasser, explained this perspective: "I might not be able to vote, but my sister can vote. And I might not be able to vote, but my aunt can vote. My professor can vote. . . . And they will vote on behalf of me and my family. And they will vote with our DREAM principles and our DREAM values."[60] But the understandings of undocumented canvassers often go beyond this notion of virtual representation to a more direct sense of participation in the political process. Phoenix canvassers came to see the enlistment of voters as another way to be involved in that process, very much on a continuum with the vote itself. "Even though I might not have the right to vote," Reyna Montoya declared, "I have made the choice to empower those who can."[61] This sense that new voters are casting ballots as a result of their efforts gives some canvassers a sense not simply of participation but of influence in the political process. As Élias, the LUCHA canvasser, put it: "Every single time I go to a house and I manage to get their vote, I feel like I'm voting; and so I feel like I've voted a thousand times."[62]

Canvassers also learn about the accountability of elected officials. Accountability is the flipside of electing a representative who shares one's views; it allows voters to hold electorally responsible an official who has failed to respond to his constituents' preferences. The Pearce recall and the Adios Arpaio campaigns focused squarely on accountability, because they aimed to remove officials who had terrorized Latino and immigrant communities. As Eduardo said of the Pearce recall: "This is the guy who started it. This is the man who has been passing on policies that are affecting our community. We need him out. And bam, we did it."[63] But canvassers also learn that officials are answerable to voters for a variety of choices. Many canvassers become familiar with issues facing their "territories" that are quotidian but important: Do they have accessible parks? Paved streets? Streetlights? They come to see elected officials as the conduit for remedying these problems. As Élias explained, "Voters have a right to say to their elected officials: '[Our streets] need a stop sign, and there's not a stop sign. *We need you to fix this, or else, if you don't fix this, we will hold you accountable and the same way that we bring you in, we have the right to take you out of office.*'"[64]

Some canvassers come to see the accountability of electoral officials as running not simply to the voters they empower but to themselves as well. Through the experience of canvassing, they come to feel an affinity with voters and to see themselves as comparable to voters, along many dimensions that shape accountability. Like voters, they live in the neighborhoods that elected officials served. Like voters they are directly—sometimes more directly—affected by the decisions of those officials. Like voters—and more than many voters—they are engaged participants in the political process. This leads some of them to feel that they, too, can hold elected officials accountable. Élias, the LUCHA canvasser, exclaimed:

> I can go to any street, and I can tell you . . . this neighborhood wanted this. And when I see that . . . the roads are cracked; they're old, they need fixing. . . . I want to go up to somebody and tell them, "You know what? This is going on, and this community wants this, this, and this. How do I know? I knock on these doors. . . *[T]his is what's burning inside of me. I want to hold somebody responsible for what's going on.*"[65]

Abril Gallardo put it succinctly: "*At the end of the day, you work for us. You work for the community.*"[66] It is not a large step from this concrete sense of local officials' accountability to residents in their neighborhoods to a broader sense of the accountability of national actors. When DREAMers demanded that Obama enact deferred action for childhood arrivals, or when direct action protesters sought to hold Obama accountable for the separation of families through deportation—campaigns that are discussed in more detail in chapters 4 and 5—they were expressing the same sense that he was answerable to them: not only as those affected by his policies but as engaged participants and as residents of the nation he governed.

STRATEGIES OF PERFORMATIVE CITIZENSHIP IN THE UNDOCUMENTED IMMIGRANTS MOVEMENT

The factors that made Adios Arpaio a success not only as a campaign but as an example of performative citizenship are not difficult to discern. The familiarity of voting and the strong and uncontroversial association of the electoral process with political membership are vital starting points. But it is also key that participation in electoral processes involves not simply a right that is exercised by those with membership but a responsibility that is carried out by them:[67] the fulfillment of an expectation the polity places on its citizens. Through their involvement in the electoral process—particularly involvement as arduous as canvassing in the Arizona summer—undocumented immigrants, wrongly stigmatized as "takers" from their adopted nation, demonstrated that they are, in fact, contributors. They visibly carried out the kinds of responsibilities that formal citizens bear when they are living out their commitment to their political communities.[68]

This enactment of a familiar example of civic responsibility is crucial not only for members of the observing public but for activists themselves. Beyond the knowledge, expectations, and attitudes that they draw from their participation, undocumented canvassers, too, feel that they are fulfilling a kind of responsibility that they associate strongly with citizenship. "We are the future of America," one canvasser declared, "and if we don't get involved, then nobody else is."[69] As I explain in chapter 6, when undocumented activists reflected on what should make someone entitled to citizenship, as a normative matter, they cited precisely the fulfillment of such collective responsibilities: for informing oneself and for helping one's community.[70]

Finally, participation in electoral processes—like other forms of institutional participation, such as testifying before, or speaking with, members of Congress—signals immigrant activists' commitment to the formal political processes of the nation and its subdivisions. As proponents of change that may exceed extant legal frameworks, immigrant activists may in fact feel ambivalent about the promise of institutional processes, a point I examine later.[71] But as participants whose lack of status may complicate their belonging for at least some observers, Phoenix campaigners' embrace of tactics that showed their commitment to institutional processes helped to legitimate them in the eyes of the public.

This kind of "institutional" performative citizenship may be distinctively compelling for these reasons, but it is not the only mode of performative citizenship through which Phoenix activists have demonstrated what it means to be an active public participant. Sometimes—when they have encountered delay or unresponsiveness in formal institutions—they have moved outside these processes to assume a more oppositional stance. The tactics used in these efforts—from vehement public protests, to attention-seizing direct action tactics, to dramatic instances of civil disobedience—can be described as "oppositional" forms of performative citizenship. Oppositional tactics are often empowering for activists, sometimes in ways that enhance their investment and sense of belonging in their political communities. The physicality and extremity of a hunger strike or long-distance march can express indignation or frustration, fortify connections among activists, and sharpen opposition to an official target. Civil disobedience enables activists to face down law enforcement, and take control of their greatest fear, by purposefully risking arrest, detention, and deportation. These tactics connect undocumented protesters to participants in movements past, from the civil rights and Farmworkers movements to the LGBT struggle.[72] Moreover, challenging the state in such a direct and visceral way, may, paradoxically, amplify a sense of stake and belonging in the polity.

There are also varieties of performative citizenship through which activists have confronted hostile state officials by asserting rights, either in individual encounters or by bringing claims in court. In Arizona, rights assertion by undocumented immigrants has occurred most frequently in the context of individual encounters with law enforcement officials. The KYR trainings, for example, described in chapter 1, taught activists what questions they could decline to answer, or when they could demand a translation or a consultation with a lawyer. This gave some activists a sense of recourse, or a feeling that they, too, were protected by the Constitution. Undocumented activists also asserted rights when they enlisted the courts to curtail the excesses of state officials. For example, undocumented organizations, such as ADAC and Puente, served as named plaintiffs in constitutional challenges to enforcement officials such as Joe Arpaio and Governor Jan Brewer.

Yet as the experience of activists in Arizona has demonstrated, these additional forms of performative citizenship may be less predictable in their impact on undocumented activism. For example, the very aspects of "oppositional" performative citizenship that root and empower activists may evoke ambivalence in their audiences. Oppositional tactics do not share the wide recognition enjoyed by activities such as electoral participation or jury service as indicia of political membership.[73] Though they may be strongly resonant with some audiences, because of their association with First Amendment rights and venerated social movements, other observers may be wary of their extremity and skeptical of efforts that work so far outside institutional channels, particularly when those who undertake them lack formal status. Civil disobedience is a particular source of controversy. While some audiences admire proponents' willingness to break the law—and endure the consequences—in order to move the nation toward greater justice, others view it as beyond the scope of legitimate protest. Some members of the public become particularly irate when it is performed by undocumented immigrants, as Arizona activists learned following some highly publicized actions.

Strategies of performative citizenship based on rights assertion can also be equivocal in their effects. Rights assertion is less obvious as a strategy of performative citizenship because it is less visible than institutional or oppositional modes. Phoenix activists who asserted their rights during law enforcement stops often described a sense of empowerment or legal inclusion, but their rights bearing was rarely witnessed by anyone who understood its import. Court challenges, too, often flew below the radar of public awareness, particularly before they reached the appellate level. Moreover, whether feelings of empowerment and legal inclusion arose from the assertion of rights proved to be a contingent question, even for the activists involved.[74] Some immigrants were emboldened and affirmed by the rights they learned they could assert in encounters with law enforcement; others found the admittedly modest array of rights secured to undocumented residents to be confusing or uninspiring. Still other activists experienced recourse to courts—which might seem to affirm a sense of membership and empowerment—as a passage to a technical, largely inscrutable world, in which they were outsiders, deprived of even that agency available through political action.[75]

These potential trade-offs in using "oppositional" or rights-claiming forms of performative citizenship can create complicated choices for the movement, as subsequent chapters discuss in more detail. Yet in Phoenix, the "institutional" performative citizenship embodied in voter engagement campaigns was a clear boon to the movement. It enabled large numbers of participants in the movement—particularly those who were becoming politically active for the first time—to undergo a transition in their political understanding, their self-perception, and their sense of relationship to the polity, that enhanced the capacity of the movement and the personal agency of those involved. It also began the slower but essential work of transforming the way that members of the public perceived undocumented immigrants.

The next two chapters turn from the movement practices that fortified activists and enlisted members of the public to movement practices that more directly engaged the state. They explore a series of campaigns that reflect the gradual confluence of the youth and adult wings of the movement and show how activists used Arizona issues as a template or hook for national campaigns. They also illustrate the increasingly oppositional stance with which undocumented activists confronted the ambivalence of the Obama administration. Finally, these campaigns demonstrate how activists took practices of storytelling, emotion culture, and performative citizenship into the political field and adapted them to the contingencies of state response.

PART THREE

Engaging the State

Self-Reliance and Opposition

CHAPTER 4

The Oppositional Awakening of the "Undocumented and Unafraid"

On July 24, 2012, a small crowd milled about on a sun-baked plaza outside the Sandra Day O'Connor federal courthouse in central Phoenix. Sheriff Joe Arpaio had just completed his testimony in *Melendres v. Arpaio*, a civil rights lawsuit charging unconstitutional racial profiling by the Maricopa County Sheriff's Office.[1] In a fiery statement to the press, Arpaio defended the legality of his actions and pledged to fight to vindication. Immediately following his words that day, Puente-Arizona, a community-based immigrant rights organization, called a "people's press conference." Four undocumented adults in their twenties and thirties stepped up to a microphone to share their stories. The statement of Leticia Ramirez was typical: "I've been undocumented for 18 years. I am a mother of three kids. . . . Arpaio [has] been chasing our community, he's been chasing our people. And I'm here to tell him that I'm making his job easy. . . . I'm not going to stand for what he is doing to our community, [so] come and get me."[2] The four speakers unfurled a banner bearing the words "sin papeles, sin miedo" ("without papers, without fear") and carried it to the middle of the busy adjoining street. As supporters marched in a circle around them, they sat down on its four corners. A phalanx of police officers assembled, issuing warnings as they stepped in formation toward the protesters. Moving to the four corners of the banner, they pulled the protesters to their feet and led them to an awaiting wagon.

This protest, one of the earliest incidents of civil disobedience by undocumented adults, sought to rivet public attention on the trial of

98 | Chapter 4

Arpaio, the longtime nemesis of the county's undocumented community. It also hailed the departure of the Undocubus, a retooled 1970s-era tour bus that would leave Phoenix several days later, taking several dozen undocumented activists on a six-week freedom ride from Phoenix to the Democratic National Convention (DNC) in Charlotte, North Carolina.

Chapters 2 and 3 examined the formation of activists through the practices of storytelling and emotion cultures in undocumented organizations and through campaigns, like Adios Arpaio, in which tactics of performative citizenship played a role. These chapters focused on Phoenix organizations, like Arizona DREAM Act Coalition (ADAC), Living United for Change in Arizona (LUCHA), and Puente, that had coalesced and mobilized in response to Arizona's policies of "attrition through enforcement." The next two chapters explore how activists in these organizations engaged with government actors and how this engagement changed over time. The focus in this chapter is on two national campaigns in which Arizona activists played prominent roles. These campaigns sometimes contested anti-immigrant state action (i.e., policies modeled on SB 1070), but they sought primarily to influence the federal government, in its legislative power to enact rules regulating citizenship and its executive power to grant relief from deportation.

The first of these efforts is the long campaign for DACA, waged by immigrant youth between 2010 and 2012.[3] The campaign had its roots in the mobilization of immigrant youth for the DREAM Act, which offered a path to citizenship for undocumented immigrants brought to the United States as children. When this act was narrowly defeated in the US Senate, youth activists shifted focus and pressed President Obama to protect them from deportation. Obama responded in June 2012 with Deferred Action for Childhood Arrivals (DACA), which protected eligible youth from deportation and granted them working papers for a limited, renewable period.

The second campaign examined in this chapter is the Undocubus campaign. This six-week bus trip, which took a mixed-age group of undocumented immigrants across southwestern, plains, and southern states en route to the DNC in Charlotte, North Carolina, had two objectives. It publicized and protested state policies modeled on Arizona's by organizing and mobilizing with undocumented communities in a series of immigrant-hostile states. And it challenged President Obama to fulfill his commitment to undocumented immigrants through comprehensive immigration reform by staging visible acts of protest at the DNC.

These campaigns enlisted activists from local organizations across the country; they also involved national organizations such as United We Dream (UWD) and National Day Laborers Organizing Network (NDLON). These organizations advocated for pro-immigrant priorities at state and federal levels and worked as movement mentoring organizations with local groups, including the groups I studied in Phoenix. In these campaigns, UWD and NDLON played an organizing role: offering coordination, logistical support; and publicity for specific actions; and advice and training to local organizational participants.[4] Yet despite the broader range of activists and organizations involved, these campaigns were not detached from the Arizona context. Arizona activists predominated on the Undocubus and played leading roles in both campaigns, fortified by their years-long struggle against "attrition through enforcement." Resistance to Arizona's policies also helped to frame these campaigns. The onslaught of hostile policy and enforcement patterns at the state level demonstrated why federal action to protect undocumented immigrants was vital. Moreover, exposure to the strategies of anti-immigrant state officials primed undocumented activists for the skepticism of governmental actors that became central to in these campaigns. In chronicling these national campaigns, this chapter demonstrates how Arizona activists converged with, and occasionally diverged from, patterns of undocumented activism in other jurisdictions or in national organizations like UWD or NDLON.

The campaigns explored in this chapter, as well as the Not1More Deportation campaign examined in chapter 5, illustrate the impact of activists' experience in Arizona on the national movement for immigrant rights. They also depict key patterns in the movement nationwide, as it evolved between 2010 and 2014. These patterns may have been more pronounced among Arizona activists because of the hostile environment and the greater, ongoing threat of deportation for undocumented residents, but, as these chapters demonstrate, they were evident among activists organizing in other states as well.

The most significant pattern was a growing posture of opposition on the part of activists toward government actors and institutions. Following the failure of the DREAM Act in late 2010 and the proliferation of state laws patterned on SB 1070 in 2011 and 2012, activists increasingly positioned themselves as engaged adversaries of the state.[5] This shift was reflected in changes to the way they narrated their experiential stories as undocumented immigrants and in the emotions they were willing to project as they addressed governmental actors. It was also signaled, and fortified, by more oppositional forms of performative citizenship. These tactics operated outside formal institutions, although the tactics still aimed to reach those institutions by mobilizing the public. Sometimes these tactics approached or exceeded the boundaries of law, as in acts of civil disobedience, and participants voiced critical views of federal institutions. Because they functioned outside of institutions and pressed the boundaries of legality, these tactics were not always recognizable as practices that exemplified the roles and responsibilities of citizenship, although they resonated with audiences who associatd organized protest with committed citizenship. Although they evoked mixed reactions among the broader public, these tactics nonetheless had powerful effects on the political consciousness of participants: they bolstered he confidence of activists and fueled feelings of investment in and connection to the polity.

Underlying and reinforced by these tactical changes was an increasingly "oppositional consciousness" on the part of both youth and adults. Political scientist Jane Mansbridge has argued that "oppositional consciousness" emerges when members of a marginalized group develop four kinds of understanding, when people: (1) "claim their previously subordinate identity as a positive identification"; (2) "identify injustices done to their group'; (3) "demand changes in the polity, economy, or society to rectify those injustices"; and (4) "see other members of their group as sharing an interest in rectifying those injustices."[6] As this chapter discusses in more detail, these new forms of understanding emerged among activists in both groups over the course of these campaigns—albeit in different ways and at different times. The "oppositional consciousness" that they reflect demonstrates the growing confidence and independence of this movement, which, despite the status of its activists, was becoming capable of confronting the government to advocate for its demands.

The youth activists began to manifest these elements of oppositional thinking beginning in 2010—they did so explicitly in their public pronouncements, and more implicitly in the story lines they emphasized when they shared their experiences. Between the 2010 DREAM Act campaign and the contentious push for DACA that occurred in its wake, the undocumented participants in these efforts moved from trust in federal actors as the architects of reform, to state skepticism that approached federal institutions as unreliable allies in the quest for change, to a critical view that framed the federal government as a source of injustice. At the same time, advocacy of specific changes moved from a posture of petition to one of demand. Adults took a different path to the same destination. Their experience with "attrition through enforcement" helped them to grasp state injustice, but political confidence robust enough to animate demand was slower to emerge. Yet through community-based education and observation of youth protest, some adult activists arrived at a similar place.

The increasingly shared perspective on state injustice demonstrates a second feature of these two campaigns: the cross-fertilization and gradual convergence of youth and adult activism. These groups had been separate, in their goals and their tactics, as they mobilized against state hostility in Arizona: youth fought for access to higher education and for pro-immigrant voice in elections as they modeled de facto citizenship; adults used mutual defense and protest as they pushed back against Arpaio's raids and SB 1070. But in the campaign for DACA (a youth campaign) and the Undocubus (a mixed-age campaign in which adults provided the public face), activists embraced similar tactics—"coming out" as "undocumented and unafraid" and engaging in direct action and civil disobedience—and staked out similar positions of impatience and demand. They called on the Obama administration, which presented itself as an ally of immigrants, to make good on its promises. When its failure to do so became clear, with the collapse of Comprehensive Immigration Reform (CIR) in 2013–14 and the continuing pace of deportations, youth and adults joined together in the Not1More Deportation campaign, which is explored in chapter 5.

THE LONG CAMPAIGN FOR DACA: THE POLITICAL EMERGENCE OF THE UNDOCUMENTED AND UNAFRAID

The long campaign that culminated in the announcement of DACA introduced changes in narratives, tactics, and emotional expression, each of which contributed to a broader shift in the way that youth activists understood their relationship to the state. Beginning in early 2010, as youth activists asserted autonomy from pro-immigrant nonprofits[7] and shifted focus from a stalled effort at CIR to a stand-alone DREAM Act,[8] they took a more adversarial stance, stressing the urgency of congressional action. The narratives and tactics for this effort signaled a growing oppositional consciousness, which fueled new and challenging forms of protest as the DREAM Act failed in Congress, and the movement turned its pressure toward the White House, seeking executive relief.

One early expression of this new moment was the practice of coming out as undocumented and unafraid. Fusing a powerful emotional directive with a public act of self-revelation produced an emblematic tactic that engaged new audiences.[9] The practice was introduced to undocumented activism by participants in Chicago's Immigrant Youth Justice League (IYJL) in March 2010. Their Coming Out of the Shadows action drew on the experience of IYJL leaders in LGBT politics, where the practice of coming out had been a mainstay of the movement since the late 1970s. But this action also tapped the distinctive power of self-disclosure for undocumented activists. Public self-revelation fought the silencing effects of stigma, while activists' declaration that they were "unafraid"—and sometimes "unashamed" or "unapologetic"—challenged the stigma itself.[10] But for undocumented activists, this was not only a defiant or "stigma-philic" stance,[11] as it had been for LGBT activists; it also announced their arrival as political subjects.[12] The revelation of status in the course of public advocacy challenged the assumption that claims making is an activity of citizens. As such, it was a dramatic, disruptive form of performative citizenship.

The act of coming out as undocumented was performed by sharing brief, "kernel" stories. These stories revealed some part of the speaker's experience as undocumented—often a part that involved difficulty or struggle—and conveyed the speaker's emotional response to that experience. These stories pushed back against anti-immigrant stigma by publicly acknowledging and embracing a socially stigmatized identity (i.e., being undocumented). Yet they also diverged from the narrative of the "good immigrant"—the upwardly mobile striver, who complied with dominant social and legal norms—that had shaped stories shared in Congress in the early 2000s and predominated in some youth organizations. In part because the IYJL had been contesting the deportation of a youth leader with a misdemeanor charge, in part because they saw the limits of the "good immigrant" narrative in representing a diverse community, the stories at the inaugural Coming Out of the Shadows event took a different tack.[13] They drew less strongly on the exceptional accomplishment that infused early DREAMer narratives: education, for example, was referenced only to exemplify barriers to a productive, satisfying life.[14] The coming out stories described the fear and uncertainty of living as undocumented, without a path to citizenship, even as the storytellers confronted that fear by revealing their status.

Moreover, these storytellers set aside the cheerful optimism of early DREAMer narratives to acknowledge feelings of frustration and grievance against the government as their status remained unresolved. Early DREAM advocates seemed conspicuously to avoid accusations of injustice or frames of demand, just as they avoided contentious tactics—those that worked outside of, or even disrupted, institutional processes or pressed the boundaries of legality. Particularly in the Dream Act advocacy of the early 2000s, youth and their national nonprofit sponsors approached the federal failure to create a path to citizenship for youth as a kind of remediable error or category mistake, displaying confidence that Congress, having glimpsed the character of the claimants before them, would make it right. Whether this posture stemmed from earnest belief, strategic decision-making, or an ambivalent sense that those without status lacked an entitlement to indignation or demand—all of which find support in my research—a critical, demand-based view was rarely visible in early national campaigns for change. This began to change with coming out narratives, which acknowledged impatience and frustration with the ongoing impasse and approached the government in a posture of demand.

Many of these differences can be glimpsed in the coming out speech of Tania Unzueta, a co-organizer of the Coming Out of the Shadows event:

> Every time I take a step forward in my life, I have to consider that my options are limited, because in this country, I am not free. We are not free. I believe that this is the only life that I get to live, and I am tired of hiding. My name is Tania and I'm undocumented.[15]

These differences can also be seen in the coming out speech of another activist that day:

> I refuse to think about what another ten years of not knowing whether I will be able to come home to my mother and brother will feel like. I refuse to think about what another ten years of dreams shut down will feel like: dreams of a good education, dreams of a normal life without fear. I am undocumented. I am not afraid. I will not hide any longer. I will come out of the shadows every day if I have to. I'm a human being. I deserve to be happy.[16]

These new narrative and emotional elements appeared not only in the act of coming out but in other tactics that emerged in this period. As youth activists sought to shift the focus to a stand-alone DREAM Act, they moved from conventional efforts at legislative advocacy to leveraging the attention of the public to increase pressure on Congress. A good example of this can be seen in the Trail of DREAMs, a four-month walk from Miami to Washington, D.C., undertaken by four undocumented activists to raise consciousness about the need for the DREAM Act. On their arrival in May 2010, they presented President Obama with a petition for an executive order protecting undocumented youth. Although the stories they shared in the course of their journey sometimes leaned on familiar DREAMer images,[17] and they largely delegated acts of civil disobedience to allies,[18] the difficulty of their undertaking and the insistence with which they addressed the president seized the attention of the public and motivated other immigrant youth.[19]

As the furor over SB 1070 claimed national attention, Arizona became the site of a tactical escalation by DREAMers. In May 2010, a group of youth activists often referred to as the "DREAM 5" organized the first act of civil disobedience by undocumented students: a sit-in at the Tucson offices of Senator John McCain, a key vote in a possible DREAM Act coalition.[20] For undocumented activists, civil disobedience meant more than simply breaking the law in order to change it; it meant delivering themselves into the hands of law enforcement, a fate their community otherwise worked strenuously to avoid. When the DREAM 5 described their plan to engage in civil disobedience at a meeting of ADAC, it sent shock waves through the organization. "We had never seen anything like that before," Erika Andiola recalled. "Oh my god, everyone was crying. Everyone was like 'you're going to get deported.'"[21] Nevertheless, warming to the daring and the clear message conveyed by the plan, ADAC leadership offered help to the organizers and accompanied them to Tucson for the action. An ADAC cofounder who was with the DREAM 5 in Tucson explained the factors driving the escalation:

> A lot of people have said these were acts of desperation. . . . I would call them acts of anger. People are angry that nothing has been done, people are angry that these deportations are happening. . . . When we have been working for this issue for so long and we know that we have done it the "right" way, and not [] ruffled anyone's feathers, and not done anything that's given us a bad image, six years, seven years, eight years, nine years, and we still don't see any change. . . . [Protesters] just think, I need to put myself out there, I need to be the catalyst for this change, in order for me to motivate other students.[22]

This statement highlights feelings of anger—an emotion only beginning to be publicly articulated—and describes these feelings as a response to legislative failure. Neither advocating in Congress nor carrying themselves in a way that legislators found acceptable had led Congress to act. A feeling of skepticism about whether the state could be a viable partner in making change moved activists to embrace more self-reliant, extra-institutional tactics.

When the DREAM Act failed to pass Congress in December 2010, undocumented activists entered a period of introspection and reconsideration.[23] Although activists viewed it as a painful blow—"it was like a family member had died," one ADAC leader observed—most saw it less as a thoroughgoing defeat than as a moment for reassessment.[24] They were proud that the campaign had placed DREAMers on the national agenda and developed the political resources of undocumented youth. Yet the failure to pass the DREAM Act deepened doubts about the state—and specifically, about the national legislative process. For many Arizona activists, who had been made vulnerable by state laws and enforcement practices, it was the moment that they recognized that Congress could not be relied upon to vindicate their interests, and that immigrants could be betrayed by Democrats—who had failed to muster the votes for cloture in the Senate—as well as by Republicans.[25] Facing no short-term political openings, some activists, both in Arizona and across the country, left the movement. Those who remained sought to vent the frustrations of a hard-fought but inconclusive campaign and support each other in finding a path forward.

Storytelling provided a vehicle for this reevaluation. Turning to online platforms aimed specifically at undocumented communities, youth began to share new kinds of stories, which reflected their uncertain moods and allowed them to question the demands of publics they had previously accommodated. They challenged the "perfect DREAMer" narrative so resonant with lawmakers and the public, not only for its failure to represent their parents' generation but for its failure to represent themselves.

Some were tired of curating their self-presentation or of serving as standard-bearers for an entire community. Many sought to express the full, flawed human personalities that other youth could manifest without hesitation, as they moved through their daily lives. They also sought to voice the range of emotions and moods produced by the undocumented experience: not just the pride, hope, and resolve reflected in traditional DREAMer stories, or the indignation expressed by direct action protesters, but a variable mix of doubt, frustration, outrage, irony, and humor. They resisted the flattening of variation produced by the need to project a publicly appealing image. This narrative homogenization muted differences not just in educational achievement or cultural assimilation but also in attributes such as gender and sexuality. The narratives of the "undocuqueer" epitomized the human diversity that had been hustled "offstage" in the effort to accommodate legislative or public expectations.

Youth also sought new vehicles for sharing their stories. They stepped back from the first-person, linear narration that had become a staple of

DREAM Act organizing and turned to graphic arts, videos, and spoken word as a means of exploring undocumented identity. Cultural forms became a respite from political protest and a means of reinvigorating it. "Artivist" collectives, such as Dreamers Adrift (cofounded by the undocumented graphic artist Julio Salgado)[26] and CultureStr/ke,[27] supported the emergence of complex, ambivalent, artistically rendered stories that began as internal vehicles for mutual support and reassessment and became instruments for transforming public-facing politics.

Dreamers Adrift's video series *Undocumented and Awkward* exemplified this effort. This series troubled the dichotomy between the heroic and the suspect that early DREAMer stories seemed to trail in their wake, highlighting instead the uncomfortable, yet indelibly human, moments produced by illegalization.[28] In this series, for example, the refusal of states to award drivers licenses to DREAMers is framed not (simply) as a civil rights issue but as a source of social discomfort and stress.[29] *Undocumented and Awkward* also scrutinized the vision of transformation through political mobilization that was central to the DREAM Act campaign. One episode depicts a humorous but telling exchange between a citizen-ally and two undocumented youth, in which the citizen lectures them on the "gift" of anger and the need to get arrested, while the undocumented "artivists" try futilely to explain to their self-absorbed colleague that they are pursuing innovative forms of communication and protest.[30] These plural, ambivalent depictions helped make the image of the DREAMer more inclusive and more human.

Artivists soon began to implement this view of cultural representation as political strategy. Undocumedia Workshops, designed by Dreamers Adrift, taught DREAMers how to organize through visual imagery and social media.[31] Culture Str/ke staged Undocunation, an event of "art and activism dedicated to immigrant artists" adjacent to the site of the 2012 Democratic National Convention.[32] This siting was a self-conscious effort to spark conversation about the lives of undocumented people, at a venue where major political players would be setting agendas.

Youth organizing in Arizona did not directly incorporate the ambivalent, ironic stance of Dreamers Adrift. This tone, embraced by artivists living in more politically receptive states, may have felt ill-suited to the hostile, culturally conservative environment of Arizona. Yet many of the elements captured in artivist explorations inflected Arizona youth activism in the post–DREAM Act period. At ADAC, these shifts manifested not only in individual stories but also in organizational structure. Two new chapters of ADAC reflected a growing pluralism in identities and modes of self-representation. QUIP (Queer Undocumented Immigrant Project) sought to highlight and support queer sexual identity in a community whose religious traditions and conventional gender norms made sex and gender dissidence an uncomfortable topic. Double Coming Out events supported youth in the difficult task of explaining their sexuality to their families.[33]

Another new chapter called iDREAM utilized the arts, particularly photography, to give a visual dimension to undocumented storytelling. It formed initially around the work of Alejandra, a visual artist based in Phoenix who saw in photography a valuable medium through which to communicate the stories of undocumented activists. As a graphic designer, Alejandra sought to use people's faces to share a key part of their stories. "We all had different . . . dreams and goals and aspirations," she observed, "but our focus and where everyone met was being able to be a part of this US." These musings ultimately led her to photography, a medium she had not previously used. "You could do a lot with words," she allowed, "but when you see a person [in a photo] it could be like, 'Oh, it's my neighbor,' 'It's the person down the street.' . . . I decided I would use photography, just because it would be . . . a stronger message."[34] Her inaugural project presented images of undocumented youth, including many ADAC members, with the colors of the American flag emblazoned in small patches of grease paint on their cheeks or hands, their belonging to America made visible on their bodies.[35] Visual images thus became part of the performative citizenship of youth activists. When Alejandra's images sparked enthusiasm on the internet, she arranged in conjunction with ADAC to sell versions of the most popular photographs, raising funds for scholarships for undocumented students.

ADAC members also pluralized their images and efforts in another way: by incorporating parents and other adult community members in their organizing. Some DREAMers still felt stung by the accusation of national advocates that they had abandoned or implicated their parents through their support of a stand-alone DREAM Act. Others saw a means of sharing the transformative experience of activism with family members, who sometimes failed to grasp the import of youth-based activism. Elena, a cofounder and leader of ADAC, recalled:

> I remember telling my parents, "Oh, I'm going to go [to McCain's office], and I'm going to be sleeping on the sidewalk." And they were like, "What are you talking about?" And "You're lying. You're probably partying somewhere." And I think there was a gap. So some of us started inviting our parents to our actions so they can see what we were talking about.[36]

ADAC members found that parents who understood the stakes of activism could provide moral support; they could also provide logistical support, such as driving, food, and other supplies. After the failure of the DREAM Act, ADAC formed a new chapter called DREAM Guardians, which organized parents of youth members. As parents became increasingly active within the organization, both generations felt a greater convergence in their perspectives. As Elena concluded, "You desire your parents to take a more active role and . . . [be] civically involved. [T]hey start understanding you, and it's like . . . you see what you went through is some of the stuff that they're going through right now. So it's really fascinating to see that and very *satisfactoria*."[37] This bridge between DREAM activists and their parents not only exposed a growing number of adults to youth organizing tactics; it also pluralized the youth movement: ADAC, for example, began holding meetings in both Spanish and English, to accommodate monolingual Spanish speakers.[38]

By mid-2011, youth began to organize around their next political goal: if they could not presently secure a path to citizenship, they would press for relief from deportation for youth brought to the United States as children. Through a UWD program called Education Not Deportation, youth activists had begun the practice of defending individual DREAMers who had been placed in deportation proceedings.[39] This practice, in which ADAC participated, was familiar to Phoenix activists because of the prevalence of deportation in their communities. These efforts exposed activists to the role of executive discretion in the enforcement of immigration laws. Learning how discretion could be mediated by broad priorities, such as those expressed in the 2011 Morton memorandum, as well as by individual decision-making at many levels of ICE or DHS, led youth activists to focus on President Obama and the goal of categorical relief from deportation for DREAMers.[40]

As youth activists regrouped for this challenge, their interventions bore the traces of their DREAM Act struggles and their post–DREAM Act reassessments. Storytelling shifted in tone and content from even that offered in the campaign for the DREAM Act. Experiential stories became more intersectional, narrators insisting, sometimes explicitly, that belonging in America did not require hiding one's sexuality or rejecting one's native language or culture.[41] Storytellers also assumed a more critical stance, challenging political actors for their inconsistent, opportunistic treatment of DREAMers. Elena, speaking in 2011, challenged politicians, even as she called for greater self-reliance by activists and their communities: "We're tired of politicians playing with the lives of Dream activists. . . . I have hope, not in the politicians, but in the people working every day to fight for justice. We have learned that we cannot expect one person to create the conditions for change. We have to ask ourselves, 'what are we doing to fix the problem?'"[42]

Activists also drew on varied media, using cultural expression to incite political action. In a widely circulated, spoken word–style video urging deferred action, the cofounders of Dreamers Adrift addressed the president:

> This video's for you: you know who you are. Yeah, we saw your speech. Yeah I guess you did have some valid points. We get it, you're informed about our broken immigration system. We get it, we know that you support DREAM Act students. But what we don't get, what doesn't make sense to us, is why you refuse to use your executive powers to *end our pain*. There are DREAMers right now who are about to get deported. And what are *you* doing to help them? *Mean what you say. Say what you mean.* Simply saying you support the DREAM Act is not getting us anywhere. Oh, and by the way, we are not your political pawns, so don't use us for ad space on your campaign trail. Obama, don't deport my mama, Obama don't deport my mama.[43]

This video lodged a claim of injustice against the president himself: it called out his hypocrisy in coupling a public embrace of DREAMers with a continuing stream of deportations, including those of youth. It also invited the platform's growing body of young viewers to press the Obama administration for relief.

Above all, activists sought to exploit the circumstances of the upcoming presidential election.[44] At a session of the 2011 UWD national congress, organizers strategized about how to bring Obama to the table. "What do we have that he wants?" Ileana Salinas, an ADAC member who attended the congress, recalled, because "power is about what resources [you] have that others want."

> We said okay, we do not have money, we cannot vote, but we have people; and if we do it right . . .we can shift the Latino vote . . . *if we convince President Obama that without our support, the Latinos were not going to vote for him to get reelected in 2012, then we could pressure him to give us something.* That was pretty much the "theory of change." We are not going to [argue against] one deportation of one person, we are going to ask for categorical relief.[45]

For UWD's activists, lack of status was not a disqualification from engaging the president with an assertion of power; it simply required that they think strategically about the resources at their disposal. The Latino voters that President Obama hoped to carry could be a potent means of forwarding the agenda of undocumented youth. Although activists enlisted these voters through registration and turnout efforts, their growing comfort with oppositional tactics and their growing discomfort with Washington led them to supplement those efforts with more confrontational forms of action.

The most visible confrontation occurred in Colorado, in June 2012.[46] When a protest walk from San Francisco to Washington, D.C., brought a group of youth activists to Denver, participants staged a rally outside Obama's campaign headquarters. Two members of the group, Veronica Gomez and Javier Hernandez, entered the headquarters and commenced a sit-in, which later escalated into a hunger strike, as remaining walkers maintained a vigil outside the building.[47] Hernandez made the connection between Obama's reelection and the youth demands:

> We are going directly to his Obama for America offices because they are the offices reaching out to the community, and they are the ones strategizing and executing . . . how are we going to get the Latino vote? Obama has offered fixes in the past, but these changes are not working. We need something more concrete.[48]

A statement from the National Immigrant Youth Alliance echoed the protesters' posture of demand: "If the Administration does not issue an executive order, we will be forced to respond with direct action in the coming days. The administration, by not taking action by means fully within its power, keeps our lives on hold. That position, for us, is no longer acceptable."[49] When Gomez and Hernandez emerged after six days, their fellow protesters, energized by publicity and support for the action, announced plans for a series of rolling sit-ins, to be staged throughout the nation until the election. "Undocumented youth will be escalating in other actions. They are going to be arrested in some states," Hernandez explained. "The message is: we want an executive order."[50] Two days later, President Obama announced his program of DACA.

Youth tactics were reinforced by several influences, from political pressure from senators to the legal opinion of the immigration professoriate. Yet the timing of the announcement, following the very public occupation of the Denver office and the threat of rolling strikes, suggested that DREAMers may effectively have exploited a presidential vulnerability. Organizers highlighted their role in Obama's decision, encouraging activists to feel a sense of ownership in the hard-won, if limited, victory. As Monica Sandschafer, the first director of LUCHA, declared:

How do you think we got deferred action to begin with? We talk about the Dreamers who chained themselves to the Obama campaign offices, and that's the only reason we have deferred action. And the Dreamers who went in with their attorneys and said, "Oh, no, Mr. Obama, you can actually do this." Otherwise we wouldn't have it, right? . . . [I]t's not just because Obama's a great guy. It's because of power. It's because of campaigns. It's because of organizing.[51]

Tactics mobilized during this long campaign ran the gamut from recognizably institutional practices (meeting with or testifying to members of Congress) to efforts to incite institutional accountability through extra-institutional action (sitting-in or staging cross-country walks). They ranged between the more instrumental (all of the preceding) and the more expressive or self-representational (Coming Out of the Shadows events or the video for Obama). But these tactics increasingly conveyed a stance of opposition: a willingness to be more candid and less complicit in describing and expressing themselves and a resolve to demand action from a state whose failings they more bluntly exposed. At the same time, these tactics contained a thread of performative citizenship: they demonstrated to the public—and affirmed for activists themselves—that undocumented youth possessed the knowledge of and commitment to the polity that one might expect of its most responsible formal members. They showed the risk and sacrifice youth activists were willing to endure to bring their de jure membership into alignment with their de facto belonging. This demonstration differed in some ways from the performative citizenship of the Adios Arpaio campaign. Modeling membership may have been less explicitly a goal among activists who were more urgently focused on outcomes. And its vision of citizenship drew on distinct cultural currents in defining the meaning of "citizenship." But these tactics similarly endowed participants with a sense of institutional knowledge, tactical confidence, and some sense that they belonged—whether to the nation as a whole or to a tradition of committed dissent that threaded through its history.

SIN PAPELES, SIN MIEDO: THE UNDOCUBUS

As youth organizations in Arizona and across the country were savoring a victory with the announcement of DACA, back in Phoenix, Puente was planning another kind of campaign. The Undocubus would take a group of undocumented community members on a six-week organizing and public consciousness-raising voyage across the country.[52] The

Undocubus departed from Phoenix in late July 2012, shortly after the civil disobedience at Joe Arpaio's trial. It traversed eight other states that had enacted or proposed laws like SB 1070 or had entered into 287(g) agreements with the federal government, before arriving at the DNC in Charlotte, North Carolina. Declaring that Obama must decide "which side of history" he was going to be on, the riders sought to demonstrate the human costs of the administration's inconsistency by highlighting the effect on immigrants of enhanced state enforcement or collaboration between state and federal authorities.[53] But Obama, while crucial, was not the only target of the ride. Riders sought to accelerate nationwide resistance by organizing in communities facing enhanced enforcement. And with a daring, innovative campaign of direct action, across the country and at the DNC, they sought to shape public views on immigration policy.

For Puente, which worked with NDLON in planning the campaign, the journey marked the maturation of several strands of organizing.[54] The oppositional stance of its adult activists, fostered in the struggle against Arpaio and SB 1070, had been fortified by an expanded program of community education and deportation defense in 2011 and early 2012. Many of those who had learned their rights and how to defend their neighborhoods now felt ready to take on more visible, public roles. The Puente community, which had utilized direct action in response to SB 1070, was also inspired by youth coming out as undocumented and unafraid and sought to integrate their contentious tactics and defiant stance in its adult protests. Finally, organizers at Puente were eager to share their "open hand, closed fist" approach with other communities struggling with adverse enforcement.[55] Leaders at Puente understood attrition through enforcement as a broader, national pattern. The group had sponsored gatherings for organizational leaders; its director, Carlos Garcia, had advised organizations in other states. But those most at risk from enforcement in Arizona had rarely had the opportunity to share their hard-won lessons through face-to-face engagement with members of other communities. A bus trip through the most immigrant-hostile states in the nation, which would integrate community organizing with self-revelation, direct action, and civil disobedience, could enable activists to pursue all of these new directions. The idea, which was coordinated and publicized by NDLON, drew riders from California, Texas, and Illinois as well as Arizona.

On the Undocubus, physical hardship and political risk-taking fostered solidarity among a diverse group of undocumented protesters.

The Undocubus itself was a partially retooled, 1970s-era tour bus.[56] It had no air-conditioning, no plumbing, and no facilities for food preparation; several dozen passengers crowded, and sometimes slept, on couches placed in the empty body of the bus. The physical challenges reminded riders of their purpose; they also created powerful emotional bonds among participants. "We had difficult times, moments of long trajectory and long hours," recalled Ximena, a mother in her forties, who became active with Puente after watching police arrest her young adult children for civil disobedience:

> [We would go] two to three days without showering, sometimes without eating [breakfast.] . . . [T]hose hours seemed eternal and it would get dark and we slept in the same bus, on the two sofas that we had. It was something very uncomfortable but also very beautiful because we were a family—men, women, students, fathers, mothers. It was a different group of people there and it was living together [that] made the trip tranquil.[57]

Organized around the goal of preserving family bonds, Sin Papeles, Sin Miedo encompassed undocumented community members of all ages, including some groupings of parents and their children.[58] Undocumented adults, who described themselves as workers, parents, and community members, established the tone and content of self-presentation. Their stories gave a new face to the undocumented immigrants' movement, further pluralizing and democratizing its images and narratives. They did not draw on the legitimating attributes of DREAMers, and youth participants followed their lead. Although the youth who were students, for example, would occasionally identify themselves as such, they avoided the exclusive discourse of accomplishment or assimilation that had sometimes reemerged in the wake of DACA.[59] The mix of ages gave the group's events a bicultural feel, blending music and visual imagery from their countries of origin with American political discourse and offering public statements in both Spanish and English.

The Undocubus also highlighted a strong queer presence in the movement. From the earliest phases of organizing, in Arizona and elsewhere, substantial numbers of undocumented activists had also identified as LGBT or queer.[60] The influence of these activists had been prominent in the move to "come out" as undocumented and unafraid, and in artivists collectives such as Dreamers Adrift. But highlighting the intersection of immigration status and sexuality had often been sidelined as a "distraction" in the most visible public campaigns. On the Undocubus, queer riders spoke openly of their sexuality, of the influence of queer activists such as Harvey Milk and Bayard Rustin on their politics, and of the experiences of marginalization some had suffered in earlier un-documented organizing.[61] Marco Flores, an undocuqueer student and artivist from California who traveled to Tuscaloosa, Alabama, to join the riders, described this difference:

> Within the undocumented movement, our queerness is often pushed aside, and at times, even erased. . . . We are asked to downplay our *jotería* for the public, because there is no room for sexual politics in the undocumented movement. . . . We can never be queer *and* undocumented, because to be both simultaneously would be a "sort of distraction" that would weaken the movement. But in the midst of the UndocuBus riders, I could for once exist as my undocumented *and* my queer self. It meant piecing myself together for the first time; I felt whole within my own fragments.[62]

On the Undocubus, riders integrated storied tactics of earlier libera-tion struggles with innovative forms of direct action. The structure of the ride mirrored in many ways the Immigrant Worker Freedom Rides of 2003, in which nine hundred immigrant workers and allies on ten buses rode across the nation to Washington, D.C., sharing stories and meeting with labor groups along the way.[63] But its more explicit refer-ent was the political and tactical legacy of the civil rights movement, from the Freedom Rides, to the lunch-counter sit-ins, to the Mississippi Freedom Democratic Party's trip to the 1964 Democratic convention.[64] Riders self-consciously explored these practices and their history, in statements and blog posts.[65] In Memphis, they toured the Civil Rights Museum; in New Orleans, they met with organizers in the Congress of Racial Equality (CORE).

Participants also featured the tactic of coming out, which had been pioneered by LGBT activists and reintroduced by undocuqueer par-ticipants in the undocumented and unafraid campaigns of 2010–12. Yet self-revelation had a different resonance when utilized by undocu-mented adults. Youth who came out as undocumented and unafraid drew, if implicitly, on the legitimacy of DREAMers—education, ac-culturation, some level of achievement—to expose a more candid and critical story of thwarted opportunity. Adult speakers, in contrast, face a different prospect.

Lacking in formal education, English fluency, secure employment, or other forms of privilege, theirs is not an experience out of which politi-cal voice is expected to arise. Their narratives highlight features of im-migrant life that may be less familiar to the general public: exhausting and exploited labor, fearsome law enforcement encounters, impounded vehicles, and struggles to provide their families with food and shelter.

When undocumented adults challenge expectations by speaking out about their lives, it can produce many powerful effects. As with youth who surmount stigma when they learn to share their stories, adult storytellers may experience greater self-acceptance in relation to their status and also to those intersectional elements of identity, such as poverty, sexuality, or lack of formal education, that can deepen shame or immobilization. The narratives of adult community members can also challenge prospective allies, and other members of the public, to reconsider what they thought they knew about this group. They humanize and concretize an experience that involves more struggle, fear, and dehumanization than familiar "good immigrant" narratives. Finally, adults who come out publicly can also offer a potent invitation to undocumented immigrants who enjoy greater relative privilege to join them. All of these effects—but particularly that of inspiring other immigrants—motivated the riders on the Undocubus. "I want to be that motivation that if I can do it with no education, with no resources," Ximena declared, "then so can someone who has an education, who in in a better position, and [has] a better promising future."[66]

Legacy tactics like coming out were also combined with new initiatives that excited participants and captured public attention. One key innovation was the riders' organizing with undocumented immigrants in impacted states. These efforts brought the lessons of the "open hand and closed fist" to undocumented communities that had experienced little organizing in the face of enhanced enforcement. Undocubus riders did Know Your Rights (KYR) trainings with local community members; they shared information on tactics of enforcement and on local collaboration with ICE. Over meals and at gatherings, riders expanded practices of storytelling, recounting the oppression they had endured at the hands of state officials and the support they had drawn from their communities. The "open hand" dimension of organizing was strengthened not only through shared meals and storytelling but also by incorporating the arts. Marco Flores recalled:

> Art is being able to re-create our humanity in the face of people who deem us only as "illegal." The power of art to nurture collective activism is immense, and such were my nights with the UndocuBus riders, who would stay up until sunrise to complete banners, posters, speeches, *cuentos*. . . . Together, we, as undocumented artists, create the tools necessary for each day's struggle. *Art became more than a language; it too becomes our instrument of growth and empowerment.*[67]

Thus visual representations, including the graphic art of Julio Salgado of Dreamers Adrift, became prominent in the campaign.[68] The bus itself was painted a bright aqua color and bore images of the monarch butterfly that the group embraced as the symbol of natural, unencumbered migration.[69] Music also served to relieve stress and forge bonds between riders and local communities. At sites such as Knoxville, Tennessee, riders shared traditional songs, offered rap improvisations, and danced joyfully to music provided by host communities.[70] As the Undocubus gained visibility, riders were sometimes joined by well-known artists, such as Jornaleros del Norte or Salgado, who came to pay tribute to the journey.

Amid these emotionally fortifying celebrations, riders also modeled the "closed fist." Focusing strategically on cities with unfriendly sheriffs or 287(g) agreements, riders executed tactics of defiance and invited local community members to join them. Coming out events were themselves novel and provocative in many of the localities the Undocubus visited, but riders also engaged in more explicitly contentious tactics. Unlike the original Freedom Rides, on which inflamed members of the public met arriving riders with violence, Undocubus riders were rarely met by angry opponents. Instead riders took the initiative in raising issues central to the communities they visited, particularly 287(g) agreements between local law enforcement and the federal government. The riders visited sheriffs' offices with petitions protesting collaboration with ICE and staged rallies and sit-ins in public spaces, self-consciously running the risk of arrest in communities where they could not predict the consequences of coming into police custody.

One of the most innovative actions of the campaign was an intervention in a meeting organized by the US Civil Rights Commission (USCRC) in Birmingham, Alabama.[71] The USCRC visited Alabama, home to a draconian policy of "attrition through enforcement," to hold a hearing on state immigration laws. The USCRC invited Kris Kobach, the architect of SB 1070, to address them, but invited no representatives of undocumented communities to join the discussion, either as speakers or as members of the audience. Declaring "si no nos invitan, nos invitamos solos" ("if they don't invite us, we'll invite ourselves"), four riders, including two members of Puente, staged a dramatic interruption of Kobach's testimony. Wielding banners reading "undocumented," protesters called out from the audience, in both Spanish and English, introducing themselves as undocumented and unafraid and describing hardships they faced as a result of state enforcement practices. Warned from the podium against interruption, then forcibly removed by security, protesters continued their statements to media assembled outside the hearing and a growing crowd of observers. Finally, one USCRC member grasped the significance of the intervention and negotiated their return to the proceedings, giving two riders an opportunity for brief testimony before the commission.

This action not only combined a new tactic of disruption with "kernel" storytelling about undocumented lives. It also embodied a new claim about the value of undocumented experience in immigration politics: that the perspectives of the "most affected" offer a necessary substantive vantage point on immigration policy making. To Undocubus riders, the flaw of a USCRC hearing on state immigration enforcement that did not elicit their experience was self-evident and glaring. "They live in a world where they don't know what it is to be undocumented, what it's like to live in a barrio," one Puente rider declared following his removal from the proceeding. "Therefore they don't have a right to have an opinion about our lives. They don't understand what we're feeling. That's why we're here, shouting our truths."[72] This position staked out new epistemic ground, even for a movement that had elevated the role of experiential storytelling. Organizers had long taught activists that the concreteness and emotional valence of stories made them more persuasive than other forms of political claims making.[73] But the riders were saying something different: that undocumented experience brings substantively distinct and irreplaceable perspectives to immigration policy making. While this position was consistent with the more autonomous role that undocumented youth began to assert in the campaign for the DREAM Act, Undocubus riders made more explicit the claim that the experience of those directly affected was essential to sound decision-making. These positions previewed the argument made by participants in the Not1More Deportation campaign that undocumented activists must be not only be heard but included in formal processes of governmental policy making.[74]

Finally, when the riders reached Charlotte, they used a highly visible instance of civil disobedience to issue a challenge to President Obama. Ten riders from the Undocubus sat down in the public space immediately in front of the convention hall. Holding aloft signs that identified them as "undocumented," they blocked the entry to the DNC until they were arrested by law enforcement. When they were released, without being handed over to DHS officials, protesters issued the following statement about their tactics and goals:

> We came out because we are tired of the mistreatment. We are tired of waiting for change and we know that it never comes without risk or without sacrifice. . . . We know that the Republicans have decided to completely turn their back on our communities. We also know that President Obama's legacy

on immigration is undecided. We want him to be on the right side of history. And we know that it is the effort of our organized communities that will make that happen. . . . We want President Obama to use his executive authority to provide relief for our entire community, students, parents, and all of us.[75]

Recapitulating the theory of power that ADAC had embraced in the DACA campaign, the Undocubus riders invoked the electoral pressure fueled by "organized communities"—communities they had helped to bolster throughout their trip—to move Obama to the "right side of history."

As a campaign marked more by its innovation than by its scale, in a summer that saw two presidential nominating conventions and the announcement of DACA, the Undocubus did not become a flashpoint for national controversy. Yet supporters of immigrant rights tracked its progress avidly, and journalists, advocates, and academic commentators debated it publicly, with varying assessments. Conservative commentators distinguished it sharply from those civil rights protests on which it drew. "This is no Freedom Ride," one exclaimed. "It is a movement intended to celebrate the flouting of the law. What is at stake is . . . the right of a sovereign people to determine the terms on which others may join their political community and enter their territory."[76] Others saw it as an amplification of the coming-out tactic originated by youth activists two years earlier. While some analysts regarded this as a grave step with uncertain implications for those who take it (even after the enactment of DACA),[77] others hailed it as an innovation that made visible "the harms felt by a particular group,"[78] and as a way of showing the public that "we are, in fact, one of you."[79]

PERFORMATIVE CITIZENSHIP IN AN OPPOSITIONAL MODE

The Undocubus signaled the growing convergence of two streams of the movement on an oppositional yet solidaristic strategy. It entwined the distinctive experiential stories of adults—stories of fear, targeted enforcement, and material struggles to survive—with the oppositional tactics of self-revelation and civil disobedience that had been honed in the long campaign for DACA. Even the riders' credo "sin papeles, sin miedo" (no papers, no fear) mirrored the stance of the undocumented and unafraid. The emotional tenor of the journey, as well, combined the adamant, dignified carriage of Puente's anti-Arpaio campaigns with the defiance that fueled the campaign for DACA.

Moreover, both of these campaigns made strategic use of Arizonans' experience resisting "attrition through enforcement," within a broader, national movement. That experience primed the more skeptical stance toward government that emerged in the DACA campaign: it was not a reach for youth in Arizona, who had watched state actors curtail their access to higher education, to conceive government officials, whether state or federal, as obstacles or even adversaries. For riders on the Undocubus, the harsh enforcement that Arizonans had faced at home motivated them to organize with communities in other immigrant-hostile states and to demand a federal solution.

The oppositional posture that emerged in these campaigns, above all, brought a new dimension to the performative citizenship of undocumented activists. Both campaigns embodied, to varying degrees, more traditional elements of citizen-like conduct, but both also highlighted more contentious forms of civic commitment, less familiar to public audiences and more adversarial in their engagement with the state. If these latter forms of de facto citizenship could be challenging for some observers, they, like the more traditional elements, contributed powerfully to the political subjectivity of participants.

The more conventional performative strategies of the long campaign for DACA—the storytelling in Congress or the use of rallies, online campaigns, and other forms of organized speech—fueled the growing confidence of immigrant youth as institutional, political actors. This was signaled not only by their greater involvement in legislative advocacy but by their assertion of autonomy from national nonprofits and redirection of their efforts in 2010 toward a stand-alone DREAM Act. As they moved from the DREAM Act to seek executive relief from deportation in 2011–12, the strategy developed at the UWD conference—to pressure Obama by wielding influence over Latino votes that he needed for victory—showed activists' ability to think in pragmatic, "insider" terms about the accountability of elected officials and how to activate it. Youth activists did not hesitate to engage the president through an assertion of power, despite their lack of status. They may have had fewer resources than others who sought to influence the president, and they could not exercise the franchise. But their experience with voter engagement campaigns, like the 2011 Pearce recall campaign in Arizona, had taught them that those deficits could be overcome through the force of numbers and by enlisting citizen-allies.

The riders on the Undocubus also gained from the more conventional aspects of their performative citizenship. Like the canvassers who took part in the Adios Arpaio campaign, they experienced a rapid growth in their civic knowledge and understanding. Traveling through affected communities, participants learned about state laws shaping the treatment of immigrants and agreements between states or counties and the federal government that facilitated federal immigration enforcement. This knowledge helped participants understand the many contexts in which enhanced enforcement operated and how states and counties could be implicated in federal policies of detention and deportation. One rider explained this benefit:

> Having lived in Arizona for 10 years, and experiencing the harsh immigration laws there. . . . [S]ometimes I don't think about the fight that other states are going through. . . . Being in Colorado . . . was a real eye opener for me. . . . I got to learn about SB 90, a law that has been in effect for the last 6 years and that is pretty much the same as Arizona's SB 1070. . . . [I also heard] about a raid that took place . . . at a community party where ICE took six undocumented people who were there with their kids, families, and friends. . . . [This] affirmed that immigration laws affect people in a lot more states, and [that] this fight doesn't belong to just one community but to ALL of us.[80]

Participants in both campaigns also developed a keen sense of the accountability elected officials to those they served, including undocumented communities. This appreciation had also emerged among youth canvassers in the Adios Arpaio campaign, but it functioned differently in these campaigns. This was partly a result of growing state-skepticism. Having witnessed years of federal inaction—against a backdrop of frank state hostility—riders on the Undocubus, for example, did not trust that accountability to immigrants would be triggered solely by the electoral process. This belief helped to fuel the turn to contentious tactics. Ximena explained:

> During their election [representatives] offer to help us with immigration, and when they are in power . . . they no longer give us what was promised. And it is then up to us to go to them with other tactics so that they can remember we are waiting for what they promised us. We need to pressure them so that we will be heard and treated equally because we are a very important part of this country . . . so that they take us into account and they see our value.[81]

This demand for accountability, as Ximena suggests, sometimes drew on comparability or proximity to voters. Youth demanding deferred action—like youth in the Adios Arpaio campaign—saw the president as accountable to them, because they could mobilize Latino voters on their behalf. Riders on the Undocubus, however, did not always describe their role as comparable to, or vindicated by, the role of voters.[82] They some-times described voting as an act specifically foreclosed to them, though they did not view this exclusion as delegitimating.[83] Their challenge was to identify means outside the usual institutional channels, to amplify voice and demand accountability. As Kemi Bello, a rider from Texas, explained: "When you are shut out of the process, you have to create new forms of entry. Whether or not they lock the front door to political participation because of our status, we will create a window and climb through it."[84] The sit-in at the threshold of the DNC, like other pub-lic confrontations, offered such a window. "These actions serve as a friendly accountability reminder to those in power," Bello warned, "that we may not be able to vote at the polls this November, but we will con-tinue to find our own ways to participate within the electoral system."[85]

These novel "accountability reminders"—situating participants out-side formal institutions, in more confrontational roles—sent strong, if challenging, messages to the public about the civic commitment of undocumented immigrants. They also powerfully shaped the political subjectivity of participants, building a sense of confidence and recourse, and fostering feelings not only of connection but of membership among activists. From the broad strategy of interruption and demand that characterized these actions, activists glimpsed their capacity to use their truths to engage institutional actors, sometimes with concrete results. Some riders described this in terms of "gaining voice": a sense of an entitlement to speak and of having something important to say. One Puente rider said of his Undocubus resistance: "I remember feeling like I was taking [back] the power they had taken from me without me knowing that I had lost it. The power to defend myself and speak for myself."[86] Participants also drew lessons from specific practices that were deployed frequently over the course of these campaigns.

Coming out as undocumented and unafraid—whether in youth-led ral-lies or at a hearing of the USCRC—posed a series of powerful, reorienting challenges to the public. It made visible the indelible human faces of an often-hidden identity. Activists' defiant embrace of that identity pressed the public to revisit the stigma many had assigned to it. And the risk and commitment reflected in that self-revelation challenged citizens to accept undocumented immigrants as active, contributing political subjects.[87]

Despite its impact on the public, however, the action of coming out may have achieved its most potent effects on the subjectivity of the actual participants. Activists had noted its bolstering effects, even when they voiced their status in organizational settings. Tania Unzueta, the youth activist who organized the first Coming Out of the Shadows Day, in Chicago, explained: "We found that when we said we were undocumented, even in our own private spaces, it was . . . empowering to us as individuals."[88] This effect became more potent when activists came out in public settings. Martín, who came out as both undocumented and queer during his time with the Undocubus, described the effects of this revelation and its acceptance. It was "one of those changing moments of my life that I realized that I was a whole person," he recalled, "I felt complete. . . . I was me for the first time in my life."[89] But the impact of the practice went beyond its effects on individuals: the declaration also served to knit activists together as a collective. When protesters say they are "undocumented and unafraid," Roberto, an ADAC activist, explained, the message is "that we are going to be strong and we are together . . . that we are not alone. That's what being not afraid is."[90] As Unzueta concluded: "It connected us, created community, and allowed us to organize in ways we hadn't before."[91]

Civil disobedience touched off even stronger responses among both participants and their audiences. Challenging an unjust law by breaking it—and being willing to suffer the consequences—is one of the most controversial acts of civic participation.[92] The willingness to risk one's freedom to expose an unjust law may be seen as a potent form of political responsibility. Or it may be seen as a form of lawlessness that undercuts one's standing to offer a critique. This tension escalates dramatically when the participant is undocumented, and the possible consequences include deportation, family separation, and the disruption of entire lives. Among audiences, it may prompt admiration, as the ultimate act of civic commitment by participants not yet recognized as citizens. Or it may trigger unease, even indignation, as an act of lawlessness and disruption by a group that critics may associate with both.[93]

For the undocumented participants themselves, the effects of civil disobedience were also heightened. Like coming out in its earliest days, this tactic could be daunting for undocumented protesters, because its novelty made it difficult to predict the official response. Making themselves subject to arrest through the knowing violation of laws could feel perilous even for experienced activists, after years of avoiding encounters with law enforcement. Elena, an ADAC leader, described the culmination of a day-long sit-in at Senate offices in Washington, D.C., shortly before the vote on the DREAM Act:

As things were getting closer and we started getting our warnings, then it was like . . . I was in Disneyland, because when you go into this roller coaster, how you start feeling. . . . It felt like, oh, we're going up. You see the entire seaport from top and they drop you. And so that's how I felt.[94]

Despite or perhaps because of these emotional demands, civil disobedience, a frankly oppositional form of performative citizenship, produced a sense of empowerment, and sometimes—paradoxically—a sense of political belonging, for undocumented protesters. Those individuals who took part experienced a sense of liberation from confronting and surviving their fear of detention, deportation, and family separation. As Elena put it, "When I got arrested, that was the first time I felt free in a very long time."[95] Some protesters also experienced a change in their relationship to ICE and law enforcement. By "taking ownership of the same fears that are going to exist no matter what," a member of the DREAM 5 explained, they showed that officials could no longer "hold our status over our heads." [96] This gave them a feeling of greater recourse in an encounter of radically unequal power.

Undocubus riders experienced this sense of recourse after their civil disobedience at the DNC. When they were arrested and held for processing, the feeling of power they gained from holding their ground at the convention doors, fused with the KYR training that had become second nature to them in Phoenix. "That's what we are teaching our members of the community here," Martín observed, "that you don't have to become [the officer's] best friend. [B]y law, you don't have to answer every question they ask."[97] As riders implemented these lessons in detention, they felt resourceful rather than vulnerable. Martín recalled:

> We noticed the change [in] the way [the officer] was treating us up there. We were resisting. He got tired of us. . . . So he started playing the mind game and bec[a]me nasty to us. And we decided to not talk to him anymore, and we told him, and he got more pissed. . . . [W]e knew that we [had] him by his hair [then], that we had the power to control the situation. . . . [A]fter all the pressure and all that, he came out to talk to us, and he told us that [based on] the investigation that they did . . . they didn't find that we were any terrorists, we weren't criminals . . . we weren't being looked for by the government of our countries. I mean, we were laughing afterwards.[98]

As with the youth who sat-in at Congress, taking the risk of deportation and seeing the action through created a sense of fortitude and mastery, in this case reinforced by the lessons of KYR training. When these protesters collectively applied their training, it enabled them to assert some control in their interactions with the official holding them. They felt that they were no longer at his mercy and could even negotiate the situation with a touch of humor or play. The experience of relief and triumph Martín experienced afterward emboldened him to engage in civil disobedience going forward: "It makes me a little bit more secure, more stronger, every time I do [it]."[99]

The sense of confidence, and of enlarged capacity to act, that arose from civil disobedience also emboldened participants' larger communities. It motivated those who had not been part of the protest to envision and execute new forms of political action. Erika Andiola, who took part in the Capitol Hill sit-in, recalled its effect on other members of ADAC:

> When we came back from DC . . . one of the really awesome things that I saw was that a lot of other youth were starting to be a lot more empowered. . . . You started to see a lot of the youth being like, "I would do this; I would do that." I mean, they were willing. . . . A little bit after that . . . we literally slept outside of McCain's office for almost a month. And folks were willing to do it. And that was not the case in 2009: I mean, we were arguing about putting [out] a freakin' newspaper [article about DREAMers] at ASU.[100]

Finally, these contentious tactics produced in many participants a sense of responsibility for and connection to a larger political community. For some, the commitment to act on behalf of others was directed to immigrant communities. Describing their stops on the Undocubus, Consuelo, a Puente rider, observed: "They were organized a bit less than us, but when we'd get there . . . we'd give them strength and wisdom so that they could continue organizing."[101] For others, the sense of commitment was more general. Thinking back on her travels with the Undocubus, Ximena mused: "I now feel like that person who cannot live without helping others. I feel responsible to be the representative, and to support others."[102] The feeling of responsibility for others, and the efforts that it fuels, are more robust than those typically manifested by citizens, and the emphasis on organizing against dominant injustices signals a more oppositional practice.[103] But the pull to inform oneself and serve the well-being of a broader community is a hallmark of engaged citizenship.[104] Elena experienced this feeling as she awaited arrest on Capitol Hill: "I felt like, 'I have done everything possible for me to fix this situation . . . so if I get deported tomorrow, it's fine.'"[105]

Some activists also felt a greater sense of belonging to the very polity whose laws they contested. This feeling was mediated less by a sense of affinity with the nation as a whole than by a potent connection to those who have struggled to change it. Tania Unzueta, a Chicago youth activist who was both undocumented and queer, saw in her work the legacy of Harvey Milk, who advocated coming out as a political strategy, and the Southern Non-Violent Coordinating Committee (or SNCC), which envisioned "young people taking more radical actions."[106] As they developed their strategy for the first undocumented civil disobedience in 2010, the DREAM 5 discussed Martin Luther King Jr. and the lunch counter sit-ins; they planned their action to coincide with the fifty-sixth anniversary of *Brown v. Board of Education*.[107] Undocubus riders spoke publicly about their connection to figures such as Martin Luther King and Bayard Rustin (an icon from both the civil rights and LGBT movements). One Puente rider blogged a tribute to the civil rights movement, which she claimed as a source not only of oppositional tactics but of inspiration:

> While I am looking at the pictures and learning about the history, I feel like I am living those same moments right now. Each picture, each song, each protest, is being reflected in the work that I do. . . . Without knowing, I think we are forging a similar path to the one fought for 50 years ago. African-Americans stood up for their rights, they came together with their white allies, and have been able to make gains.[108]

Ximena shared with me a similar feeling when she summed up her time on the Undocubus. "Something very beautiful has stayed [with] me," she mused, "that I have formed part of this movement, being part of change, being part of history."[109] That history is a specifically American resistance story.

The inclusive narratives, defiant emotions, and contentious modes of performative citizenship inaugurated in these campaigns brought new energy and new directions to the movement, in Phoenix and across the nation. This oppositional posture would become more adamant, and its substantive demands more systematic, as activists weathered the ill-fated fight for comprehensive immigration reform and pressed the Obama administration to end deportations.

CHAPTER 5

The Oppositional Citizenship of the Not1More Deportation Campaign

On August 21, 2013, four members of Arizona DREAM Act Coalition (ADAC) chained themselves to the gates of ICE's Removal and Detention Facility in Phoenix. This action represented a new tactical turn for ADAC, an organization primarily known for community education, voter registration, and legislative lobbying for undocumented youth. Chained to the gates and impeding traffic in and out of the building, the four activists held their ground until law enforcement officials eventually arrived, cut the chains, and placed them under arrest.

Later that evening, as ADAC activists held a prayer vigil outside the facility, one of them glimpsed a deportation bus beginning to move. Several activists raced across the parking lot and knelt in front of the bus, halting its progress. The standoff, which began near midnight, lasted for more than two hours, with activists chanting and praying while those on the bus raised shackled hands in solidarity. Two more undocumented activists were ultimately arrested as police ended the demonstration.[1] "I was worried about my dad," said Reyna Montoya, a participant whose father had been in deportation proceedings. "This [was a way] of telling him that this is not okay and we're going to fight back, because of course that could have been my dad" on that bus.[2]

The ADAC bus protest marked a new phase of undocumented activism, spurred by a national campaign called Not1More Deportation. This campaign, which began in mid-2013, emerged at a critical moment in the immigrant rights struggle.[3] The path to citizenship promised by the CIR bill had been freighted with border security requirements in the Senate and stymied by Republican leadership in the House. The Obama administration, which had escalated immigration enforcement as a "down payment" on bipartisan cooperation on immigration reform, continued to move thousands of undocumented immigrants each month through its apparatus of deportation. The Not1More Deportation campaign sought to end deportations in the face of legislative stalemate, through executive relief for those not included under DACA. But this goal—albeit ambitious—belied the extent of the campaign's reach and vision. Undocumented youth and adults, who largely followed separate paths in activism, found common cause in this campaign. Painful narratives of family separation took center stage, their unmediated anguish and outrage framing a moral accusation. Participants utilized novel and risky forms of direct action, including physical intervention in the machinery of immigration enforcement. The sharp contentiousness of this campaign revealed a changing self-conception among activists and a frankly adversarial relationship between protesters and state actors. It also pointed toward a vision of justice for migrants that challenged the assumptions of a sovereign, carceral state. Schooled by years of resistance that incubated key elements of this campaign, Phoenix activists played a leading role in this nationwide effort.

FROM CIR TO NOT1MORE: INTIMATIONS OF A NEW TURN

Toward the end of 2012, Phoenix activists felt a current of new hope as Congress began to consider a blueprint for immigration reform. The grant of DACA, the swelling ranks of Latino voters in the state, and the reelection of Barack Obama, who had pledged to take up immigration in his second term, led even the state-skeptical to wonder if their voices might now be heard and the moment for change might be at hand. Organizations in Phoenix coordinated their efforts to support the bill and prepare immigrants for the successful outcome of the campaign. A CIR Table, which enabled collaboration among local organizations, national pro-immigrant nonprofits, and supportive members of Congress, formed under the direction of Petra Falcon of Promise-Arizona. Meeting weekly, group members received briefings from Washington, devised strategies for pressing local members of Congress, and coordinated canvassing and public events designed to rally public support for legislative change. Somos America, another pro-immigrant umbrella organization in Phoenix, planned Estamos Listos, a program that would prepare a large and varied population of immigrants for the detailed logistical work of applying for legalization or citizenship. Powering these efforts was a sense of pride and commitment: as the youth mobilizations of spring 2012 had moved Obama toward the grant of DACA, this moment of institutional promise, too, would be fueled by community education and organizing.

Yet even as new possibilities emerged at the national level, local governance and enforcement continued to loom large in the lives of Arizona's immigrants, and organizations directed efforts to these targets. While Puente participated in the CIR Table, a primary focus for the organization in this period was a public campaign against Arpaio's workplace raids. These raids were fueling prosecutions by Maricopa County attorney Bill Montgomery, who used state forgery and identity theft statutes to render undocumented workers who were arrested and whose files were seized during raids immediately deportable. When political interventions aimed at Montgomery and his charging practices failed to bear fruit, Puente became a named plaintiff in a federal lawsuit. *Puente v. Arpaio* challenged the raids and statutes that turned undocumented workers into felons.[4] (This lawsuit is discussed in more detail in chapter 6.)

Living United for Change in Arizona (LUCHA) also took part in the CIR Table, but after the successful engagement of Latino voters in 2011–12, the organization redoubled its efforts to serve immigrant communities by mobilizing the vote.[5] With the creation of an affiliated 501(c)(3) organization, Arizona Center for Empowerment (ACE), LUCHA activists could campaign for specific ballot issues and for pro-immigrant and Latino candidates. Under the leadership of new executive directors Tomas Robles and Alejandra Gomez, LUCHA also organized around issues of low-wage labor. LUCHA became active in the minimum-wage Fight for 15, targeting local fast-food employers with direct action tactics and occasional civil disobedience.

ADAC was active in the campaign for CIR, collaborating with the nationwide efforts of United We Dream (UWD) and drawing on the legislative experience of ADAC leaders to lobby Congress in Washington. Erika Andiola was hired as a staff member by newly elected representative Kyrsten Sinema, and ADAC members participated in demonstrations and congressional visits at the Capitol. Yet as the campaign wore on, differences in focus and strategy emerged among ADAC members. A core of its members sought to advance reform through means that simultaneously highlighted the suffering produced by deportations. One example of this was in June 2013, when Reyna Montoya, whose father had been detained, helped to coordinate Operation Butterfly, a program that brought undocumented youth to the border fence at Nogales, Arizona, for emotional reunions with relatives deported to Mexico.[6] Another example was the effort by several members of ADAC who had relatives in detention or deportation to initiate an antideportation project, which featured ADAC's first campaigns against the deportation of adult immigrants.[7] In summer 2013 the organization also introduced United4Families, a program that trained members not only in lobbying Congress but in fighting individual deportations and engaging in acts of civil disobedience aimed at increasingly stagnant political institutions.

As these varied strategies circulated, two highly visible actions with roots in Arizona cast a national light on deportations and showcased new tools for resisting them. The first was a video made and circulated by Erika Andiola to fight the deportation of her mother. Filmed in early 2013, immediately after the seizure of her mother and brother by ICE, the video shows Andiola, distraught and weeping, as she says:

> Hello, my name is Erika. . . . [M]y mother and my brother were just taken by Immigration. They just came to my house, they knocked on my door. . . . My mom came outside and they took her, for no reason. And then . . . they just took [my brother]—they didn't want to tell me why. They just said that they needed to go because they were here illegally, and that they shouldn't be here.
>   This needs to stop. We need to do something. . . . We need to stop separating families. This is real, this is so real. This is not just happening to me, this is happening to families everywhere. We cannot let this happen anymore. *I need everybody to stop pretending like nothing is wrong, to stop pretending that we're just living normal lives, because we're not. This could happen to any of us at any time.*[8]

Undocumented activists had been fighting individual deportations for several years at the time of Andiola's video. Efforts by UWD to fight the deportation of DREAMers had fueled the effort to secure DACA. At Puente, a campaign called Uno Por Uno (One by One) fought deportations by appealing to the discretion exercised by the Department of Homeland Security (DHS) to close individual cases. Yet Andiola's video offered new tactical fuel for these efforts. Her decision to film herself at the moment of greatest impact, before she had the opportunity to assimilate her fear, anger, and grief, vividly conveyed the costs of administration policies. The viral response, which leveraged Andiola's national visibility and the power of social media to amplify antideportation messages, made it a model for future antideportation efforts.

A second campaign called Bring them Home and its inaugural action, the return of the "DREAM 9," demonstrated the potential of innovative direct action.[9] Three DREAMers traveled to Mexico to join six other undocumented activists who had previously been deported; all nine then marched to the US-Mexico border at Nogales, where they presented themselves to immigration officials and sought humanitarian parole or asylum. Like the Undocubus, which had traveled a year earlier, this action included youth and adults and combined new narratives with dramatic, symbolic action.[10] DACA-eligible DREAMers, unlikely to be deported from within, sought instead to be admitted from outside, where their lack of papers presented a more acute problem. The action not only created dilemmas for the Obama administration, which had to decide how to handle the protesters' petition; it also publicized the plight of transborder families. The administration, the DREAM 9 argued, confronted undocumented migrants with a cruel choice between the life they had established in the United States and loved ones who had remained in or had been deported to countries of origin.[11]

The DREAM 9's challenge also encompassed the conditions of immigration detention. When the DREAM 9 were arrested at the border, they were placed in immigration detention at Florence, Arizona, where they organized internal protests over the conditions in which immigrants were being held. After several days of media contention, in which mainstream immigration advocates protested the "distraction" of this unconventional action, the protesters passed the "credible fear of persecution" screening and were released to rejoin their families as the years-long asylum process ground forward. But the novel tactics and broader substantive claims of the DREAM 9—for the legislative consideration of transborder families and against the inhumanity of immigrant detention—set the stage for more ambitious appeals.

These developments shaped discussions of strategy in Phoenix, as S. 744 cleared the Senate but almost immediately encountered opposition in the House. Conversations at the CIR Table became less tactical and more contentious. ADAC's representatives, who had returned from lobbying and demonstrating in Washington, were disillusioned by the lack of action and transparency on CIR that they had witnessed in Congress. They questioned what they saw as activists' deference to the strategies of congressional Democrats and national pro-immigrant nonprofits.[12] Some ADAC members began to ask whether the legislative strategy of citizenship as a sine qua non of reform was helping or harming a community plagued by ongoing deportations.[13] Perhaps, they suggested, immigrant activists should table the push for citizenship and press for executive action that would stop the deportations. Carlos Garcia and Puente had already reached this conclusion. In early August, at a sober and subdued meeting of the CIR Table, Garcia proposed a more decisive transition. He noted that even if Congress was making progress on legislation, which was far from clear, immigrant communities were paying an unacceptable price in continued deportations. "We're losing 40,000 people this month," he declared.[14] By October, he argued, it would be time to set aside the push for CIR and move to an "administrative ask": deferred action for those the president had aimed to legalize through CIR.

The response from many Table members to these growing doubts was deeply ambivalent. One called it "a disaster" to move to an administrative ask "when we're trying to tell [the House] we won't take no" for an answer.[15] Another member decried the shift from a demand for full citizenship as "cowardly."[16] The Table ultimately focused on planning a major event, designed to rally public support for legislation. The march, which took place on October 5, was a full-throated if politically ambiguous event. Assembling on a bright Saturday morning, more than five thousand participants shouted "Reforma Ahora!" ("Reform Now!"), as they marched toward the Sandra Day O'Connor Courthouse. Yet with few signs of progress from Washington, it was not clear if the boisterous good spirits of the participants marked a renewed effort for reform or a tribute to a vanishing hope of full membership.

Meanwhile, driven by the urgent need to stop the flow of deportations, Puente began the pivot to the "administrative ask." Organizers commenced this effort under the logistical umbrella of Not1More Deportation, a campaign initiated in spring 2013 by National Day Laborers Organizing Network (NDLON). Consolidating a focus on deportation that had persisted throughout the campaign for CIR, Not1More highlighted tactics of direct action to publicize the administration's ongoing deportations and demand administrative relief. With NDLON's support, Puente organized an October convening for community leaders from across the country. Organizers at this event would argue for a conclusive shift to an administrative, antideportation focus and train participants from across the country in direct action tactics. The power of self-reliant, local communities to challenge the political stalemate in Washington and fight deportations would be the message of the nascent campaign.

NOT1MORE DEPORTATION: A CAMPAIGN SPEAKS FOR A CHANGING MOVEMENT

The Not1More Deportation campaign combined the public pressure of direct action tactics with appeals, both particularized and general, to executive discretion over immigration enforcement. The first branch of the campaign was a fight against individual deportations, exemplified by Puente's Uno Por Uno program. This effort applied grassroots pressure, mobilized through the circulation of family separation videos, to sites of discretion within immigration enforcement agencies. When an undocumented community member was seized by ICE, Puente worked with that person's family to locate the family member, establish channels of communication, enlist legal assistance to assess prospects for relief based on legal rights, and conduct its own assessment of whether the case might provide a basis for the official exercise of discretion.[17] Where the detained community member presented a compelling case for the exercise of discretion—a lower priority for deportation under the Morton Memorandum,[18] a cohesive family with young children, robust contributions to neighborhood, church or other organizations— Puente commenced a more extensive public campaign.

The organization filmed a video, similar in concept to Andiola's, which introduced the detained person through the eyes of his or her family, describing the circumstances under which she or he was taken, the role of the person in the family and community, and the painful efforts of the family to continue life without the loved one.[19] Videos were then circulated through social media, with a petition directed to an ICE or DHS official, or member of Congress, pressing that person to seek the release of the detained family member. Puente worked with a changing array of officials and channels of command to identify specific offices or officials who might exercise discretion in favor of a detained community member. Garcia explained:

> Sometimes it was pressuring the local ICE office and that would do it. When that person wouldn't do it, we would go to D.C. . . . [A]t that time we pushed so hard they [began to rely on] a program called Headquarter Review . . . where they assign someone in D.C. [to oversee the decisions of] the local ICE office.[20]

This practice resulted in many victories: Puente estimates that they secured release from detention or termination of deportation proceedings for more than 150 community members.[21] But the constantly changing cast of characters—which made Garcia wonder if DHS had been "made that way . . . [so that] you never know who's actually making those decisions"[22]—showed the need to address the one actor with consistent control over deportation policy: the president.

President Obama was targeted by a second branch of the campaign, which sought more comprehensive relief from deportation. This effort proceeded through an urgent, innovative direct action campaign. Activists engaged in extreme versions of familiar tactics, including weeks-long hunger strikes or multiday endurance marches. They staged sit-ins or formed human chains at the entrance to ICE offices. In the most dramatic actions, they blocked the exits at detention facilities or tied themselves to the chases of deportation buses. These novel protests expressed activists' sense of urgency about the ongoing suffering of families in their community. "[The government and nonprofits] didn't understand the urgency of it all," said Camila, a leader in ADAC's ICE action: "We saw that we needed to make it urgent, that we needed to 'be in their face.' So we planned an action at ICE, and we chained ourselves to the gate."[23] These unconventional protests also expressed a newfound self-reliance, demonstrating that communities would act on their own behalf until government ceased its oppression; as activists put it, "If you don't stop deportations, we will."[24] The actions sometimes had an immediate focus: an individual being detained, a locality with a history of collaboration with ICE, a detention facility with a particularly brutal record of inhumane practices. But these actions also aimed to make visible to the public the institutional pipeline running from police encounter to deportation, supported by a president who claimed to be a friend to immigrants. And they sought to thwart the operation of that pipeline, making it more difficult and costly for the administration to continue its deportations. The tactics employed in Not1More Deportation were more immediately disruptive, and more confrontational in tone, than even the oppositional campaigns that had preceded it; they challenged what the public was willing to accept as a tactical expression of protest.

The Not1More Deportation campaign made one initial demand: that President Obama grant deferred action to adults not covered by DACA ("DACA for all"). As the campaign continued, protesters also sought assurances that the administration would provide undocumented communities a "place at the table" in subsequent immigration policy making. Yet Not1More framed for public debate a series of wider issues—about the power of the state to establish and defend borders and the legitimacy of detaining and deporting immigrants—that earlier campaigns had only obliquely referenced.

Viewed one way, the bold tactics and broad demands of Not1More Deportation had roots in the increasingly defiant campaigns explored in chapter 4: the campaign of the undocumented and unafraid for a stand-alone DREAM Act and for DACA and the voyage of the Undocubus. But they also staked out new ground for the movement, reflecting its growing confidence and increasingly self-sufficient, oppositional character. This new ground spanned several dimensions of the campaign: the convergence of youth and adults on a single campaign, the reframing around narratives of family separation, the tactical and emotional innovations of the campaign, and activists' frankly adversarial relation to the state.

GENERATIONS CONVERGE IN THE STRATEGIES OF THE NOT1MORE CAMPAIGN

In Not1More Deportation the activism of youth and adults converged around a federal antideportation campaign. This confluence was particularly striking in Phoenix, where the activism of youth-focused organizations and community-based organizations had often run on complementary rather than conjoined tracks. Although protection from deportation was one focus of DACA, it was also viewed as a vehicle for the political and economic incorporation that had evaded youth with the failure of the DREAM Act. Youth campaigns, such as those organized by ADAC, aimed primarily at such incorporation, focusing on affirmative measures such as scholarships, civic engagement with Latino voters, and legislative reform entailing a path to citizenship. Community-based organizations like Puente had been more systematically committed to fighting deportations and preventing forms of enforcement—such as SB 1070 or Joe Arpaio's raids—that terrorized undocumented and mixed status communities. As 2013 and the campaign for CIR wore on, the goals and tactics of the two groups converged.

While the adult activists of Puente remained focused on deportation, they moved toward an emphasis on federal action—an arena long dominated by youth—through their efforts to address local challenges. This transition happened differently for Puente's leaders and for its grassroots members. Puente's leadership had targeted the federal government early on, as a vehicle for limiting the excesses of state officials like Arpaio, yet they saw federal power as a double-edged sword.[25] Federal intervention against state officials was often grounded in a claim of federal preemption:[26] a fight, as Carlos Garcia put it, about which level of government "has the right to deport us."[27] The Not1More Deportation campaign allowed activists wary of such risks to confront federal enforcement practices directly. Uno Por Uno efforts targeted the discretion of federal enforcement agencies such as DHS. Winning a release from detention or a termination of deportation proceedings did not simply free an individual to resume life with his or her family; it could also clarify DHS priorities in ways that other organizations could exploit.[28] Seeking categorical relief from deportation through presidential action was a more systematic way of limiting the scope of federal immigration enforcement.

Puente's grassroots members moved more gradually from a state and local to an interstate, to a federal, focus. The Undocubus enabled this transition. The riders on this multistate trip to the Democratic National Convention (DNC) first learned to look beyond their individual states by glimpsing the parallels between their states and other immigrant-hostile jurisdictions where they stopped and organized. As one Phoenix rider observed, organizing with people in other states taught her that "[restrictive state] immigration laws affect people in a lot more states. . . . [T]his fight doesn't belong to just one community but to all of us."[29] Riders also came to see how state hostility was engendered or exploited by the federal government, whose 287(g) program turned local sheriffs' departments into a "force-multiplier" for federal immigration enforcement.[30] The heightened vulnerability triggered by these programs, and the contrasting protection recently secured through DACA, helped them grasp the deep implication of the federal government in local security or suffering. By the time they reached the DNC in Charlotte, they were ready to challenge President Obama, demanding to know "on which side of history is he going to be."[31] The Not1More campaign extended this emergent federal focus with an explicit demand for a broad grant of deferred action.

Youth organizations, which had previously targeted the federal government in their search for a legislative solution, moved toward a focus on ending deportations. In many ways, this was a more complicated transition. The desire of youth activists for the de jure recognition of their de facto citizenship—a prospect offered by CIR—had diverted many from a focus on antideportation work. During 2013, however, this balance began to shift; this transition was led locally, and nationwide, by a group of ADAC activists.

One factor that fueled a shift was the disillusionment of these activists with the politics of CIR in Congress. Those members of ADAC who witnessed congressional machinations firsthand grew frustrated by the partisan, careerist posturing of legislators in the face of the tangible, urgent concerns of their families and communities. Andiola, who spent fall 2013 in the D.C. office of Representative Sinema, was struck by the contrast between external messaging and internal disarray:

The first eye-opener was the meeting that I had with [House] leadership . . . literally with the chief of staff and their advisor, and they straight-up said,

"We're going to introduce a symbolic bill [HR 15].... It's not going to pass...." But the worst thing is that I continued to see them doing press conferences [and] all this public outreach on the actual bill, knowing that it was not going to happen.... I was working there when they shut down the government. And Syria was happening. *So there was absolutely no work for immigration reform [going on] inside.* But they could swear to the public that they were doing something. So it's like, this is not right.[32]

This not only made these youth activists skeptical about the prospects for a legislative solution; it led them to seek a more direct voice and self-reliant strategy for undocumented communities. Summing up her time in Congress with a group called AZ2DC, Reyna Montoya observed: "I was able to see the politics and how cynical DC is. But then at the same time, the power our people have, and [how] we underestimate them.... [W]e need to have undocumented people speak for themselves."[33]

What ADAC members heard as undocumented people spoke, and as they reflected on their own families' experiences with deportation, contrasted sharply with the debates in Washington. It made, instead, a case for new priorities. Montoya explained:

Many parents especially [are] saying that what they want is relief. I could care less about citizenship, to be honest, if my mom gets deported. How is she going to become a citizen if she gets deported? ... [M]y family cannot really afford a citizenship-or-nothing [stance] and ... it's good to be challenging our thinking, to be reevaluating what [has] happened in 2013.[34]

In January 2014, ADAC members led this reassessment at a national level. In an open letter to the Immigrant Rights Movement, ADAC as an organization, and some two dozen of its individual members, including Andiola, Montoya, and others who had lobbied in Washington, joined other activists in declaring:

Despite all the hard work that we did last year, we cannot ignore that we did not win a legislative policy change. In the same year we lived through close to 370,000 undocumented immigrants being deported by the Obama administration.... We don't know what's going to happen in 2014, but we know that the status quo is unbearable.... We do want citizenship rights.... We do want to be able to vote and voice our opinions ... [but w]e can't ask our communities to wait for "citizenship" while we see our mothers, our fathers and our children being taken from our homes by immigration.... Fight with us for immediate relief for our families. Let's together hold President Obama accountable for every deported parent.[35]

Underlying this rejection of a failed politics of legislative reform was a subtler shift in self-conception: a recognition of persistent vulnerability created by the threat of family separation. Undocumented youth had long negotiated a hybrid or intersectional identity, shaped by law, familial experience, and the demands of movement campaigns. The legal guarantee of K–12 education established by *Plyler v. Doe* allowed undocumented youth to spend their early years in the United States as functional "insiders": mastering the English language, becoming fluent in American culture, and experiencing the feeling of being largely indistinguishable from their peers.[36] But what Supreme Court doctrine fostered, federal or state legislation often impeded. Those who came to feel like any other American youths often hit a wall of exclusion in late adolescence, because they lacked federal authorization to work or were barred by state law from attending state universities or paying in-state tuition. For youth involved in activism, adaptation to this new reality, which Roberto Gonzales has called "learning to be illegal," could be interrupted or deferred by the anticipation of change or the immersion in challenging, meaningful work.[37] But the extent to which undocumented youth activists identified with the "insider" or "outsider" facets of their identity proved to be variable over time, the oscillation shaped by familial and activist experiences and by external political developments.

If the grant of DACA and the promise of CIR summoned the "insider" identities of youth, by highlighting the path to integration, the collapse of legislative possibility reactivated a sense of "outsider" status. And led by those who had experienced family separation firsthand, youth activists declared publicly what they had long understood: that their own sense of security was inextricably bound up with the fates of family members made vulnerable by enforcement priorities and the spaces in which they worked. This deep connection made the life of any DREAMer decisively different from a person living in a family of citizens.[38] "I could care less about citizenship," Reyna Montoya declared, "if my mom gets deported."[39] For some, this perception fueled a belief that, as beneficiaries of DACA, they had a special responsibility to unprotected family members. Camila, a leader of ADAC's antideportation efforts, who had faced her own father's deportation, expressed this view: "If we have DACA, we're somewhat protected, so then why would we not protect our parents, who sacrificed so much to get us to where we're at?"[40] For others, the intractable vulnerability of their parents demanded a radical reappraisal of their own situation. Andiola, in her video, took this position, saying pointedly to her fellow DREAMers:

"I need everybody . . . to stop pretending that we're just living normal lives, because we're not. This could happen to any of us, at any time." For many youths during this period, the unresolved prospect of family separation incited a reassessment of strategic options. Acknowledging that however accomplished or culturally integrated they might be, undocumented youth could not live normal lives when their parents were threatened, young people embraced the antideportation priority advanced by Puente's adults.

NARRATIVES OF FAMILY SEPARATION AS A NEW MOVEMENT FRAME

Consistent with these shifts in focus and self-conception, the narratives offered in this campaign evolved as well. The specter of family separation had been a recurrent thread in the storytelling prevalent among undocumented youth. Even in DREAMer narratives, the fear of family separation sometimes emerged: the stories of youth canvassers and the Dreamers Adrift plea, "Obama, don't deport my mama!" are examples. Although early adult mobilizations did not rely explicitly on storytelling, fear of family separation was present in those statements they made against SB 1070 and the enforcement efforts of Joe Arpaio. In the Not1More campaign, however, family separation became *the* narrative, the unifying definition of what it meant to be undocumented or a member of a mixed status family. The Not1More campaign also changed the *way* that family separation was narrated in the movement: family members described it not as a looming threat but as a reality they were living through, described in an anguished present tense. A change in the dominant narrative helped activists shift the leading frame of the movement to how the need for change for undocumented immigrants was conceptualized for the public. Relief from deportation became the way to address a practice of family separation that was disruptive and painful, and that implicated the government in stark inhumanity.

Embracing family separation as the dominant narrative of the campaign required a change in some familiar features of undocumented storytelling. First it marked a further divergence from the long-standing, if sometimes implicit, practice of distinguishing between "good" immigrants and less-than-good immigrants in undocumented narratives. The DREAMer narrative, which invoked the hardworking aspirant to economic and cultural assimilation, had a corollary: it made others into "nightmares," who should be deported or detained.[41] This focus eased somewhat as activists declared themselves to be undocumented and un-afraid: they turned the focus from academic achievement and affirmed the language and culture of their countries of origin. Yet their identification as students deprived of higher education referenced a narrative of upward mobility and economic contribution, and the official discourse surrounding DACA reestablished DREAMers as exceptional among un-documented immigrants.[42]

Those who presented themselves as family members torn from their loved ones, in contrast, claimed no distinctive or privileged identities, for themselves or for those who had been taken. In this sense they were similar to the adults who had come out against Arpaio or traveled with the Undocubus. They might be hardworking or devoted to their communities—characteristics that resonated slightly with the "good im-migrant" narrative—but their most salient, unifying characteristic was their vulnerability to rupture in their family lives. Leading with this vul-nerability, rather than with innocence or upward mobility, challenged citizens to understand and accept a broad swath of undocumented ex-perience, not just the most conventionally accomplished parts of it.

Family separation stories also reflected a shift in narrative structure: from stories of triumph over adversity that sought formal legal recog-nition for their completion, to stories of tragedy that required dramatic state action—reversal of a deeply flawed state policy—for their resolu-tion. Even the narratives of the undocumented and unafraid, which were less triumphal than the early DREAMer narratives, featured a de-gree of agentic self-help that made the federal role one of recognition or assistance rather than transformative intervention. The narrators of the Not1More Deportation campaign presented themselves and their sequestered kin as more painfully and systematically impeded. Though they struggled ahead with their lives—single parents raising households of children, older siblings caring for younger brothers and sisters—the essential message delivered by family separation narratives was that life, as a family knew it, would remain suspended until an end to inhumane governmental policy enabled family members to reunite. This narra-tive, of course, conveys only part of activists' experience: participants who moved from a strategy of reliance on Congress to a strategy of confronting the president did not lack for agency or self-reliance. But the experience of family separation, as narrated in the campaign, high-lights neither triumph over adversity nor the personal agency of family members. It foregrounds the imperative of state action to end a state-imposed harm.

There is also a change in the emotional valence of the narrative and the demands it makes on storytellers, organizers, and audiences. The narratives of Not1More, particularly in the fight against individual deportations, confront their audience with raw, unmediated anguish, as family members grieve the seizure, detention, and deportation of their loved ones. Andiola's wrenching video provided a key model for this form of expression. She is captured weeping and wiping tears from her face as she struggles to grasp the fact of her mother's seizure. Her organizing instincts have not deserted her; by filming herself, she is reaching out to a community capable of assisting her. Yet she mobilizes others not by offering a plan but by showing them what it is like to live through ICE's seizure of a loved one. In this sense Andiola's video resembles those made by Puente for its Uno Por Uno campaigns, which capture the grief of family members who are not activists. The videos aim to make visible the rupture created by immigration enforcement, even as families struggle to continue their daily lives.

The publicization of private forms of suffering was not inaugurated by Not1More; this kind of revelation lies at the heart of undocumented storytelling. But the pain expressed in the fight against deportations is more intense and personal than the indignation of Undocubus riders or the frustration of the undocumented and unafraid. It is also less resolved by time or reflection, which means that the demands of sharing it are particularly acute. Organizers recognized the burden this imposed on narrators, even as they grasped the value of sharing this kind of pain. Carlos Garcia explained:

> So everyday, we['d] have these people come into our space or we'd be outside the jail and we'd run into these people. . . . They're just [crying] to us, we would swallow it and then we would go into this mechanism and come up with a strategy to fight it. [Finally, we said] we need to share that. We can't be swallowing it and making these political arguments. We needed to put that [pain] out there. And we also put it back on the people, that this is going to help your loved ones get out. People need to see what you're going through. That's how we're going to get the people engaged and involved in fighting for this.[43]

By explaining to family members that the public communication of private suffering was the best way to help their loved ones, organizers helped them to assume the burden of this more demanding form of self-disclosure.

Narratives of family anguish also place new demands on prospective allies. DREAMer stories offered listeners familiar, even comforting, narratives of triumph over obstacles; narratives of family separation may strike audiences as unfamiliar and their pain unrelieved. They also lie bafflingly beyond the personal experience of many citizens, though those with incarcerated loved ones may recognize the stark disregard for the integrity of families. Most viscerally, the raw, unresolved grief expressed in these statements or videos can be excruciating to observe.[44] But participants judged these demands to be worth making, if they could awaken the public, the bureaucracy of executive enforcement, and President Obama himself to the anguish unleashed by inhumane enforcement practices.

TACTICAL INNOVATION: BODILY EXTREMITY AND OUTRAGE AS EXPRESSIONS OF PERFORMATIVE CITIZENSHIP

In Not1More, activists innovated not simply by introducing new narrative frames and emotions but through their choice of tactics. The campaign orchestrated a cascade of direct action events in cities across the country, some involving starkly disruptive acts of civil disobedience. Many of these actions crossed an implicit boundary between tactics that were familiar and largely tolerated (though they were perhaps more controversial when they were performed by undocumented protesters) and tactics that ventured into unknown and potentially dangerous territory.[45] In the Not1More Deportation campaign, protesters intervened bodily in the processes of immigration enforcement, sometimes risking physical harm to themselves, and framed their actions not simply as an appeal to institutions from outside them but as a robust form of self-help ("If [the administration] won't stop deportations, the community will"). These actions departed even from past oppositional tactics, in several ways.

As in the coming out of youth activists or the civil disobedience of the Undocubus, activists targeted potentially receptive members of the public. Protesters sought to expose the devastating extent of detention and deportation, effected by a president who was perceived by many supporters as a friend to immigrants.[46] But these protests also targeted DHS leadership and Obama himself, creating vexing dilemmas for the administration. How would it handle the stream of negative publicity at a time when the administration itself felt thwarted by House Republican opposition to reform? How would it navigate the ongoing standoffs, which forced the administration to balance temporary publicization and disruption of immigration enforcement against politically damaging conflicts with a group the president claimed to support? And as the human costs of close to two million deportations were conveyed ever more vividly, what action would the president take to protect undocumented adults and their families? These confrontations were designed to expose and embarrass the Obama administration before constituencies who supported immigration reform and to prod the conscience of a president who seemed prepared to use immigrants as pawns in his negotiations with Congress, yet publicly affirmed their belonging and aspirations. To claim the attention of these vital targets, the campaign combined familiar direct action tactics such as hunger strikes and long marches with novel bodily intervention in the machinery of immigration enforcement.

Beyond the larger purposes of awakening the public and creating conflicts for the administration, these tactics served shorter-term goals. Direct action events bolstered the fight against individual deportations. Events that were extreme in their duration or bodily demands kept a case before the public and allowed those directly affected to voice their pain and demonstrate their commitment to their loved ones. In February 2014, for example, seven activists from Puente staged a three-week hunger strike to protest the detention of their adult children. They were led by Fernanda, whose adult son had been detained for more than two years, and who declared that she had "nothing else left but to sacrifice herself and health for her son, and to end all the suffering in our communities."[47] Like many actions of Not1More Deportation, the strike combined willingness to endure suffering with strategic siting and political self-assertion. The hunger strikers created a sidewalk encampment outside the Phoenix ICE office, resisting an order to decamp when Phoenix police claimed they had encroached on privately owned property. The ensuing police raid, and the arrest of Erika Andiola and Carlos Garcia (who were occupying the site as strikers rested at Puente), presented new opportunities to claim visibility and articulate demands.

Direct action events were also staged as a form of escalation, as Puente claimed more ambitious targets for its individual campaigns. Uno Por Uno, as Carlos Garcia explained, sought a categorical progression of cases.[48] When a series of releases made clear that detainees with a particular profile—no criminal record, for example—could be the beneficiaries of executive discretion, Puente then turned to more difficult cases, such as detainees who had recrossed the border to reunite with their families, or who had been placed in deportation proceedings following a minor vehicular or drinking offense. As cases became more challenging, Puente used dramatic direct action events to generate publicity and place additional pressure on DHS decision makers.[49] By April 2014, for example, Puente was engaging in public campaigns for detainees who had committed minor alcohol offenses. To demonstrate the commitment of the community to such cases, Puente organized the sixty-mile Walk to End Deportations, which culminated in a vigil at the notorious private detention facility at Eloy, where many community members supported by Puente had been and were being held. The most prominent faces and voices of the walk and the strike were undocumented adults, many of them middle-aged parents who had suffered the extended detention of their adult children. But Phoenix youth activists participated as well, joining in walk and vigil, publicizing the effort, and posting their support.

Youth played a more prominent role in a second set of tactics: bodily intervention in the processes of immigration enforcement. These dramatic events became the hallmarks of Not1More Deportation, in Arizona and across the country. Because protesters inserted themselves in contexts where their physical presence was not only unexpected but often legally prohibited, these actions functioned as a form of civil disobedience, which exposed protesters to arrest and to the risk of detention and deportation. The ADAC actions, which blocked entry to an ICE building and halted a deportation bus, exemplified this kind of protest. These actions spotlighted the sites and sequences of immigration enforcement while impeding the functioning of this apparatus. Protests blocked access to ICE buildings, delayed and sometimes prevented the transportation of immigrants across the border, and sparked protests among those held in detention centers.

Though civil disobedience and feats of physical suffering were not new to the movement, the more dramatic or disruptive application of these tactics communicated new messages to the public, the administration, and immigrants themselves. The feats of physical endurance, for example, helped to externalize and concretize suffering that the public might not fully understand. The Puente hunger strikers conveyed in a currency members of the public could grasp—the familiar experience of fasting or hunger—a kind of pain or longing for which many had no point of reference. More defiant protests countered this anguished testimony with physical demonstrations of agency and resolve. Physical intervention in deportation processes, for example, sent a potent message of self-reliance and helped to preserve a delicate emotional economy for a group of protesters who remained ambivalent about unqualified vulnerability.[50]

The physical demands of these transgressive actions also reflected a kind of performative citizenship. Public protest, as we saw in chapters 3 and 4, claims a central prerogative of the citizen: the power to dissent or to engage in demonstrations seeking redress of grievances. But these tactics reflected a kind of super-citizenship: participants demonstrated their willingness to endure physical hardship and expose themselves to the possibility of arrest—with its daunting immigration-related consequences—to lodge their protest in the most pointed and vivid way. The public response to this extreme version of citizenship was not knowable ex ante: some observers might be less impressed by the commitment reflected in such actions than by its transgression of legal boundaries, particularly when those acting lacked legal status. But in bringing an element not only of transgression but of bodily hardship to their protest, activists allied themselves with iconic citizens—including Cesar Chavez and Martin Luther King Jr.—who had placed their bodies at risk to protest laws they regarded as unjust.[51] This bolstered their resolve and enhanced the positive resonance of their actions for some observers.

Finally, activists' vivid, disruptive tactics helped to communicate a feeling of outrage, an emotion that reflected a sense of de facto membership. This feeling, captured through the bodily extremity of blocking roads with human chains or tying protesters to the chases of deportation busses, was given voice by a participant in an action to shut down the Boston ICE building:

> My mother crossed the border to this country some thirty years ago. She existed twenty-seven years as an undocumented person . . . as this government would like to label her . . . an illegal human being, something that is incomprehensible, something that is inhumane. . . . That was the woman that birthed me, that was the woman that raised me to be the person that I am today, to stand . . . here demanding justice, to stand here and say to this country: *you* are the one that is inhumane, *you* are the one that is breaking rules, *you* are the one that is breaking laws, *you* are breaking laws of humanity, *you* are breaking laws of dignity, *you* are breaking laws of respect.[52]

This expression of frank outrage was a new development in undocumented politics. The range of emotions related to anger—frustration, indignation, outrage—was slow to emerge in undocumented activism. The cheerful determination manifested by early DREAMers, or the proud resolve expressed in the first marches against enforcement by attrition, distinguished immigrant activists from participants in many social movements, for whom anger is the "fire in the belly" that transforms injury into mobilization.[53] One factor shaping this affective stance may have been the status of the protesters. "Undocumented people feel that it's not okay to express your outrage," Reyna Montoya explained. "It's not okay to express how things are not right, because *you're not supposed to have rights*, right?"[54] Yet as undocumented youth became more empowered political participants—as they came to feel that political actors were accountable to them yet saw only a slow, equivocal response—they gradually shed this inhibition. Part of being "undocumented, unafraid, and unapologetic" was acknowledging and voicing frustration at the opportunism and delay of elected officials. On the Undocubus, adults too began to express indignation at their treatment: unjust deprivation and surveillance imposed on those who come only to work and to support their families. "We are undocumented, but we are human" declared one activist at an Undocubus action. "We are not animals."[55]

In Not1More Deportation, these anger-based feelings verged on outrage, as what was once a political critique came to be infused with a moral impetus. Family separation, protesters suggested, is different from thwarted opportunity. It is not simply unfair, given the attributes or expectations of those involved. Tearing parents from children, siblings from siblings is categorically unacceptable: it is arbitrarily cruel and denies the deeply human imperative to make a shared life with loved ones. But the expression of outrage, while clearly sparked by governmental inhumanity, also implicated a feeling of desert. The "right to have rights," invoked by Montoya, has been raised as a central dilemma of stateless individuals by theorists dating back to Hannah Arendt.[56] But statelessness or lack of membership, as Montoya's rhetorical question suggests, is a frame that undocumented activists no longer apply to themselves. Their commitment, their ongoing work, their willingness to sacrifice for collective gain, and the knowledge they have drawn from their efforts give them a claim to behave like those with a formal stake in American politics. This claim is both the product of more conventional forms of performative citizenship—such as voter registration or legislative advocacy—and a feature of its more oppositional expression.

THE OPPOSITIONAL POLITICS OF NOT1MORE

Finally, the Not1More campaign signaled the development of a more mature oppositional stance on the part of activists toward the formal institutions of government. For the first time, undocumented activists faced the state as an adversary: no longer merely a dilatory or inconsistent ally but an entity charged with violating the humanity of undocumented communities, that should be engaged in a fully oppositional spirit, either within or outside its institutions.[57]

The trajectory of undocumented activism in Phoenix between 2010 and 2013 reflected the gradual, sometimes episodic, emergence of oppositional consciousness. This functional level of oppositional consciousness, as political scientist Jane Mansbridge explained, involved "identifying with the group, recognizing injustice, demanding rectification, and seeing shared interest."[58] The oppositional thrust of this period was nevertheless muted slightly in late 2012 and early 2013, as activists approached the campaign for CIR; the magnitude of the stakes, the optimism produced by DACA, and the revived promise of Obama's second term may have softened elements of oppositional consciousness. Although activists' pride and determination persisted during these months, their accusations of injustice and posture of demand temporarily eased slightly, as they worked with national pro-immigrant organizations and members of Congress toward a strategy for CIR. Phoenix organizations persisted in antideportation and other state-skeptical projects at the state level, yet they also retained enough hope in the federal legislative process to collaborate with mainstream organizations and offer narratives that, if more generationally inclusive, echoed the aspiring tropes of the "good immigrant."

But as legislative actors advanced partisan interests and national nonprofits pursued their own visions of a pro-immigrant agenda, the reality of continuing deportations forced a reckoning for activists. Their decision to rely on their growing arsenal of skills, frame an inclusive image of undocumented identity, and confront the president as a means of producing change marked their transition to a more robust oppositional stance.

The Not1More campaign moved from what Mansbridge identifies as a functional oppositional consciousness to a "full-fledged" or "mature" oppositional consciousness. Mature oppositional consciousness, according to Mansbridge, goes beyond embracing a marginalized identity and coalescing with others to struggle against group-based injustice. This full-fledged oppositional consciousness involves grasping the systematic character of a dominant group's use of power, condemning that domination in a moral register, and developing a set of strategies for ending that domination.[59] Through their argument that family separation entails not simply injustice but inhumanity, and through their frank expressions of outrage, participants signaled a shift to a moral register of condemnation. But a systematic critique of governmental power over immigrants and an ambitious set of proposals for ending that oppressive power were also defining features of Not1More Deportation.

The Not1More campaign began by framing the Obama administration as a false ally: it supported immigrants when it glimpsed electoral advantage but deported far more extensively than even bipartisanship required. Exposing the hypocrisy of the Obama administration had always been a challenge, given the popularity of the president with progressives who also favored immigration reform, but this task became immeasurably more difficult after the announcement of DACA. "After he did DACA, the president was an amazing hero for a lot of people," Erika Andiola reflected. "Turning that into 'Deporter in Chief' took a lot of work."[60] The campaign accomplished this not simply by publicizing the staggering numbers of deportations and the range of those deported (which did not always conform to the administration's stated priorities), but by rendering visible and concrete both the machinery of detention and deportation and the lives of those who were affected.

The campaign's focus on the "apprehension to deportation pipeline" also demonstrated the systematicity of the government's efforts. It exposed the scope of the administration's investment in ongoing deportations: the network of institutions and relationships that it has created and maintained in order to insure the movement of immigrants out of the country. And it uncovered the role of immigrant detention in the functioning of the US economy, highlighting the rise of actors whose motivation to detain immigrants stemmed not just from the search for political influence but from the search for profit. These revelations connected immigrant detention with preexisting systems of mass incarceration that disproportionately confine Black and brown persons and with patterns of overpolicing and abusive policing that affect their communities.

The full-fledged opposition of this campaign was also illustrated by the scope and systematicity of its agenda for change. The campaigns of the undocumented and unafraid, though rhetorically and tactically adverse, made demands that worked largely within existing legal and institutional frameworks. The DREAM Act, had it been adopted, would have extended the path to citizenship to a publicly appealing group of youthful immigrants. DACA enlarged the established practice of executive discretion over deportation through a bounded, categorical grant of deferred action. In Not1More, activists pressed these established legal frameworks to their limits, opening substantive vistas that lay beyond the assumptions and goals of extant institutions.

In March 2014, after President Obama called for a review of DHS's deportation policy, aimed at making it "more humane," NDLON, the formal sponsor of the Not1More campaign, announced the formation of its Blue Ribbon Commission, which would advise the president in this effort.[61] The commission, which included Phoenix youth activist Erika Andiola, was composed of currently and previously undocumented individuals. The use of an organizational form traditionally employed to marshal professional expertise, and the decision that the commission would be self-appointed, when blue ribbon commissions are conventionally convened by government officials, made clear that this effort was based on a claim about knowledge. The form of expertise most germane to immigration policy is experience as a person directly affected by immigration enforcement.[62] In addition to making this epistemological point, the commission's report provides the clearest available statement of the goals of the campaign and of the antideportation wing of the movement at that time.

The campaign's insistence on the need to reach beyond existing legal remedies is clear in its primary demands: that the government stop separating families through deportations and include undocumented people in policy-making processes. Though one description of the first demand, "DACA for all," seems simply to extend a preexisting program of executive relief, its scope is actually far broader. DACA, while exceptionally valuable, is a modest program, which has granted relief to fewer than a million people.[63] Even the incomplete relief afforded under the Deferred Action for Parents of Americans (DAPA) program that President Obama announced in November 2014—which granted deferred action to undocumented parents of American citizen or legal permanent resident children but not to the undocumented parents of undocumented youth[64]—would have extended deferred action to three to four times as many people as the DACA program.[65] If DACA were to be provided "for all," it would cease to be a categorical exemption from deportation and would become a systematic change in deportation policy.[66] More revealing, however, is the alternative formulation of this demand: to "end deportations." As Carlos Garcia described this demand: "[We're] not trying to change a policy, not trying to change an elected official, *but trying to change a mindset: trying to change the idea that it is okay to deport people.*"[67] Ending deportations—as opposed to suspending some deportations under a program like DACA—would curtail the power of the state to act against those who are present without authorization within its boundaries. This change implicates the power of ostensibly sovereign states to include and exclude through the establishment and enforcement of geographical boundaries.[68]

The claim for inclusion in policy making, similarly, exceeds a conventional demand for voice. Not only does the commission make a powerful epistemic claim about its experiential knowledge, but it describes inclusion in policy making as a performative means of integration:

> Democracy and active citizenship are built upon full participation in the democratic process and we would like the opportunity to represent ourselves in the negotiations that will affect our lives. . . . *The effort for inclusion of immigrants can already begin to be realized by including us at the table as our own advocates.*[69]

The broad implications of the commission's prioritizing of experiential knowledge became clear in summer 2014, when undocumented activists learned that President Obama was appealing to national pro-immigrant nonprofits to "manage the expectations" of undocumented activists prior to his announcement of a change in deportation policy. Indignant at the president's failure to engage a group that possessed the vital experiential perspective on immigration enforcement, Blue Ribbon Commission members issued a statement declaring the following:

> Now is the most important time for President Obama to meet with undocumented people, it is not enough for immigration lobbyists in Washington to be the sole group of stakeholders meeting with President Obama to discuss the timing and scope of pending administrative changes to immigration policy. This is why members of the Blue Ribbon Commission, a group composed of undocumented people in deportation proceedings and families of people in immigration detention, ask our allies in Washington to press President Obama to meet with us.[70]

Activists punctuated this message by protesting outside the White House and visiting the offices of pro-immigrant nonprofits, demanding that they refrain from meeting with the president in any convening that did not include undocumented representatives.[71]

The campaign's most prominent demands demonstrated its reach beyond the scope of existing legal frameworks; however, the report of the Blue Ribbon Commission signaled an even more comprehensive agenda that could transform the terms of the immigration debate. The inhumane conditions of immigrant detention—inadequate heat, nutrition, and outdoor time, and separation of parents from children—had long been an issue in the movement; Not1More activists also focused on the use of solitary confinement and the threat of force-feeding to respond to hunger strikes and other prison mobilizations. But the commission's recommendations demonstrated a further shift in its remedial goal: they aimed not to "fix" immigration enforcement or related institutions of immigrant detention but to radically reduce their footprint and funding, with the ultimate goal of eliminating them. The demand to "end" integral features of this regime[72] announces an abolitionist goal that diverges sharply from dominant legal frameworks.[73] The asks embodied in the report that serve this end are numerous and extensive: "**end** programs that extend DHS/ICE enforcement through official deputization of local law enforcement," "**eliminate** the bed quota (i.e., the mandate of funding for a minimum number of beds for detained immigrants)," and "**terminate** federal contracts with private prisons."[74] These decarceral demands make clear, as Garcia also put it, "that people shouldn't be detained and that it's not ok to be detained."[75] Similarities between immigration detention and criminal incarceration, and the growing role of private prison corporations whose bottom line incentivizes detention without clear channels of public accountability, highlighted problems that were pervasive among, but not exclusive to, immigrants. These commonalities, reinforced by the critique of overpolicing and racial profiling that had become central in Phoenix, enabled efforts at coalition building with the Movement for Black Lives (MBL) and other abolitionist organizations.

A demand that may be equally consequential, but more inchoate, concerns the control over borders in the nation's immigration regime. From the DREAM 9's claim that undocumented people should be able to cross borders to support those they love, to the commission's demand that Obama allow the return of those previously deported so they can be with their families in the United States, these views gesture toward a more constrained role for the nation-state in setting and enforcing its geographic boundaries—and deciding who lies inside or outside them.[76] Not1More offered the most systematic critique of the role of the state in deportation and the most challenging programmatic proposals for ending detention and deportation that the movement has thus far advanced.

A CONTINGENT LEGACY

On November 20, 2014, President Obama ended months of effort and speculation by announcing a new program of deferred action. DAPA extended temporary relief from deportation to parents of US citizens and legal residents, a group estimated to number more than three million.[77] It did not, however, extend deferred action to parents of DREAMers or to undocumented immigrants living in the United States without children. Organizations from Puente to LUCHA wrestled with their ambivalence about the outcome of a campaign in which "1% of our people [fought] for 100% of our people, and then g[ot] something for 40%," as Carlos Garcia put it.[78] They worried about the potentially divisive effects of this partial relief and of Obama's freighted distinction between "families," who would receive protection, and "felons," who would become more focused targets of federal enforcement.[79] Yet these debates were short-lived; within months of Obama's announcement, a federal district court enjoined the implementation of DAPA, a decision that was affirmed by the Court of Appeals and allowed to stand by a divided Supreme Court.[80]

With no relief forthcoming, the new ground broken by Not1More Deportation—in its demands, narratives, tactics, emotions, and consciousness—would be the primary legacy of the campaign. Yet if the systematic critique and mature opposition of the Not1More campaign were accomplishments that would continue to fuel the movement, the innovative tools it pioneered seemed less likely to serve as new defaults for the movement than as hard-won resources to be deployed selectively in the future. As became clear over the course of the campaign, these were demanding, sometimes costly tactics that would work best in specific contexts.

Participants were frank about the energy and gratification they drew from their contentious engagement. The campaign's anguished public appeals and feats of bodily extremity allowed family members to express their deep commitment to their loved ones. Activists also found in these protests a sense of agency. Recalling her own experience with her father's detention, Montoya reflected:

> Even though . . . it's hard, . . . it's a moment of ownership, too, because you're doing something. You're doing something instead of just weeping and crying and remaining alone in your own grief. But it gives you that sense of, like, "I don't know if this is going to work, but . . . I'm doing everything I know and everything I can to help my loved ones."[81]

Even those activists whose loved ones were not immediately threatened experienced a sense of moral impetus in the campaign that brought them energy and meaning. Reflecting on her decision to take part in

ADAC's bus action, though she had previously been placed in deportation proceedings, Ileana Salinas affirmed:

> "It was always in the back of my mind, like what if they can reopen my case? . . . But it made sense for me in that time. I wanted to do it . . . if I would ever get arrested that I would do it in front of the bus. . . . Because it was a sense of like if I am able to stop somebody's deportation, I'm okay with being deported, because I know that my community is going to be there for me, regardless.[82]

Because this campaign was so entwined with personal anguish, the feeling that participants drew from it differed from the buoyant aftermath of civil disobedience in the campaign for DACA or the Undocubus. Yet they felt affirmed and motivated by voicing loss as it had been experienced or expressing their commitment to their family or community. "Their love for their loved ones matter[ed], and . . . that's what kept them going" as Reyna Montoya put it.

But even buttressed by this powerful commitment, the ongoing, public expression of private trauma could be excruciating and exhausting. This was evident at public events at which family members experienced difficulty in voicing their pain or were overcome by the experience of sharing their anguish.[83] It also surfaced during more private efforts to use storytelling to bolster energy and morale. The toll that the ongoing expression of personal pain could take on protesters became clear, for example, during Puente's Walk to End Deportations in April 2014.[84]

Completing sixteen miles of the planned sixty on their first day, protesters arrived at Florence, Arizona, home to a large immigration detention center. In a parking lot near the prison, a group of marchers held a vigil to celebrate their journey and remember those for whom they walked. It was a difficult night for Fernanda, an adult leader at Puente whose son Ruben had been detained for more than two years at Eloy, the final destination of the march. That day, as Fernanda walked, she had received a call from Ruben from inside the detention center. A guard who disliked him had denied him, for the second time in a month, the small portion of meat that prisoners were served once a week. Ill and malnourished, Ruben cried in frustration over the denial of his most basic needs, and Fernanda was devastated by her powerlessness to help her son. As the vigil began, I was struck by Fernanda's despondent appearance. She was usually vocal and engaged: she had proposed the idea for the Puente's earlier hunger strike and had fasted through three weeks, and a hospitalization, to try to free Ruben. That night, however, she was subdued and silent. An organizer mentioned Ruben's predicament and asked Fernanda if she would say a few words to share her experience and buttress the resolve of the marchers. Eyes downcast, unable to speak, Fernanda began to weep. The vigil participants rallied gently around her, murmuring words of encouragement. One participant, who had herself been detained, reminded Fernanda that "stay[ing] strong" and continuing the fight was the only way to help Ruben; she noted that "[m]y family never gave up while I was in detention and that's why I am here today."[85] As Fernanda struggled to collect herself, the group continued to give her space, bolstering her with hugs, touches, and expressions of support. But she remained silent, her eyes downcast, throughout the vigil. Two days later Fernanda rallied and brought an assembled crowd to tears, calling out an impassioned message to Ruben over a public address system outside the detention center where he was being held. She then boarded a bus for Washington, D.C., for yet another hunger strike. But that night, her exhaustion offered a window on the cost of a campaign based on transforming private pain into public protest.[86]

Perhaps a greater threat to the campaign than the exhaustion of its activists—who remained buoyed and impelled, despite their fatigue, by the goal of liberating their loved ones—was the emotional fatigue of its allies. After Obama's announcement, and the injunction against DAPA, Puente continued its Uno Por Uno escalation, taking on more ambitious cases to challenge the conceptual distinction between "families" and "felons." Yet, Garcia acknowledged, it was not an easy time to organize. Not only was the Obama administration, which had been rebuked by the courts for even its limited plan, tapped out, but the burden of grief and desperation as new videos arrived, and new press conferences were called, was taking a toll on supporters. Numbing, a product of emotional overload or a self-protective mechanism for those less familiar with the risk of deportation, was curtailing response. In spring 2015, Garcia mused about whether the campaign against deportations could continue in its current form:

> The risk in all this . . . is that people become numb to it. . . . As we [began] putting petitions and videos out there, . . . we were getting thousands of signatures and views earned a year, [but] it just started diluting, people just getting numb to it like oh, it's another family crying. . . . [F]or us it's a really frustrating thing. As people who are committed to it, I hear another story and I want to fight for it as much as the other one, but we're not getting the same response.[87]

If numbing was the challenge for supporters, then ambivalence, or even resistance, was the risk for less committed segments of the public. Participants in this campaign did not simply sacrifice their bodies; they deployed them against a president who had positioned himself publicly on their side. In some cases, they placed their bodies in purposeful violation of offending laws. When even mainstream allies like immigration lawyer David Leopold branded the DREAM 9 a "publicity stunt that doesn't do anything to move the ball forward," this raised the possibility that the audacity of this campaign could press too hard on public ambivalence about undocumented participation.[88] Would viewers who had cheered the performative citizenship of the voter engagement campaigns view the contentious protests of Not1More as an intensification of civic commitment, or a bridge too far? The peaceful violation of unjust laws would evoke King or Chavez for some, but might it also evoke the claims of lawlessness raised by Kris Kobach or Russell Pearce for others?

Conservative columnist Ruben Navarette voiced the latter view in a series of columns castigating DREAMers for their activism. Writing caustically of Erika Andiola's video ("Did you hear about the DREAMer who got a rude awakening?"), Navarette declared:

> [Most] young people, brought to the United States as children by their parents, are wise enough to not draw attention. But a group of activists, succumbing to the narcissistic culture of their adopted country, thrives on it. These activists think of themselves as full-fledged Americans who can get away with the kind of in-your-face agitation that has been prevalent since the 1960s. But . . . their arrogance and radicalism alienates supporters and puts them in jeopardy.[89]

For Navarette, this kind of performance is not a sign of courage or commitment but a sign of "arrogance": it goes too far for people without status. Part of the problem with activists is that they've assimilated *the wrong* aspects of American political culture (the "narcissism" and "in-your-face agitation . . . prevalent since the 1960s"). This argument disdains contentious politics, even as undertaken by full-fledged citizens. But such tactics are more problematic, for Navarette, when performed by those without status: those who should be "wise enough not to call attention," a clear reference to the deferent, "good immigrant" posture he sees as normative. Although Navarette's condescension and failure of empathy are particularly stark, his tirade raised the prospect of less extreme scenarios, in which tactics that sparked ambivalence could lead to public disengagement from a movement already facing potent institutional barriers.[90]

Finally it became clear, particularly in retrospect, that the efficacy of a contentious, oppositional campaign depended in part on the singularity and political predilections of its ultimate target: in this case, President Obama. The fact that categorical discretion could be directed by a single official, rather than a more numerous body, meant that the campaign did not have to appeal to a "least common denominator" of immigration-related assumptions. Activists did not have to rely on the DREAMer narratives that remained the safest course with Congress; because President Obama, who remained susceptible to this imagery, was also receptive to the contributions of families, activists could appeal to him with more inclusive stories.

Obama was also a distinctive target in that he could sometimes be reached by critique but could, in any case, hear it without repressing or retaliating against the movement. Despite the betrayal they saw in the administration's ongoing deportations, activists viewed Obama's public support for immigrants, and his status as a progressive, a person of color, and the son of immigrants, as attributes that could at least be leveraged to induce intermittent intervention. His grant of DACA demonstrated this pattern, and his concern with his legacy, as his second term drew to a close, offered a new opportunity. Obama could be shamed, Ileana, a longtime youth activist, observed, because he "wanted to have a legacy and . . . wanted to have a good history with immigrants."[91] Just as important, he could be shamed without prompting public derogation or punishment of his unexpected adversaries. Although Obama complained loudly and defensively that Not1More protesters were targeting the wrong party and sought the assistance of national nonprofits to "manage [protesters'] expectations" as the campaign wore on, he did not publicly disparage protesters or enforce against them. Obama proved to be a well-chosen target for this kind of campaign, despite the subsequent action of the courts. Yet it was not clear when a president with this distinctive set of attributes would come again.

Thus, the kinds of tactics, and approach to officials, that would have most purchase moving forward would depend, at least in part, on the signals coming from the federal government. In the waning months of the Obama administration, Phoenix activists turned their focus to state-level campaigns. Puente mobilized around *Puente v. Arpaio* and continued its campaign to get ICE agents out of local jails. ADAC mounted successful efforts to secure drivers' licenses and persuade the Maricopa County Community College District Board (MCCC) to grant in-state tuition to DACA recipients.[92] LUCHA organized ultimately successful civic engagement campaigns: Bazta Arpaio, which resulted in the defeat of Sheriff Joe Arpaio, and Proposition 206, which increased the minimum wage and provided sick leave for the state's workers. But the direction of the national movement, to which Not1More had so eloquently spoken, would await the outcome of the 2016 presidential election.

PART FOUR

"America Woke Up in Arizona"

Navigating the Trump Years and Beyond

CHAPTER 6

The Asset Map of the Movement

"AMERICA WOKE UP IN ARIZONA"

On January 26, 2017, I landed in Phoenix, filled with a mixture of apprehension and curiosity. During the five years I had spent speaking with people active in the Phoenix movement and tracking the development of their approaches to activism on shifting political terrain, Barack Obama had been president. Obama's policies had been a source of frustration and mounting anger for immigrant communities: his professed concern with the rights of immigrants, which yielded DACA and the failed initiatives of 2013–14, was paired with an enforcement policy that swelled the ranks of the detained and deported, and separated families. But now Donald Trump, an avowed antagonist to immigrants, was in the White House, having taken office less than a week earlier. The day before my arrival in Arizona, the administration issued two sweeping executive orders on immigration that portended an effort, consistent with his campaign promises, to subject all those present without authorization to indiscriminate immigration enforcement.[1]

Since November, I had exchanged only short texts or emails with Phoenix activists, brief missives of concern and dismay.[2] Yet I had some sense of the movement's early efforts to regroup following the election. I had participated in two large conference calls with United We Dream (UWD), the first of which took place just two days after the election. I had joined these calls less as a researcher than as a disoriented denizen of a changed political landscape. It struck me that if there was any place where I might glimpse pragmatic adaptation, rather than despondency and inertia, it would be in this movement, for which adversity had often been the engine of creativity and resolve. And resolve was what I heard in the voices of organizers on that call, even at that bewildering moment. The determination I heard from the UWD leaders was captured in their new hashtag: #heretostay. As I listened, I thought about the performativity in that phrase. Whether they were here to stay was, after all, the question most on the minds of those who had joined the call. As I had often seen in Phoenix, the performative assertion of the slogan seemed to serve several purposes, each of which was vital at that moment of crisis. The slogan provided reassurance to those listening that the organization "had their backs" and would fight with fierce determination to defend their homes in the United States. It modeled the stance that UWD aimed to establish as normative for movement participants and other undocumented youth. It also served notice to the Trump administration that this organization, and this movement, would be implacable adversaries should the administration seek to curtail members' rights or opportunities. In addition to this multivalent resolve among the leaders of the UWD, I noticed something more complex in the dynamics of this meeting: a palpable distance between the determination of the organizers and the more confused emotions voiced by many other participants. For example, most of the questions, which occupied the latter half of that meeting, concerned the possible rescission of DACA. While listening to these questions, I was struck by the shades of doubt, anxiety, fear, desperation, and occasionally, aspiration or resolve, that I heard in the voices of the questioners. I knew that not all of those who spoke were activists or even members of organized communities; the call was open not just to those who organized with UWD but to the range of undocumented youth that it served. Now, as I returned to Phoenix more than two months later, I wondered how the movement would span the distance I'd heard during that call and what strategies organizers would develop to implement the resolve they would need in the months and years ahead.

Driving to a local coffee shop, I met first with Ileana Salinas, a longtime youth activist. Ileana had just returned from a trip to Mexico, arranged through advance parole, a policy through which youth with DACA, among others, could receive permission to cross the border and return. But with the new administration in Washington and changing immigration policies, this kind of opportunity for border crossing might not arise again soon. During our conversation that day, Ileana acknowledged that the movement had entered a different phase. With Obama, she explained, "one of our tactics was to shame the President, who wanted to have a legacy, and who wanted to have a good history with immigrants." "Shaming doesn't work" she observed, with a president whose "campaign promise was . . . to oppress this community."[3] Ileana was now working with Aliento, a new organization that helped immigrants address the traumas produced by undocumented experience, using dance, song, and the visual arts. Ileana's job was to coordinate the workshops at which community members draw, paint, dance or sing, and reflect together on the feelings that emerge. A singer-songwriter, she found this work inspiring; it was also a relief from the demands of organizing. She was tired of pressing people to do things, she said, and uncomfortable "putting myself in a position where I need to show strength . . . when I'm not sure I have that confidence."[4] This was striking to me: Ileana had been an activist and organizer for close to a decade, but the performativity of the effort seemed to be taking a toll on her. She was happy to be doing arts programming at Aliento but willing to leave the organizing to others, at least for now.

Immediately following my meeting with Ileana, I stopped by at an action at City Hall, organized by Puente and Living United for Change in Arizona (LUCHA). The goal was to press Mayor Stanton, a Democrat, for a more certain, expansive statement of sanctuary, particularly in the wake of the executive orders. A crowd of fifty to sixty people, rallied by two young activists from Puente, marched in a circle, shouting enthusiastic versions of "un pueblo unido . . ." or "What do we do? Stand up and fight!" The energy was familiar, but the shift in demand was stark: with Trump in the White House and Arpaio no longer in office, the local government was now being enlisted to protect immigrants against federal authorities. Brooding on this irony, I headed into back-to-back meetings with organizers. I was touched by their willingness to speak with me at this chaotic time and by the candor with which they shared their bewilderment and their first efforts to navigate this new terrain.

I sat down first with Carlos Garcia. He looked tired, a little shell-shocked, and no wonder. The executive orders had been coming fast and furious, and Puente is committed to defending the most vulnerable as a means of protecting the entire community. He had also been fielding calls from all over the country. "On November 9, 2016, America woke up in Arizona," as he put it later; everyone is looking for advice.[5] People in Arizona do feel like they've been here before, he observed: "total Republican control; outwardly racist officials in control of our lives. But we all recognize it's going to be worse."[6] The federal government—the ultimate authority in immigration policy and enforcement—was now a frank adversary rather than an uncertain ally; criminalizing discourse, fanned by the president himself, was on the rise. On Wednesday, Carlos had faced the community and told them it was not going to be OK: if they got caught they might be deported. He described a speaker Puente had hosted who had shared the mistakes she made when she was deported so others wouldn't make them. As they listened, people whose deportation proceedings had been resolved or suspended realized that they might now be newly vulnerable. We're back at square one, Carlos concluded, how do we protect our people? Three principles, that had been their lodestars in the past, would have to be adapted now: "First, protection: we have to think about how to do that," he said. "Second, resistance: challenge institutions that might defy Trump—the church, the city, other sanctuaries—are you with us or against us? Third, finding alternatives to better our lives."[7] As I glimpsed the reemergence of the "open hand" and "closed fist," I asked him how members of his community were coping emotionally. Hopefully they've learned resilience, he responded: "being there for each other; learning from our losses, leading with the most vulnerable."[8]

I met up next with Reyna Montoya, at another Phoenix coffee shop. She was exhausted—a constant among organizers at this time—and she didn't know when she'd have time to catch up on sleep. Reyna was doing double duty. On the one hand, she was implementing her vision at Aliento, a new organization she founded in 2016 with a grant from the Soros Foundation. Aliento helps undocumented immigrants heal from trauma through participation in the arts. Detention and deportation—and the ongoing risk of both—loom large in that experience. But Montoya sees other sources of trauma: the corrosive effects of oppressive state policy, the successive failures of federal reform, and the disenabling effects of advocacy that fails to center undocumented voices. By engaging in dance, song, and painting and other visual arts, in collaboration with supervising artists like Ileana and organizers who help them reflect on the feelings that arise, immigrants can gain greater perspective on their experience.

Since the election, however, Aliento had taken on new functions: supporting undocumented communities in the face of the administration's threats. Reyna had been fielding frequent calls from DACA recipients about its impending rescission: Would they be able to work without their permits? What should they do about the house they were planning to buy? She had also spoken with activists across the country. People don't yet have a clear direction, she said. The resolve to "fight back" felt to her "a little hollow," because "the question is how, and people haven't figured that out yet."[9] But she had noticed real differences between those who had previously organized and those who had not. Among the organized she saw less fear and more ability to focus on what to do next. In a group call with early Arizona DREAM Act Coalition (ADAC) activists—most of whom were not at that point organizing—she was struck by how smoothly they shifted to practical solutions: making sure that their families' documents were in order, saving as much money as possible, planning a responsive action for the day the announcement would come. But those DACA recipients who were younger—who didn't know adult life without it, and who might not have organized—faced greater challenges. "They've tasted equity," Montoya declared, "and now it's going to be pulled away."[10] The first step for all groups was "to have broad participation: people have to show up. . . . We don't have answers, but we're not alone," she said. Solidarity was, for Montoya, the foundation from which other answers would flow.

In the late afternoon, I headed to LUCHA, where I met with Abril Gallardo. She, too, seemed exhausted, though she retained the thread of stubborn optimism that I'd witnessed in her activism. Recalling the November election, she began not with Trump but with LUCHA's landmark victories: the defeat of Joe Arpaio (with 150,000 new voters registered by the Bazta Arpaio campaign) and the victory on Prop 206, a ballot measure providing a minimum wage increase and sick leave for Arizona workers—LUCHA's first statewide effort. These victories "were built on strengths developed through defeats," she declared. "We know what it's like to have a Trump. . . . [He] can take DACA away, but [he] can never take away our learning how to fight, to protect each other. We've grown in skills . . . [and in] our pride."[11] Abril also shared a story from her own experience. Although she had worried about her parents' response to becoming newly vulnerable to enforcement, in the week after the election her family had remained positive, ready to support her as she moved through a period of inertia, of wondering what would come next. "When my dad hugs me, or my mom gives me coffee, or my brother jokes [finding humor in all of this], that makes me feel safe because they feel safe," she summed up. "We can embrace our loved ones, organize, keep fighting."[12]

TRACING THE ASSET MAP OF THE MOVEMENT

"Asset map" is a term used by organizers and community-engaged policy makers to describe the resources available to those who seek to organize a community.[13] I first heard the term during "Una Luz, Un Aliento," a fundraiser hosted by Aliento during that January 2017 trip. That evening, a guest artist, Stephanie Gamba, encouraged the assembled group by talking about the asset map of their strengths. A movement like the one in Phoenix draws on financial, logistical and tactical assets, but as previous chapters have demonstrated, they also draw on identifiable emotional resources that should be considered part of the larger map. By 2017, these emotional assets included powerful responses like resilience, resolve, and a sense of belonging in both the movement and the country. These emotional resources, which arose from a years-long engagement with Joe Arpaio and Arizona lawmakers, shaped Phoenix activists' response to institutional and political obstacles and helped to form their broader political consciousness.

Organizers referenced these emotional assets repeatedly as they described their early grappling with a new enforcement horizon. They observed that familial love and political solidarity were vital resources from which fortitude and more concrete strategies would flow, that those who had "been here before" manifested a kind of resilience that could help sustain them and others, and that participants had developed not just strategies but pride and confidence that would stay with them in facing this newest challenge. More than this, organizers manifested these emotional resources themselves as we spoke. Despite their fatigue and dismay, I glimpsed in the responses of Carlos, Reyna, and Abril an underlying thread of poise: a subtle, reemergent form of confidence or resilience. These organizers might be depleted and apprehensive, they might be unable to see beyond the next days or weeks, but they were moving forward: they would draw their communities together, they would take steps toward their immediate protection, and workable answers would emerge in time. Some element of this poise might be performative: as with UWD, organizers were modeling the confidence required to reassure their communities and signal their resistance. Yet when I considered their circumstances and their history alongside their words, I gained a clearer picture of the experience that grounded their assertion.

Part of their poise came from having seen close at hand a kind of adversary who seemed strange and frightening to many undocumented communities. They were familiar, not just with the contempt and stigma sowed by a leader like Arpaio or Trump, but also with navigating the environment of enhanced enforcement and pervasive fear that that kind of leadership creates. "We know what it feels like to be discriminated against, to have raids, to see families being torn apart with anti-immigrant laws, [to be] pulled over for the color of your skin," Abril Gallardo explained. "We've seen and lived this."[14] Some level of confidence arose simply from having confronted such challenges and survived: withstanding an experience that one fears or dreads brings a sense of greater strength.[15] They could see an Arpaio—or a Trump—as a force that could be endured and, like the ADAC veterans Reyna spoke with, begin to think more practically about responses. But this poise also stemmed from a more tangible sense of capacity: an awareness of what movement-based resources—from the tactics of campaigns to the culture of organizations—had provided, when they had used them to contend with this kind of adversary in the past. And it stemmed from the political self-understandings that they had gained from their experiences of mobilization and resistance: that they belonged, not just in this country, but in this fight and in their local communities.

In the following sections, I discuss in more detail the key resources on which these organizational leaders explicitly and implicitly relied at this time—what we might call the asset map of the movement—as they sought to respond to the new threat posed by the Trump administration. These resources—from concrete skills, to adaptability, to a sense of belonging—arose from the experience of past campaigns and from the practices of undocumented activism and would prove essential to the way the movement developed in the months and years ahead.

A SENSE OF CAPACITY BUILT ON PAST STRUGGLES

One of the most important assets that organizers relied on after Trump's election was a sense of capacity that would enable them to negotiate an uncertain future, even if they could not yet glimpse the precise path they would follow. This sense of capacity relied on several discrete strengths. It comprehended the organizational, tactical, and human resources that undocumented leaders had honed through a decade of mobilization. It also encompassed a hard-won ability to adapt to changes in immigration policy, government leadership, or the enforcement landscape through reappraisal and adjustment.

Leaders could rely on a deep toolkit in responding to the new political environment; they were, in the words of one activist, "resourced" in terms that extended far beyond the material.[16] To return to the typology introduced in chapter 1, they could rely on a broad array of organizational, cultural, moral, and human resources in confronting the threats posed by the new administration.[17] In the first category, undocumented leaders could draw on the resources of dedicated organizations, which had both cadres of activists and networks that enabled outreach to the larger community. These organizations had the capacity to recruit widely for public campaigns or actions, to train new volunteers, and to plan community-facing programs. In terms of cultural resources—the repertoire of tactics and practices on which organizational leaders and participants could draw—the varied experiences of the past decade had served them well. Undocumented organizations commanded a rich array of tactics that ran the gamut from the institutional (registering voters or lobbying legislators) to the demonstrative and oppositional (vigils, marches, hunger strikes, sit-ins, civil disobedience). Activists had mastered the challenge of sharing private pain in public settings and drawing out different elements of their experiential stories to address different circumstances and audiences. They had learned how to bolster each other through the development of robust emotion cultures. They had also built credibility and legitimacy—moral resources often presumed to be in short supply among those present without authorization—through the citizen-like roles they were prepared to take on and the conspicuous sacrifices, including risk of apprehension, detention, and deportation, that they were willing to make, as they staked their political claims. This moral authority bolstered their confidence and won the respect of some audiences, though how it would fare under the renewed assault of stereotypes and dehumanizing treatment was harder to ascertain.

Organizational leaders had also cultivated in their volunteers and activists a distinctive set of "human resources." Many activists had reliable skill sets, honed in varied campaigns, that ranged from the ability to speak with prospective voters on a doorstep, to the knowledge necessary to lead Know Your Rights (KYR) trainings, to the capacity to navigate institutional settings like legislative hearings or meetings. They had absorbed, from the emotion cultures of organizations, a kind of emotional discipline that enabled many to persist in the face of fatigue, uncertainty, or risk, and to share with their audiences inward emotion states ranging from hope to urgency to outrage. Organizers also understood that the ability to experience and communicate emotions was not simply a tactical resource to be projected outward. The human capacity to experience solidarity with those similarly affected was a vital resource, a current that could flow among community members, easing fear through mutual support, fortifying the bonds among them, and emboldening them for collective action. Because solidarity played a key role in this work, leaders had made a pointed effort to rekindle it now—"being there for each other,"[18] "embrac[ing] our loved ones,"[19] and remembering that "we're not alone"[20]—as they considered what strategies and tactics would be most productive in the changed environment.

But beyond this robust set of resources, Phoenix organizations, and their activists, had also developed a capacity for adaptation and reassessment that would equip them to respond in a new political landscape. Adaptation had long been the coin of the realm in immigrant activism as organizers confronted a shifting array of hostile policies and elusive opportunities at federal, state, and local levels. Activists had learned to respond quickly to crises, whether Joe Arpaio's neighborhood raids (met with alerts to a growing network, cop watch operations, or hotline calls), the unexpected passage of SB 1070 (met with vigils, marches, and the organization of a boycott), or the detention of a beloved community member (met with videos and social media outreach). They became skilled at recalibrating their stories and emotions as prospects and audiences changed, modifying individualistic "DREAMer" stories to create the more collective narratives of the civic engagement campaigns or shifting the tone of their emotional appeals from the cheerful aspiration of the early DREAM Act campaigns to the impatience of the 2010 campaign's final months. They had also become masters of the stark pivot, changing the target of their campaigns, the sites of their activity, and the posture in which they engaged officials or the public, when they confronted larger obstacles. This sometimes meant moving outside institutions to engage a larger public when institutional action proved unavailing, as in the 2013 impasse over CIR. It sometimes meant shifting the institutional target altogether, as when youth, after the legislative defeat of the DREAM Act, sought deferred action from President Obama, or when organizations that had seen their hopes of a federal solution dashed by the injunction against Deferred Action for Parents of Americans (DAPA) redoubled their focus on the Bazta Arpaio campaign. As Lena, an Eastern European DREAMer who mobilized with ADAC, explained, when barriers arise, "they just find [other] ways to go about it, different avenues. It's like water. It will find the path of least resistance."[21]

This capacity for adaptation went beyond adjustment to changing circumstances. Organizers had also begun to turn the lens of scrutiny on their own organizing practices when they discovered unmet needs in their communities. This kind of adaptation was demonstrated by the founding of Aliento. Through her own family experiences with detention and threatened deportation, and through her organizing of family-based campaigns at local, state, and federal levels, Reyna Montoya had become concerned with the extent of unaddressed trauma in immigrant communities. The lives of many immigrants —particularly in hostile environments like Arizona—were shaped by harrowing experiences of fear, anxiety, and grief. And these painful experiences remained unaddressed for many immigrants as they managed the many challenges of their daily lives.

Focusing on enforcement-related trauma faced headwinds in immigrant communities. Discomfort with mental health treatment created barriers, as did a potent, pragmatic survival instinct: "[It's] like we're strong . . . we got it. We have to keep going, I have to look out for my children," Montoya explained.[22] A focus on trauma also created tension with some strands of activism, Montoya observed, which encouraged people to see themselves as "fighters": "If you are in tune with your emotions . . . that's a sign of weakness because people either can use you, or people can not take you serious, or not think you are strong."[23] Yet, convinced that the weight of unaddressed pain could have a corrosive effect on the community, Montoya and her colleagues at Aliento began to explore a new form of community-based organizing: using supervised participation in the visual and performing arts to address painful feelings produced by experiences of immigration enforcement.

Utilizing painting, music, or movement could enable participants to express, and reflect on their feelings, in the company of fellow community members and trained facilitators. Moreover, they could do so without expectations or pressure to conform to any particular organizational agenda. Montoya explained:

> We're not forcing people to do specific art about their detention story. It's more about what do you want to express that is holding you back, or what do you want to express that makes you happy? What are the emotions that you have? . . . [P]eople are making different choices that I [as the leader of Aliento] am not in control of.[24]

This way of expressing experience not only responded to the needs of the individual community member; it could also support their agency. By producing dance, or song, or visual images, Montoya explained, "pain is transformed into an artifact"; the process of creating something new helps participants to see that "this [traumatic experience] is not who you are but this is just a part of you."[25]

The practice of addressing immigration-related trauma through the arts recognized that community members—even those who would be activists—carry with them injuries that require collective attention. A patient, nonstrategic focus on these injuries, Montoya made clear, was necessary to a movement that aimed to improve the lives of immigrants. A capacity for reappraisal that could extend even to central assumptions of immigrant organizers was a resource that organizers could draw on as they entered a new political landscape.

A SENSE OF DE FACTO MEMBERSHIP
AND THE IMPORTANCE OF BELONGING

Activists were bolstered not simply by a sense that they possessed a range of tools to navigate a newly threatening political landscape but by a feeling that it was right for them to use those tools. Their resolve to remain—in the jurisdiction and in the fight—was animated by feelings of familiarity, investment, and legitimacy that gave activists a sense of a place in the political community, be it the United States, Arizona, or Phoenix. These feelings, as this section demonstrates, have been fostered by the varied forms of activism in which they have taken part. They are, in some sense, a measure of the efficacy of their performative citizenship. As we saw in chapter 3, performative citizenship works not only to help citizens view undocumented immigrants as those capable of the obligations and rights of citizenship but also to help activists—through the roles they perform and the skills and perspectives these roles confer—internalize this sense as well. A feeling of being at home, not simply where one is comfortable or familiar but where one belongs and plays an active part, makes being #heretostay an external expression of an interior state, rather than simply a performative assertion. Several experiential tributaries have fed this sustaining sense.[26]

For the largest group of activists, feelings of de facto membership flow from their participation in political processes and their reflection on that role. Another, smaller group of activists derive a sense of membership from understanding and exercising rights that protect them in contexts of protest or in law enforcement encounters. Finally, many of those who have engaged in face-to-face organizing—most often in the context of electoral canvassing—develop a sense of social belonging to the communities in which they have worked. In highlighting these feelings among undocumented activists, my claim is not that these are the same feelings of membership or belonging that citizens enjoy, if we could specify with any coherence or determinacy what those feelings are.[27] It is that these feelings among activists arise without the warrant of formal legal status, from the activities that undocumented participants perform and their reflection on them. Also, these feelings seem to have informed or shaped the political consciousness activists brought to their struggle with the Trump administration. In the remaining part of this chapter, I explain how each of these forms of membership and belonging—which I refer to as *political membership, rights-based membership,* and *social belonging*—emerged among the activists in Arizona, and how this emergence equipped them with resources for an uncertain future.

Political Membership

Undocumented activists, in Phoenix and elsewhere, quickly grasp the fact that their political participation is constrained in ways that do not affect citizens. They cannot vote, nor can they stand for office, in the vast majority of jurisdictions.[28] Their outward-facing political participation is shadowed by the possibility of immigration enforcement, although whether and how that possibility will materialize in practice is almost never clear ex ante. Yet many Phoenix activists have drawn from their experience the conviction that two central dynamics of democratic political participation that apply to citizens also apply to them: first, that it is both legitimate and essential for them to exercise political voice; and second, that elected officials are accountable to them and to undocumented communities. The path through which they reach these conclusions may be different than for citizens, who can reflexively rely on their formal membership. But these claims nonetheless fuel a conviction that they are legitimate participants with a vital role to play in electoral and political processes.

Activists describe the legitimacy of their voice in several ways. Some make an implicit comparison to citizens: like their neighbors who have formal status, undocumented residents are subject to, and may be injured by, the consequences of governmental decision-making.[29] They express this not simply with respect to immigration policy but with respect to routine decisions that affect their daily lives. Consuelo, an adult activist with Puente, explained:

> We need street lighting, we don't have any. We need sidewalks, because the ones we have are made of dirt . . . as *activists and members of this community [we] suffer and we see the effects* . . . [and we] say, 'Hey my community

needs this or that and we have the right to ask, whether we have documents or not."[30]

Other justifications are broader, expressing an implicit right of all persons to speak to the actors who govern them about the conditions under which they live. This is a perspective I saw arising more frequently among those who had been active over time. Martín, an adult activist from Puente, describes a right to speak out about injustice, regardless of one's status:

> These kinds of laws they're trying to pass, they're not just hurting me, but they're going to be affecting the new American generation . . . growing up without parents, growing up with the stress of not knowing if their parents are going to be home [when they get there.] . . . I mean, when something is so unfair, you have to speak out.[31]

For Ileana Salinas, a right to voice one's views—regardless of one's status—arises because human beings are prior to any particular form of government. A government, she explains is "just . . . a set of agreements between the people who live there . . . and the people who govern":

> I can criticize it because it's a form of government, and there have been so many forms of government throughout history . . . and *we* make [them] change. Like it's not that the government is our boss. It's that *we decide how we want to be organized, and our government is a reflection of how we want to organize ourselves.* But the thing is that people forget that. People forget that.[32]

Most undocumented activists, however, describe their political voice not simply as legitimate but as essential. The imperative of political voice for those most affected lies in the distinctiveness of their perspective. Experiencing migration and being subject to immigration enforcement generate a unique vantage point that cannot be supplied by those who lack this experience. A weaker version of this claim—that experiential storytelling describes the stakes of immigration policy in a uniquely vivid and persuasive way—helps to motivate participants for outward-facing activism, as we saw in chapter 2. A stronger version of this claim—that those most affected by immigration enforcement have perspectives on policy not available to citizens—has grounded activists' claim for inclusion in policy-making bodies, as explored in chapter 5. A rider on the Undocubus expressed this view when he said, of the members of the US Civil Rights Commission: "They live in a world where they don't know what it is to be undocumented, what it's like to live in a barrio. . . . That's why we're here, shouting our truths."[33] Through any of these views, undocumented participants come to see themselves as crucial contributors to important national, and subnational, conversations—a vision that fuels a sense of de facto (political) membership.

As their claims for policy inclusion suggest, activists do not view political voice as a simple matter of ventilating their perspectives. They have also come to believe that elected officials should consider and respond to these views. This perspective is noteworthy, because many Americans—at least intuitively—believe that citizens can demand accountability of elected officials primarily because they can vote. As we saw in chapter 3, there are many reasons activists see elected officials as accountable to members of undocumented communities, some of which draw on their similarities to citizens. They live in the jurisdictions these officials represent; when they suffer from the same conditions that burden other residents, representatives should respond. They also participate in the economy and pay taxes through their employment.[34] This can fuel demands for official recognition, and frustration when it is not forthcoming. Consuelo, the Puente activist, voiced this frustration: "I am contributing with my taxes so that [state actors] can have more money to do things for us, but [they] do not do them."[35]

Many organizers and participants also express the view that, particularly through their activism, they have taken on the responsibilities that *should* define citizenship, even if actual citizens often fail to meet those standards. Sometimes they simply emphasize hard work, whether it be contributing to the economy or working to improve themselves.[36] As Natalia, an Adios Arpaio organizer, observed, a citizen is "a hardworking person that provides, and wants to better themselves, and grow in this country."[37] More often, however, activists describe a practice of commitment and service to one's community that is reflected in their own actions, though not in the actions of many formal citizens. Roberto, a team lead for ADAC's 2012 voter engagement campaign, explained: "A citizen is a person that cares about their community, that stays on top of what is happening and doesn't only worry about . . . [themselves], but also looks out for others."[38] This commitment is sometimes described in a register of care, as Araceli, a LUCHA activist, framed it: "showing you are proud of where you were raised . . . [and] also taking care of your community."[39] But it is more frequently framed as engagement and service, precisely the kinds of activities in which undocumented activists take part.[40] Verónica, an ADAC activist, summed it up:

> it's about . . . [making] sure that your community is what you want it to be. Making sure that people are engaged and aware of what's going on as far as the [] policies that happen within our county, and making sure that the right

people are getting elected and are doing things [in] our interest, so that they do what they said they were going to do.[41]

These understandings sometimes support a claim that undocumented activists have met the standards of citizenship and should be entitled to its benefits. Marisol, a leader in ADAC's voter engagement efforts, declared: "We all know that we're citizens at heart. We're all doing things that would qualify us as a citizen. . . . Citizenship is more than just a status. It is a way of life, and it's what I've been working for, for so long."[42] But more broadly, these understandings ground a view that those who demonstrate this multifaceted commitment are de facto members of the polity who deserve the attention of its elected representatives.

Activists may express voice or demand accountability through channels different than those utilized by citizens. Undocumented activists cannot vote, so they inform, exhort, register, and turn out voters. They have not been permitted to serve as delegates at party conventions, so they mount political demonstrations outside convention centers. Oppositional forms of political activity are often understood as heightened efforts to incite the accountability of elected officials: to remind them, as Ximena declared in chapter 4, that "we are waiting for what they promised us" during campaigns.[43] Even civil disobedience, as Texas Undocubus rider Kemi Bello explained, is a "friendly accountability reminder to those in power that we may not be able to vote at the polls . . . but we will . . . find our own ways to participate within the electoral system."[44] But whether voice or demands for accountability are enacted through conventional channels or by means of novel institutional improvisation, activists' sense that they have a legitimate claim to both shapes their determination to preserve their place in the polity.

Rights-Based Membership

In addition to the sense of membership gained through political engagement, some Phoenix activists also describe themselves as having gained a sense of membership through their ability to assert constitutional rights. This has been a more ambivalent, less predictable source of empowerment or membership for activists. This ambivalence may arise in part because the rights that undocumented people can claim are demonstrably more limited than those of citizens.[45] The effects of rights assertion may also depend on whether immigrants can vindicate those rights for themselves, or whether they are being asserted for them by others. Yet for some activists in some contexts, understanding and asserting a set of rights they might not previously have known they possessed brings a sense of possibility and recourse. They perceive a zone of self-assertion in which they can act, and they sense that the American constitutional system protects them, even if it is not the same protection provided to citizens.

Protest activity, for example, can confer a sense of rights. Marching, or rallying at a specific site, is an activity that virtually all activists, and many nonactivists, have taken part in. It can be a vehicle for discovering voice ("Once you get that feel for it of—whoa, you do have a voice—you want more of that; you want to be heard more"),[46] or for reinforcing one's bonds with one's community ("I feel like I shout from my heart: we can do this, "si, se puede"; we are together").[47] For some activists this simply fuels a sense of empowerment.[48] Others, who experience it in the context of an organization, perceive marching not simply as a galvanizing experience but as the assertion of a protected right that they share with citizens. For instance, Ximena described how she experienced this at Puente:

> I joined an organization [where] I learned my rights . . . what rights I have here despite being undocumented. Some of those rights are freedom of speech, [the right to] express what is affecting me. That is one of my rights that made me feel strong and I decided to go out in public, and gather my community so they too could defend their rights.[49]

But if a sense of rights bearing can emerge spontaneously from some activities associated with activism, it can also be purposively cultivated by others. KYR trainings, as discussed in chapter 1, had been a staple in Arizona's undocumented communities since the start of "attrition through enforcement." After Trump's election, Phoenix organizations expanded these trainings to include a focus on home raids, a favored practice of the new administration, as similar trainings proliferated nationwide. Their effects, as trainers describe them, vary widely among community members who take part. For example, Julieta, a youth activist who has led such trainings, observed that immigrants may feel frustration with questions that have no easy answers, such as what documents, if any, they should show to law enforcement officials in lieu of a driver's license. "[If you tell them] there is no right answer to this," she explained, "they get upset, and they're like, 'But you're saying that I have rights, but these aren't really rights.'"[50] It can be difficult for adult immigrants to abandon a deference to authority, to which they may have been socialized in their countries of origin.[51] But for some participants, and for many activists who receive training, KYR can be empowering.[52] At the most basic level, KYR training creates a sense of recourse. Participants learn that there are some limits to the way they can be treated by police, and they have some power to defend themselves. Mariana, an ADAC activist, explained:

> When SB 1070 passed . . . even driving was a scary thing. . . . The fear was having a police officer right behind you and he'd pull you over. . . . [K]nowing your rights . . . you know that you just have to say your name, your first and last name, your address, your age, and that's it. And you have the right to have an attorney. . . . So now you know what you can do. There's still that risk, but now you know how to defend yourself a little bit better. So there's that comfort.[53]

For Martín, KYR training helped him step away from the attitudes he had learned in his country of origin:

> In our own countries we believe that when somebody has authority, we have to cooperate or even incriminate ourselves, even if we haven't broken any laws. . . . One of the things that I learned here in Arizona is that the only thing . . . I have to say legally, is my name and date of birth, and that's it. I don't have to tell them where I'm going or what I'm doing or anything else, even if they ask me.[54]

Learning a new set of attitudes toward law enforcement can confirm a sense that one is now part of a new culture or a new polity, as Martín's referent, "here in Arizona," suggests. For some activists, the shift produced by KYR training is not just a sense of recourse or of greater freedom. It is a sense that they are protected by the Constitution itself. Ileana Salinas described her response when she and her brother were pulled over by law enforcement:

> I was frozen, I didn't know what to do, but I remembered . . . [when they] gave us a presentation about how to talk to the police, what to say what not to say, what were our rights under the Constitution. My brother [who was driving] had not been through that training. I remember telling him, "just stop—don't get out of the car. You can tell them your name, date of birth, and your address, but if they start asking you about your social security number, don't answer those questions. You're not forced to answer those questions: *you have rights under the Constitution, the Constitution is protecting us.*[55]

Ximena drew a similar sense of constitutional protection from the contexts of her activism, declaring: "Slowly I became educated until . . . I could come go forward and say, 'I am undocumented and I have rights in the country.' "[56] This sense, that undocumented people—whether or not they have formal status—enjoy some level of constitutional protection, can create a greater feeling of membership in the political community of the United States.

KYR training was surprisingly provident in creating a sense of recourse, protection, and, ultimately, membership. But other kinds of rights-bearing activities, such as the vindication of rights through litigation, yielded more ambivalent effects. Litigation in the federal (and sometimes state) courts produced a number of victories over Arizona officials. These victories included the federal government's challenge to SB 1070, which struck down several provisions, though it sustained the "show me your papers" provision,[57] and the constitutional challenge by civil rights organizations to racial profiling by Joe Arpaio.[58] There were also two important class actions against state officials, in which undocumented organizations served as named plaintiffs: *ADAC v. Brewer*, which challenged the decision of the governor to deny state driver's licenses to DACA recipients,[59] and *Puente v. Arpaio*,[60] which challenged the sheriff's department for workplace raids that led to the prosecution of undocumented workers under state forgery and identity theft statutes.

One might predict that these lawsuits, particularly those in which organizations served as plaintiffs, would provide a sense of affirmation to activists: that they could assert rights that would allow them to hold state actors accountable. This sense has often proved authorizing, and integrative, in other social movements. Francesca Polletta has written movingly of the sense of affirmation and membership Black voting rights activists drew from watching the trials of white officials accused of violence against prospective Black registrants.[61] Though these officials were almost invariably acquitted, activists saw that they could be called to account for their anti-Black violence in a court of law. Moreover, the feeling that they could hold state actors accountable also conferred a sense of membership on immigrant activists involved in voter engagement campaigns or direct action protests. Yet the response of undocumented activists to litigation, even when they served as plaintiffs, proved to be strikingly ambivalent.[62]

Some activists complained that the litigation process wrested control from them and placed it in the hands of lawyers. This perturbed activists who believed in the centrality of undocumented perspectives and were accustomed to structuring their own campaigns. David, an ADAC activist who later became an attorney, observed: "Electorally when we have been [] claim makers, we have had a lot of control in that process.

When it comes to legal claims, we have very little control."[63] Others felt that litigation detracted from their role as storytellers, because their narratives were shaped by lawyers. Reflecting on the ADAC case, Erika Andiola recalled, "We [had] to make sure that we had the right plaintiffs, first of all . . . and [then make] sure that those stories were the right ones. . . . [I]t was a very tedious process."[64] Litigation also sidelined activists' signature tactic: political pressure.[65] "We can pressure the [state] legislature. . . . [W]e can pressure the president and Congress. These pressures work," Andiola declared, "[but here], we catch the judge on the street, we talk to him, but does that even make a difference?" Organizers also found it difficult to understand and to communicate to members what was happening at each stage of a legal action.[66] Elena described an early hearing in the ADAC case: "I remember walking out of [the hearing] very confident and saying, 'I think we got this, and we're going to win.' And then Judge Campbell's decision comes in, and I'm like, 'What does he mean?'"[67]

Some activists nonetheless remained pragmatic about the role of litigation in taming the excesses of state actors. Elena, for example, viewed the sometimes-frustrating tactic as one part of a wider repertoire:

> It shows how the movement is attacking on different fronts. And it's not just doing direct action. You need everything. And I'm very happy the organization has been able to be diverse in that aspect. . . . [W]e're trying to solve this problem from the three fronts, right? Executive, legislative . . . and with the courts.[68]

Alejandra, an individual named plaintiff in the ADAC case, also remained alert to its benefits: "I knew that it had to be a lawyer's thing, because we could only do so much. And [] we did need the help of someone who was an expert. . . . I don't think it would have had the same outcome if they wouldn't have been there."[69] Yet even for these activists, litigation seemed more like a tactical necessity than an empowerment tool. Though activists sometimes experienced a sense of integration from what litigation had achieved—"Now I get to be miserable like you at the DMV,"[70] one ADAC member told me—the process of using the courts to challenge state officials did not seem to confer a strong sense of legitimation or membership.

Social Belonging

A final feeling of membership experienced by some activists is a sense of social membership or belonging. Youth activists may enjoy a generalized

sense of social belonging, stemming partly from their childhood arrival—
they literally cannot remember another home—but more substantially
from their constitutionally mandated K–12 education.[71] They become
bilingual and bicultural, which allows for many experiences of casual social integration, and may enjoy an extended, formative period in which
they may feel largely indistinguishable from their documented peers.[72]
This was a common experience among the civic engagement canvassers
I met, as well as the cofounders of ADAC at ASU. This sense of American
social belonging can be destabilized by familial experiences with detention and deportation,[73] as well as by barriers to education and employment at the end of adolescence.[74] But particularly when it is bolstered by
DACA and normalizing experiences like obtaining a drivers' license or
higher education, this feeling of being socially American can itself buttress a determination to remain and resist and can be a predicate for a
more specific, local sense of belonging.[75]

Adult immigrants do not benefit from these early integrative experiences; many experience socialization through low-wage, exploitative
workplaces that underscore the precarity of their status.[76] But for those
adults who become activists, organizations can help create a scaffolding
of social connection. For adult activists in Puente, for example, the practices of the "open hand" seek to root them in a specific undocumented
community, whose solidarity can fuel political strength and local affinity (both of which ease the pressure to "self-deport").[77] For LUCHA,
political education courses or adult-focused meetings can create a sense
of social connection to others who may have felt similarly isolated or
unmoored in an unfamiliar political and cultural setting.

While these experiences provide important building blocks for a sense
of social belonging, a more robust, specific sense of social membership
seems to emerge from face-to-face organizing in local communities, most
typically through civic engagement canvassing. Canvassers and organizers not only experience the *political* empowerment of understanding local
institutions and electoral dynamics and helping fellow residents who are
citizens to participate fully; those who work over a series of campaigns, or
utilize similar face-to-face methods in local contexts, also develop powerful *social* affinities and strong feelings of responsibility for the neighborhoods they canvass. "These are my streets, these are our streets," declared
Elías, a young canvasser and organizer for LUCHA. He explained:

> I feel like the middle person, in a way. . . . Everybody is around me, and
> I want to know . . . what is affecting you, boom, boom, boom. And I want
> to go up to somebody and tell them, "You know what? This is going on, and

this community wants this, this, and this. How do I know? I knock on these doors. . . . Right now, I can tell you. . . . I really care about my community. I love this community."[78]

Abril Gallardo described a similar feeling: "[It's like] you start to own your city, own your state. . . . [Y]ou have to treat [your community] like your family. You inherit this and you pass it on . . . and you build every time to make it better and better."[79]

Adult participants may be less voluble in expressing this sense of local affinity, yet the more active seemed to follow a similar trajectory. LUCHA organizers described to me a successful campaign organized by Adela, a middle-aged mother, to address problems in her neighborhood.[80] At LUCHA meetings, she had worried aloud about crime and the lack of signs or speed bumps in her neighborhood. Organizers helped her to see how neighborhood organizing methods used in voter engagement campaigns could help her to address these problems. Adela became a leader, organizing her neighbors and reaching out to city council members and police to develop answers. Her organizing produced a growing sense of commitment to her neighborhood, strong ties to her neighbors, and concrete benefits for them all. Emilia, the organizer who supervised Adela, described her growth as part of a larger pattern. When prospective activists come to LUCHA, Emilia explained, they aren't sure where they belong: "This isn't my home, but neither is the place I was born."[81] Through the work they do at LUCHA, activists come to feel they are at home, that they need to be there. Emilia concluded: "When we find our power, we know we're here to stay until we make change."[82] This sense of rootedness in local neighborhoods and communities was a final resource activists could draw on as they faced a newly hostile political climate.

With the election of a starkly anti-immigrant president, Arizona activists found themselves at a new crossroads. They faced escalated enforcement and renewed stigma, at the same time that they confronted sharply curtailed prospects for large-scale, legislative change. Although organizations had no immediate answers, the territory for Arizonans was more familiar than for many of their bewildered compatriots. They had learned to organize against pervasive enforcement and anti-immigrant vitriol before, yet more than the fact of that familiarity bolstered their resolve as the Trump administration began. Their struggles against SB 1070 and Arpaio, and their deployment of that expertise against an ambivalent Obama administration, had endowed organizations like those I knew in Phoenix with critical resources that bolstered them as they prepared to meet this new challenge. Years of conflict and unpredictability had yielded an ample tactical repertoire, which they employed with growing agility and pragmatism. And their experiences in the political field—from voter engagement to direct action and civil disobedience—had given them a sense of voice, and for some of rights, an appreciation of the accountability of political actors, and a feeling of investment and integration in the social fabric of their communities. The feeling that they belonged—in the nation and in the fight—proved to be a provident, stabilizing force as organizations contemplated their next steps.

CHAPTER 7

La Lucha Sigue

*Shifting Strategies and Building
for a Post-Trump Future*

In July 2017, I arrived at the offices of Living United for Change in Arizona (LUCHA) to meet with Abril Gallardo. It was six months after Trump's inauguration, and organizations in Phoenix were working hard to counter the administration's ever-expanding antiimmigrant policies and rhetoric. I was eager to catch up with Gallardo, one of LUCHA's leaders, to hear what the organization was doing and how the leaders were navigating the new enforcement landscape. Finding a quiet place to talk, however, turned out to be a challenge, as the offices were a hive of activity. Teams of people vied for space in the main meeting room; smaller groups gathered around computer screens in the conference rooms. Posters, white boards, and sheets of butcher paper were everywhere. I was not surprised to see that LUCHA had persevered during this difficult time for proimmigrant organizations, but I had not expected to find such a busy, animated scene. Abril too seemed to be thriving. She had always had an avid energy for her work and an uncanny optimism that permitted her to see the promise in challenging situations. But more recently I had noticed a growing sense of leadership. She seemed to stand a little taller; her instructions and even her gestures—as she fielded volunteers' questions or took brief phone calls as we chatted—were more decisive. She projected bemusement mingled with evident pride at the productive chaos around her. As we spoke together that day, Abril confided that not only was LUCHA extremely busy with its day-to-day work, they were actually expanding. She told me they had been thinking about buying a new building; the organization had outgrown its current space, she said. The attention LUCHA had received after the victory in Prop 206, which raised the state's minimum wage and required employers to provide paid sick leave, had helped them to secure funding for an expansion of their staff, thus allowing them to extend their work into new areas. They would be hiring two or three new people to lead programs in economic justice, mass incarceration, and immigration. Beyond this programmatic growth, there were new members—including an energetic group of older women—and a new political education program. Recent graduates of the program were training new participants in neighborhood-based teams.

I asked Abril whether LUCHA's expanding vision of civic engagement helped to buoy organizers as they negotiated the ongoing federal threat. She nodded emphatically. "It's so heavy," she said, describing a week in which a group of state attorneys general had mobilized for the rescission of DACA, and the Republican-controlled House of Representatives had proposed "Kate's Law," which increased penalties for reentry by immigrants without authorization, particularly those previously convicted of a felony.[1] "It's easy to get discouraged." But, she continued, "actively planning gives you hope. This won't be forever. . . . [W]e'll put pain, fatigue, anger, fear into building community power. . . . Later we'll be able to look at what we've built in this moment."[2]

As the Trump administration wore on, the challenges for undocumented communities proved to be mostly as dire as organizers had predicted. Immigrants with no criminal charges or convictions became vulnerable to deportation. Undocumented communities endured a steady stream of stigmatizing vitriol from Washington, as they saw Latin American asylum seekers held in cages or crowded into wretched camps near the US-Mexico border. Mass mobilization at the federal level became more intermittent and less visible. The unremitting hostility of the executive, the Department of Justice, and the Republican-led Senate made pro-immigrant policy making virtually impossible, and mobilization itself more risky. These factors, in some respects, were the recipe for a period of social movement "abeyance": a time when opportunities for progress are limited, in which movements like the one in Phoenix cultivate networks and affirm shared identity, to preserve the possibility of collective action in the future.[3] Yet while organizers recognized the dangers and the slim prospects for federal progress, abeyance or movement preservation strategies were not the only, or even the primary, patterns of organizing that resulted. The organizations in Phoenix were focused, instead, on two primary strategies: first, careful defensive organizing that prepared the community to face an increased threat and sought leverage at a series of junctures between the apprehension of undocumented residents and their deportation; and second, ongoing engagement in state and local political processes that consolidated earlier electoral gains and found new ways of motivating voters and exercising influence in institutional settings. These strategies vindicated the confidence I had seen organizers express in the days after the inauguration that organizations could advance the well-being of immigrants amid the chaos and adversity sown by Donald Trump. Yet as they moved this dual agenda, leaders also turned the focus on their organizations themselves. They began a larger reassessment of organizing practices, which encompassed questions about the functioning of storytelling, emotions, and performativity in the movement. This period of painful yet productive adaptation underscored the exceptional capacity that had become available to this movement: capacity that enabled it not only to respond to a sharply intensified federal threat but to plan for a more promising future.

DEFENDING UNDOCUMENTED COMMUNITIES

In adapting to the increased threat of an anti-immigrant administration, the most urgent need was to coordinate the outward-facing, direct defense of undocumented immigrants. This meant equipping undocumented and mixed status communities with tools that would help them, to the degree possible, to respond to new patterns in federal enforcement. This was an all-hands-on-deck moment for organizers, one for which their struggles against SB 1070 had provided important preparation. Organizations reached out first to their memberships and then to the larger immigrant community.[4] They nurtured feelings of solidarity, reminding community members that they could rely on each other, and that organizations could provide information and support. Know Your Rights trainings, which focused on the administration's preferred tactic of home raids, proliferated throughout the region, as they did across the country. Organizations asked those who had survived law enforcement encounters or had previous experience with detention and deportation to share their knowledge with those who were newly targeted. Though members were urged to confront their greater vulnerability, they were also offered strategies for surviving it.

Individual organizations also pursued their own, distinctive ways of combatting increased risk to their communities. Puente, for example, returned to the drawing board to ask where it could intervene in the "deportation conveyer belt," as it defended a larger group of vulnerable immigrants from a more concertedly hostile administration.[5] To Carlos Garcia, it felt like facing off against Arpaio in 2007—"doing insular organizing and no leverage anywhere"—except that at that point, immigrants had a potential ally in the Obama administration and some expectation that conditions would improve.[6] Ten years later there was no federal government to appeal to; moreover, organizers recognized that the Obama administration had created many of the problems that Puente now faced.[7] Years of failed compromise had produced a huge enforcement apparatus: in Garcia's words, "a deportation machine."[8] The "families not felons" distinction favored by Obama, and the discretion his administration had employed to suspend the deportations of immigrants without criminal records, bore their own bitter fruit: there were more legally removable people in the system for Trump to deport.

The harsh implications of this fact were brought home with the first deportation following Trump's inauguration. This enforcement effort targeted a Phoenix mother named Guadalupe Garcia Aguilar. Garcia Aguilar had been arrested in a workplace raid in suburban Phoenix, and her deportation was ordered in 2013. But in the face of pressure by Puente, including the legal challenge to workplace raids in *Puente v. Arpaio*, ICE had permitted her to remain in the country under an "order of supervision."[9] Because Garcia Aguilar had no other criminal charges and posed no danger to the community, she was allowed to return to her family and report yearly for an interview with ICE officials. However, when Garcia Aguilar reported for her interview in February 2017, she was detained and scheduled for deportation later that day. Puente, which had warned her about the likelihood of deportation and counseled her about her options, staged a protest, in which several youths tied themselves to the deportation van as it prepared to depart. They were promptly detached and arrested by Phoenix police, and Garcia Aguilar was deported, leaving behind two teenage children.

One question raised by this painful example was how opportunities for leverage in the deportation process had changed under Trump. In spring 2017, a *New York Times* feature article asked whether Puente, now recognized as a national leader in fighting deportations, could retool its efforts for the new administration.[10] In this article Maria Castro, a Puente activist, identified six junctures—from police contact, to city court, to local jails, to ICE transfer, to immigration court, to deportation itself—at which activists might seek leverage. Before Trump, the *Times* quoted Castro as saying,

> Puente had focused its efforts on stopping deportations at ICE or after. But now that Trump had vacated Obama's priorities and reduced the likelihood of prosecutorial discretion, "everything from city court forward no longer works." *She drew a red line through five of the boxes, leaving only one unscathed: the initial point of police contact.*[11]

When I questioned Garcia about this assessment in summer 2017, his response was more qualified. That was what we thought when the *Times* did that interview, he said, probably between November and January. But as enforcement had continued to unfold, and they had continued to work, prospects had begun to look a little different. On the state and local side of the process, Puente worked at several sites of leverage. One was city policy governing police encounters with immigrants. Puente pushed hard with the Phoenix City Council, which had appointed an ad hoc committee to make recommendations. Puente also urged the (Democratic) mayor to increase the scope of sanctuary-style protections. A key focus for the organization—which predated the Trump administration but assumed greater urgency with its advent—was the nexus between ICE and the county jail. Since the time of Sheriff Arpaio, ICE agents had been stationed in the 4th Ave (county) jail through the Criminal Alien Program;[12] they provided early information about undocumented immigrants who were being held on state charges and helped to ensure that those released from state custody were processed for deportation.[13] Because this link delivered a steady stream of undocumented immigrants to federal custody, ICE had relied on it, in Maricopa County, to greater degree than on the home raids that were occurring in many parts of the country. Puente continued to press the new sheriff, Paul Penzone, to deny ICE access to the county jail, but Penzone—whose election in 2016 had initially been a source of hope for immigrant communities—had not reversed Arpaio's policy.

Following the transfer of immigrants to federal ICE custody, prospects of release appeared to dim, but Puente remained vigilant. The organization probed the operation of ICE discretion to release detainees even before immigration court hearings. This discretion did not halt the deportation process, but it allowed people to be with their families as they continued to fight. Garcia observed "a lot of variation" here.[14] When I asked if this might be an expression of local or individual resistance to Trump's more indiscriminate policy, Garcia was skeptical. "ICE guys are like police officers," he said. "They aren't usually partisan. They see themselves as implementers."[15] But it remained a site for careful observation and response. One glimmer of hope, Garcia observed, had been the immigration courts. Puente routinely accompanied community members as they prepared with lawyers and attended their immigration court hearings. This effort provided continuity of support and ensured that community members received responsible legal assistance. But it also allowed Puente activists to observe what was happening in immigration court. Here Garcia had seen some unexpected victories for prospective deportees. He didn't yet understand what distinguished the cases in which detained community members had prevailed—maybe in some cases courts worried about bad publicity?—but noted that Puente might learn more as they continued to accompany and observe.[16] Puente saw little prospect for leverage at the last stage of the "conveyer belt," after deportation orders had been entered. Here contentious tactics that had succeeded in some suspensions of deportation in the Obama administration had little effect; Trump continued to deport more people following the completion of the immigration court process. But organizers continued to investigate opportunities for intervention at earlier junctures.

Aliento, the organization Reyna Montoya started in 2016, took a different approach to the increased vulnerability of immigrant communities, focusing on the individual and collective emotional trauma created by escalated enforcement. Arts workshops offered a setting in which participants could acknowledge frankly the stress created by the experience of ongoing, intensified enforcement; just as important, they allowed community members to reflect on their greater precarity through the creation of visual images, movement, or music. Adult community members remained reluctant to recognize this form of emotional and psychological pain; they more often sought out these workshops for their children than for themselves,. Yet as they accompanied their young or teenage children to Aliento's arts-based gatherings, Montoya reported, many experienced the solidarity of being with others who were facing similar difficulties and spent time in a well-supported setting where they could observe trained organizers helping participants to voice and reflect on uncomfortable feelings.[17]

BUILDING STATE AND LOCAL POLITICAL POWER

The second central strategy that organizations in Arizona embraced during the early years of the Trump administration was aimed at building pro-immigrant political power at the state and local levels. As the Obama administration's ambivalence toward undocumented communities gave way to Trump's more thoroughgoing federal hostility, state and local governments now seemed the more promising institutional targets. This strategy was in part defensive: cities and states could be potential allies, as Garcia explained, providing limited protection for immigrants through policies of noncooperation with federal immigration enforcement. Yet a focus on the state and local level was not solely, or even primarily, a protective posture. State and local political processes offered organizers the chance to build on past successes and to support the sense of investment and belonging that had emerged among longer-term participants in civic engagement efforts. The removal of Russell Pearce and more recently Joe Arpaio, through robust voter engagement, and the election of immigrant-responsive Latino representatives to posts throughout Maricopa County had validated the civic engagement strategy and created institutions in which pro-immigrant voices were more likely to be heard. And the confidence that activists had gleaned from the ongoing mobilization of Latino voters made them feel like valuable contributors to local political processes. Organizers believed that they could take these strategies further.

This was particularly true at LUCHA. By the time of its victories in Bazta Arpaio and Prop 206, LUCHA had gained visibility and reputation through its successful efforts at local voter engagement. In the early months of the Trump administration, LUCHA faced a crucial choice of whether to shift gears to address federal hostility or build on its local political work. Its leadership ultimately decided that, while they would "push back where necessary," they would continue to build political strength for the longer run.[18] This choice was not easy for organizers like Abril Gallardo, who felt impelled to address the suffering she saw before her. Yet she reminded herself that LUCHA's greatest victories had been well-planned, longer-term efforts.[19] The idea, as she explained, was to work toward a time "beyond Trump; don't use all our fuel to fight him."[20] An influx of funding, sparked by the success of its campaign for Prop 206, had helped LUCHA to expand its staff, which by mid-2017 numbered fifteen, with further increases planned. The organization also planned to extend its geographic reach and its substantive focus.[21]

LUCHA's success campaigning for Prop 206 had placed the organization for the first time in the leadership of a successful statewide initiative. This victory, which increased the state's minimum wage and provided paid sick leave to workers, consolidated LUCHA's reputation as an advocate for low-wage workers; the campaign created a "bridge" to partnering with activists in Tucson. After the campaign, LUCHA established a Tucson office. "If LUCHA is going to be a force in statewide elections," Gallardo observed, "we need to build a broader base; and this moves that process."[22] LUCHA also extended its organizing among adult activists. Older women had been a force in the Bazta Arpaio campaign, organizing "Zumba vs. Arpaio" classes as a part of neighborhood canvasses and appealing to their coethnics to raise their voices in the electoral process.[23] LUCHA gradually made these "moms"—who included mothers of youth who received assistance with DACA and adult women LUCHA was preparing for citizenship—a more central part of the organization. They soon numbered close to 40 percent of the organization's membership.[24] Through an ongoing process of outreach, leaders used the substantive concerns of these new membership groups to broaden the focus of the organization, as discussed later.

LUCHA had also become visible over the past several years for running the canvassing operations for several successful campaigns for local office. As a result, prospective candidates, in the run-up to the 2018 midterm elections, began to seek the organization's endorsement of their campaigns. LUCHA took this responsibility seriously, formulating the "LUCHA 2018 Platform." This platform articulated the principles, central to LUCHA's vision, by which candidates who sought endorsement would be assessed and held accountable. Candidates' support for these principles would be examined in a closed-door meeting with the organization's membership. Those the group chose to endorse would be held responsible for action that reflected and implemented the platform's principles, through ongoing outreach after the election. This practice extended the dynamic of the early civic engagement campaigns, in which undocumented immigrants and members of mixed status families became sources of authority and leadership in the electoral process; endorsement thus became a new form of performative citizenship. Organizers also expressed hope that one day LUCHA would go beyond endorsements and see its members run for office themselves.[25] Gallardo acknowledged that as a DACA recipient, she wasn't eligible yet, but she noted, with a smile, that "some of the moms who are citizens" were making plans.[26]

Puente also built a role for itself in civic engagement processes. As part of a coalition with LUCHA and the Center for Neighborhood Leadership, Puente helped direct the BAZTA Arpaio campaign. This campaign, which sought to end the sheriff's tactics of racial profiling, and empower voters long neglected by candidates and party organizations, resonated with Puente's broader focus on mutual aid and community self-defense. Puente's role in local electoral processes became both larger and more visible when Carlos Garcia announced his candidacy for the Phoenix City Council in 2018. Garcia turned to politics in response to the same issues that animated him as an organizer: law enforcement targeting of immigrants—including six members of his own family—and communities of color.[27] Vowing that as candidate and city council member he would be "as unapologetic as I've always been," Garcia made the Phoenix Police Department's record of racial profiling and violence against communities of color a centerpiece of his campaign.[28] He was bolstered by the civic engagement of local activists, particularly a youth group called Barrio First Fellows, who knocked on sixty thousand doors in Phoenix's District 8, where Garcia was running.[29] This support fueled Garcia's ultimate victory. His inauguration ceremony in June 2019 was a festive event, packed with activists and punctuated by the performances of indigenous dancers and Mariachi bands. At the ceremony, he affirmed his commitment to the practices around which Puente had organized. "We will stand with the same fist in the air against violence towards our communities. We will fight against criminalization and deportation," Garcia declared. "But we will also strengthen community with an open hand to build together and to ensure that the city of Phoenix is a welcoming place for all."[30]

Aliento reflected yet another approach to the engagement of political processes. Because its campaigns were aimed, in part, at fostering the resilience of DACA-mented youth, Aliento remained alert for opportunities for involvement at both state and federal levels. When Trump's announced rescission of DACA sparked a brief congressional push to enact the DREAM Act, which would have created a path to citizenship for those threatened with the loss of DACA, Montoya traveled with a group of youth activists in the fall of 2017 to Washington, D.C., to lobby for its passage. Montoya deemed the trip a success even though the opportunities for legislative exposure were limited (the proposed act was shelved when a legal challenge suspended the implementation of Trump's rescission).[31] It reminded young activists that "the road to major change in immigration runs through the [federal] legislature," as she put it.[32] Despite the flaws that she and others had decried in Congress, this experience had helped youth campaigners gain exposure and develop skills applicable to the federal legislative process.[33] The knowhow and sense of agency that it provided them could be built on in the future, when legislative change might become a more feasible prospect.

Yet like other Phoenix organizations, Aliento also recognized that state-level political processes represented a more immediate opportunity for concrete impact. Thus the organization's primary legislative focus during the early Trump administration was a campaign for in-state tuition for DACA recipients or for undocumented students more broadly. Because access to higher education—which could lead to skilled work—was a vital benefit associated with DACA and a central goal of undocumented students more generally, this campaign addressed a strongly felt need and a potential source of youth agency. This campaign joined a long-standing struggle over the availability of in-state tuition for Arizona's undocumented high school graduates. An earlier political campaign by Arizona DREAM Act Coalition (ADAC) had culminated in a 2013 decision by the Maricopa County Community College District (MCCCD) to grant in-state tuition to DACA recipients. In a move that recalled the harshness of the state's policy of "enforcement by attrition," State Attorney General Tom Horne sued the MCCCD, arguing that their decision violated Prop 300.[34] A state trial court sided with the MCCCD, holding that the power of the federal government over immigration enabled it to decide who had legal presence in the state for purposes of in-state tuition; DACA recipients, who had temporary federal sanction to be present, thus would qualify for such instate tuition.[35] Almost immediately after this decision, the state regents voted to follow the MCCCD's lead, allowing in-state tuition for DACA recipients at the University of Arizona, ASU, and Northern Arizona University.[36] The court of appeals, however, reversed, holding DACA recipients ineligible for in-state tuition because of Prop 300.[37] As the parties deliberated about the next step, Aliento organized a campaign to amplify the voices of those deprived of in-state tuition by the state's intervention. I asked Montoya about the goals of this campaign, noting that some activists had voiced frustration about the prospect of achieving leverage with the courts, which were not, after all, directly accountable to the public. Montoya explained that the question was not simply about courts but about the entire "political ecosystem" in which they operated. Understanding the stakes for undocumented youth might persuade Governor Ducey to reconsider the state's position or persuade the Arizona Supreme Court to take the case, if it moved forward. The campaign could also shape the political context in which the court decided the case. Activists can't pressure a court, Montoya acknowledged—echoing the reservations of her former ADAC colleague Erika Andiola—but they can "create an environment around the Court."[38] And if the court affirmed the court of appeals decision, Montoya concluded, there would have to be a statewide electoral reconsideration of Prop 300, and "the organizing campaign will help create a base for that challenge."[39] The campaign would allow participants to explain the meaning of higher education in their lives, and it would teach them how to address an array of state stakeholders and decision makers. This effort reached partial fruition in 2021, after the state supreme court affirmed the court of appeals decision, when the Arizona legislature approved a ballot referral to repeal Prop 300, the 2006 law barring in-state tuition for undocumented students.[40] The question will be placed on the ballot in 2022.

BUILDING ORGANIZATIONS FOR THE FUTURE

In addition to building power through state and local political processes and defending undocumented communities against escalated enforcement, Phoenix organizations made a conscious effort in the years following Trump's election to focus on internal organizational practices that would help them solidify the movement for the future. As the previous chapters suggested, organizers had long reflected on the kinds of processes for socializing activists and navigating relationships in the broader community that would build a sustainable movement, particularly a movement composed of undocumented participants. But with nearly a decade of experience to assess, and diminished opportunity for productive advocacy at the federal level, organizers turned to this task with new energy and insight. Phoenix organizations adopted new approaches to training leaders and participants and expanded their substantive agendas. This section describes each of these initiatives in turn.

Training Participants and Leaders

One of the key areas of internal development that organizations turned to after Trump took office was the training of new leaders and volunteers. This effort was essentially a reconsideration of what was already a key internal development tool. Undocumented organizations had long understood the importance of training new volunteers or helping existing participants develop the skills necessary to lead teams or campaigns. Some of this effort had been programmatic: summer "fellowship" programs, for example, provided instruction and funding to young activists who demonstrated particular promise, and small cadres of paid organizers for specific campaigns received instruction in leading and motivating newer activists. Despite the need for this kind of training to build competency and confidence among participants who lack legal status, the actual practice of building skills and leadership among new cohorts of participants varied widely among organizations. Such efforts were frequently constrained by funding, by the exigencies of specific campaigns, and by the challenges of meeting inexperienced or anxious volunteers "where they are at."[41]

Over time, however, organizers became less satisfied with allowing training to unfold in ad hoc or opportunistic fashion. They increasingly understood that fostering political knowledge and specific organizing skills can broaden activists' perspectives, enhance their voices, and sustain their motivation over the longer run. During the Trump period, organizational efforts to formalize the preparation of activists accelerated. This acceleration included a number of notable innovations, such as "political education" programs, which situate campaigns in a broader political context encompassing the history of immigration enforcement and its intersection with proximate issues of inequality, and more structured mentorship opportunities, which may include paid organizing or fellowship positions.

For example, Aliento, which seeks to build voice in undocumented immigrants and members of mixed status families, established a program of youth leadership development. In this program, paid fellowships create a cohort of youth participants who receive one-on-one mentorship with Aliento's leadership; these fellows then lead teams of younger activists from their home schools or colleges in specific campaign work, under the supervision of senior staff.[42] Aliento has also established "hubs" and "partner schools" throughout the Maricopa County area, where its educational programming teaches students about the history of immigration and deportation and US political institutions. This educational program provides important opportunities for students to participate in Aliento's campaigns.

Like Aliento, LUCHA and Puente have also taken steps to elaborate and formalize their training programs over the last several years. For LUCHA, this has meant formalizing its long-term practice of one-on-one mentorship.[43] LUCHA has also established an ambitious "political education" program, which introduces youth to critical perspectives on immigration, race, and economic inequality. The inaugural program culminated with a trip to the state house, which enabled graduates to question representatives who weren't "walking the talk," as Abril Gallardo put it.[44] The "moms" at LUCHA have the opportunity to prepare for campaigns, through a Conocen Sus Candidatos (Know Your Candidates) course that explains the structure of the state and local political system while introducing them to the candidates in upcoming elections. LUCHA's executive directors, Alejandra Gomez and Tomás Robles Jr., have also sought to develop specialized skills in their senior organizers by deploying them in specific roles in large civic engagement campaigns.[45] Puente's new programs have aimed at the education and training of youth, enabling it to grow into a multigenerational organization. Its Puente Youth program offers an extended series of workshops that explain how the political system impacts youth of color, introduces participants to practices of community organizing, and offers the background necessary to participate in Puente's ongoing campaigns. More recently Puente has added the Escuelita Puente, a summer program that aims to expose youth from elementary through high school to themes of sustainability, culture, and justice that are not taught in public school and enlists organizers to train them in protecting themselves and their communities from ICE and law enforcement.

Broadening Vistas

In addition to enhanced youth and leadership training, organizations in Phoenix have also sought to broaden their substantive agendas to encompass larger patterns of injustice. These changes reflected a self-conscious effort to rethink the relationship between the core focus of the movement—the security and opportunity of undocumented immigrants—and broader issues of injustice—from the exploitation of low-wage labor to mass incarceration—that implicate the well-being of immigrants yet also extend to other groups.

Organizers at LUCHA had "known for a long time," as Abril Gallardo explained, "that we weren't just about immigration." Yet involvement in the Fight for 15 and the organization's successful direction of the campaign for Prop 206 consolidated LUCHA's identity as a leader in the area of low-wage labor. Organizers' receptivity to the interests of newer members has also led LUCHA to additional programmatic areas. The older women who have become an active part of LUCHA's membership have focused on the health of their neighborhoods, advocating for parks or public safety. The LUCHA organizers in Tucson—where the controversial Operation Streamline, a program that requires federal prosecution and imprisonment of unlawful border crossers, was located—have sought to mobilize around mass incarceration.[46] LUCHA has framed its enlarged agenda as advocating for the interests of working families, which includes the particularly urgent concerns of immigrants.

Puente also broadened its focus during these years, drawing on its experience in previous, successful campaigns to expand the focus of the organization. Puente's long-standing focus on overpolicing and racial profiling in minority communities was central to its challenges to Arpaio and SB 1070. With the Not1More Deportation campaign, the organization took on a more explicit critique of immigrant detention (with its emphasis on incarceration and incapacitation) and of the role not only of immigration enforcement but of borders themselves in separating loved ones and disrupting transnational families. The more ambitious agenda of the Not1More campaign has shaped Puente's emphasis moving forward. Since that campaign, Puente has more frankly embraced elements of abolitionism, directed both at immigrant detention and at enforcement agencies such as ICE. Puente's Chinga La Polimigra campaign, which contests the role of ICE and the collaboration of local police through Operations Order 4.48 (enacted to enforce SB 1070), is one example. This focus has also fueled broader challenges to carceral systems, through programs like Cops Outta Campus, which challenges the policing of college campuses, or Al Cien: Campaign for Re-entry, which aims to restore rights denied even to those with citizenship following incarceration.[47]

These internal, organizational changes were, at least in some sense, a species of abeyance work: they helped to fortify the movement in a period when some prospects for change had been foreclosed.[48] In a difficult period for Phoenix organizations, with gratuitous acts of federal inhumanity to migrants emerging almost daily, and opportunities for federal "progress" mostly limited to blocking the worst excesses of the administration in the courts, the resilience of organizations was manifested by preparing for a time when their work could move forward at all scales of government. Abril Gallardo captured this motivation when she said, "We use the anger we feel in this time to plan for the future. Later we'll be able to look at what we've built in this moment."[49] Yet these new emphases reflect other influences as well.

These internal changes may also have been shaped by a gradual process of professionalization in Phoenix organizations.[50] Most groups I observed retained strong elements of their original, grassroots structures. They employed loose hierarchies of supervision and mentorship, and directors might be moved among projects as needs arose. Moreover, organizations remained committed to ongoing input from all levels of participants. Yet most were, over time, subject to influences that encouraged greater professionalization. Many formed relationships with movement mentoring organizations that provided technical support and training: Puente with NDLON or Mijente, ADAC and LUCHA with United We DREAM, Promise-Arizona with Center for Community Change and the National Organizing Institute during the Adios Arpaio campaign.[51] These partnerships provided campaign- or tactic-specific training to participants; they also offered broader operational guidance to organizations.[52] In addition, some Phoenix organizations saw an influx of new funding, spurred either by successes such as the passage of Prop 206 or the wave of public and nonprofit support for immigrants triggered by Trump's election.[53] This enabled new hiring and specialization of functions.

But at least as important as these influences were the ongoing processes of reassessment and adaptation that had become second nature in this movement: the tactical adjustments tailored to institutional response, the larger changes—like Aliento's approach to trauma—that arose from a farther-reaching reappraisal of organizing practices. By the end of the Obama administration and the beginning of the Trump period, organizers had begun to reflect more critically on a central dynamic of undocumented organizations: their emphasis on performativity. This examination implicated practices from storytelling to leadership training to emotion cultures and raised the prospect of larger changes in the ways that organizations pursued their work.

REASSESSING PERFORMATIVITY

One of the most notable features of the Phoenix movement has been its emphasis on performativity: a practice by undocumented activists of modeling, enacting, or asserting emotion states or political relationships that they hope to bring into being. This approach encompasses tactics of performative citizenship, tactics through which undocumented activists take on roles associated in the public mind with citizenship. But it also includes the assertion of emotion states (undocumented and unafraid) with which activists may not yet feel comfortable, or the embrace of stances (the transparency and vulnerability of storytelling) to which they may not yet be acclimated, because this assertion or this embrace, which is ideally internalized over time, advances the larger goals of the movement. Over the last several years, organizers have taken a closer look at the varied practices that reflect performativity; some have gradually

196 | Chapter 7

been revised, others displaced. While the absence of prospects for progressive change at the federal level has created more time and space for self-scrutiny, and federal indifference to undocumented performances of membership has rendered some such performances not simply less effective but potentially less empowering, this reconsideration has been prompted less by the Trump administration than by the accumulation of experience over close to a decade of mobilization. Whatever the instigating factors, reconsideration and revision of performative practices in the movement suggests that larger change may be afoot in undocumented organizing. Building on the earlier discussion of performative practices in chapters 2 and 3, this section looks at the broader role that performativity has played in the movement, and how it is changing as the movement heads toward a post-Trump future.

Since the movement first began to take shape, "performative citizenship" has been the most visible instance of performativity. From the congressional testimony of DREAMers in the late 2000s, it infused many of the movement's most familiar, and successful, tactics. As chapter 3 explains, when activists publicly perform familiar aspects of the political membership that they aim to have formally recognized, it educates and fortifies participants and challenges public perceptions of undocumented people. During the Adios Arpaio campaign in 2012, hundreds of youthful canvassers learned to perform citizenship by engaging voters, making this visible manifestation of civic commitment and responsibility for others a central tactic of the Phoenix movement. As the movement evolved between 2012 and 2014, and the political campaigns addressed both state and national contexts, performative citizenship found a more oppositional expression in the direct action and civil disobedience of the DACA, Undocubus, and Not1More Deportation campaigns, in which participants modeled contentious citizenship evocative of earlier protest movements. More recently, performative citizenship has continued through the canvassing and electoral engagement of LUCHA and Puente and the legislative campaigns of Aliento.[54] It has even been extended by new practices, such as LUCHA's endorsement of candidates, which shows that when an organization composed substantially of immigrants without status functions as an arbiter of political fortunes, the message—not only of incorporation but of power—may affect both participants and the public.

However, in recent years the practice of performative citizenship has begun to shift in subtle ways. The buoyant, declarative enthusiasm of the Adios Arpaio period—"they are the hopeless and we are the hope";

"we are the future; if we don't do it, who will?"—has become less conspicuous among activists.[55] When I spent an afternoon volunteering at LUCHA shortly before the 2018 election, for example, I was struck by the quietly self-assured stance that young participants took toward the weighty task of engaging citizens in electoral participation. It seemed now to be part of the DNA of this organization—and of other groups, like the Center for Neighborhood Leadership or the Barrio First Fellows—that the vital role of mobilizing voters was not simply a possibility, but a valued responsibility, for undocumented participants. This shift appears to be the product of acculturation rather than critical reassessment. The tone of performative citizenship may be shifting, in large part because it has done its work: noncitizen activists, and parts of the public along with them, have begun to accept this form of participation as theirs. They can now extend and consolidate this role by orchestrating candidates' campaigns or endorsing political aspirants. There may still be times when a more explicit, declarative form of performative citizenship will be necessary, because its goal is not simply to persuade activists or allies that they can be vital participants but to change the way that skeptical decision makers and citizens see their role. But in this moment—when both participants and their local audiences have become more acculturated to their participation—the need for this declarative dimension of performative citizenship may be less.

But beyond tactics of performative citizenship, the movement has also relied on other performative practices, such as those that propel activists into the field and shape the narratives and emotions they project when they arrive there. In guiding a movement composed of undocumented noncitizens through the hostility of "attrition through enforcement" or the roller coaster of opportunity and disappointment that marked the Obama years, organizers, in some respects, constructed a movement from the outside in. They modeled and normalized an image of engaged participation that reassured the public and that conveyed the varied emotional stances, from vulnerability to defiance, that would aid in persuasion of various stakeholders.

These stances begin as aspirational: they may not fully or reliably reflect the internal states of those who adopt them. But the belief—and the goal—is that they will be internalized over time by those who perform them and by members of the public. Participants who struggle to reveal vulnerability will become comfortable with its public expression; those who are fearful in the face of law enforcement will become less afraid through collective acts of exposure and assertion. Those who feel out of place when they stand on a doorstep and urge voters to assume the responsibilities of citizenship will claim this as their pivotal role in the political process.

In each case, participants are primed for these performative acts or stances by organizational metanarratives ("stories are the lifeblood of the movement and everyone has one"), aphorisms ("feeling out of your comfort zone is the way you grow"), or emotives ("we are undocumented and unafraid") that launch new activists into the field but to which they may not yet fully subscribe. Solidarity—a feeling of connection with, and desire to commit to and sacrifice for, a larger community—is the fuel that makes this performative engine run. It is an emotion that can be readily nurtured because volunteers quickly recognize their lives in the experience of others and feel love for and commitment to their families and communities. These feelings foster identification with leaders and organizers who model participatory stances; share stories that externalize their hope, vulnerability, frustration, and anguish; and offer metanarratives, emotives and aphorisms that describe and motivate norms of participation.[56] This combination of guidance and solidaristic emulation in turn fuels in participants a confidence that—despite their shyness, their inexperience, or even their fear—they will be able to be the kind of participants that the movement needs them to be, because there are others willing to support them and to put themselves forward in similar ways.

As the groups and activists in Phoenix often demonstrate, the results of this performative dynamic can be extraordinary and affirming for those who develop the inward sense of the outward-facing confidence or courage they perform or the ability to accept the painful emotions they repeatedly share. For example, in the Adios Arpaio campaign, canvassers' outward performance of a valued political role led them to feel a sense of political membership and a social embeddedness in the neighborhoods in which they worked. This sense of belonging—to the polity and in the fight—was also notable during the direct action and civil disobedience of the Undocubus and Not1More campaigns. But these palpable successes are not the only story. This effort to perform emotions or assume stances that one does not (yet) feel may also lead to confusion for those who do not develop the internal confidence or sense of membership they assert, or to precarity for those who require more time to attain these emotion states. As we saw in the example of Fernanda, the intrepid advocate for her detained son in the Not1More Deportation campaign, repeated assumption of the roles and emotions the movement requires may be depleting and exhausting even for those whose understand the need and gain a sense of agency or empowerment from their participation. These difficulties have been the focus of critical reflection and reconsideration over the past several years.

One of the most challenging forms of reassessment has been the reconsideration of storytelling. As chapter 2 demonstrated, storytelling is a central organizational practice through which undocumented participants come to understand their own individual and collective capacity for agency, and the resources they possess for persuading others, as they approach the challenges of outward-facing activism. Once in the political field, storytelling enables activists to engage decision makers and members of the public, with the concrete detail and affective transparency that creates an emotional connection with listeners. While individual and experiential in focus, storytelling can be a vehicle for communicating unifying messages of the movement—sometimes referred to as the "story of us"—which can shift in content and emphasis as immigrants navigate a changing political landscape.

Yet as activists have found, this vital tool can also create problems for those who wield it. The repeated rendition of painful experience can be exhausting for storytellers, and sometimes—as Carlos Garcia observed toward the end of the Not1More Deportation campaign—for their audiences. But the concerns voiced by activists sometimes went further. Over the course of my research, I saw in some activists an ambivalence about storytelling, a gnawing sense of being caught between the value of their stories to the movement and the painful, even injurious, experience of telling them.[57] Natalia, an organizer for PAZ, described her struggle in doing work that she unquestionably viewed as important:

> When you tell your story of self, you have to dig into those feelings that you've blocked off to continue going . . . [so] it could be emotionally hard for someone to just stand there and say it. And then, in our field of work, we have to say it over and over and over again, because you meet different people. There comes a point where you're like, "Okay, I'll try not to cry." But I don't think it ever happens.[58]

Natalia's description of repeatedly being brought to tears by a central responsibility of her work raises the question of whether the effects of that work are simply exhausting—an issue in and of itself—or something more corrosive.

German Cadenas, a cofounder of ADAC, was more direct in his assessment:

> Telling the stories is hard. I think it can be re-traumatizing. At this point, I don't share my story all the time, because it's hard. Every time you tell it, it takes a lot of emotional effort . . . to share yourself is really personal, really

intimate. And often with strangers. And that's hard, that's really hard to do. And [the] pain sometimes . . . it may not be sustainable.[59]

The question whether storytelling can itself be traumatizing, or whether it can prevent healing from those injuries inflicted on immigrant communities, has been taken up explicitly by Reyna Montoya and her colleagues as they work to develop a new way of engaging immigrant experience at Aliento. Although they know that the painful disclosure of experience activists perform can serve the movement, they also see that the ways in which activists have learned to share their stories can risk their self-conception, by emphasizing their victimization or vulnerability and placing the needs of their audience above their need to heal from what they have suffered. Ileana Salinas saw this pattern in her own experiences, particularly when she shared her stories with white audiences. It began with the mentorship she received, in organizations like ADAC, in telling her story. She recalled, "I was taught to go into the trauma and express it in a very compelling way—with valued details and very sense-like, with the colors and everything—to be able to get people to take action."[60] The level of detail she incorporated in these revelations, and the response of her audience—sympathy without full understanding, which could lean toward pity—often left her feeling demoralized or even reinjured. "Sharing my story that way," Ileana observed, "us[ing] the pain to cause pity that causes feeling of empathy or anger . . . that can lead to action. . . . [I]t made me go into [] a victim mode."[61] Though Ileana experienced this feeling more acutely when she spoke to white audiences, she found that even telling stories in her own community—which evoked a different feeling because it described a shared experience and aimed to build capacity—could feel outward focused and strategic, lacking the inward-focused reflection that might allow her greater perspective on her experiences. She described this experience in KYR trainings:

> I would always start my story [of detention] and I noticed how eventually I stopped crying. At first . . . I couldn't even say it without crying and later on, I guess it's a process, you just start to get to know the story more, but it doesn't mean that you've healed. . . . [It was like] this is why it's important for you to know your rights, and now we're going to jump into knowing your rights. . . . [It was] more strategic, not like the healing part.[62]

As these reflections show, ambivalent activists have focused not simply on the fact or frequency of sharing personal experience but on the ways that they have been encouraged to share it. When Natalia described "dig[ging] into those feelings you've blocked off to keep going," she was referencing an organizational message: that storytellers should create emotional connection by displaying vulnerability when they share a story. Similarly, when Ileana observed that she "was taught to go into the trauma and to express it in a very compelling way—with valued details and very sense-like—to be able to get people to take action," she was referencing organizational emphases on concrete detail and emotional vulnerability, imperatives that relate directly to the needs of audiences. These forms of organizational guidance— which I describe as metanarratives or stories about stories in chapter 2—are an example of organizing that works from the outside in. Aiming to shape the consciousness of the public, organizers craft an appeal that will both meet and move the assumptions of their audiences: stories that invoke yet broaden the trope of the "good immigrant" or that open the minds of citizens by enabling them to experience an emotional bond with immigrant activists. These metanarratives—which I have come to view partly as intentional strategy and partly as exigent intuitive response—prepare activists to make that kind of appeal, by drawing out specific strands of their story or learning to share it a particular way. Yet some organizers have come to question the demands of this strategy, noting that it can sacrifice the well-being of activists to the needs of their more privileged publics. Reyna Montoya made this point succinctly:

> I know this is strategic, I know it works . . . but at the same time it's like why is it fair, is it worth it? . . . [H]ow much more to we have to keep catering to the privileged ones that don't get it, in order for them to get it? It's like we're putting [ourselves] naked in front of [them]. . . . [P]eople shouldn't feel that they have to or they need to.[63]

This reconsideration does not mean that activists will not share their stories, or even share their vivid or candid depictions of the suffering they've sustained. Storytelling plays many roles in the movement, from expressing or nurturing solidarity within organizations; to providing the text for acts of performative citizenship in legislature, on doorsteps, and in protests; to fostering emotional healing as part of a trauma-centered approach. It will likely continue to play many of those roles going forward. But the reconsideration of the more performative dimensions of storytelling has enabled activists to acknowledge the costs of sharing their stories and encouraged them to approach the communication of undocumented experience in ways that prioritize their needs as well as those of their audiences. As German Cadenas observes:

> I think it is very powerful to tell our stories, and I think it is important that we have social supports in place when we do tell our stories. It is key that we do what we need to do to feel psychologically safe and protected, and that our mental health is affirmed, when we are taking big risks such as sharing so much of ourselves.[64]

While storytelling may be the most important performative practice organizers have begun to reassess, it is not the only one. Performative aspects of organizational emotion cultures have also come under scrutiny. In chapter 2 I described how organizations used implicit feeling rules, emotives, and aphorisms to help participants adapt to manage the uncomfortable feelings that this demanding, unfamiliar form of activism can produce. For example, the aphorism "moving outside your comfort zone is how you grow" helped new participants reinterpret the discomfort they were feeling as they assumed daunting new responsibilities. Yet even as organizers employed these features of emotion culture to prepare activists, they were beginning to perceive their costs. When I remarked to Elena, a longtime leader at ADAC, about the prevalence of the comfort zone aphorism, she responded pensively, "Yeah we're definitely out of our comfort zone many times. And most of the time it's not by choice."[65] Elena then named a number of factors that made it difficult to do the training that would actually mitigate participants' discomfort: "One is, do you have the knowledge to train people; and the second question is, do you have the time to train people? . . . [And] you're going to have unexpected situations that training is not going to prepare them [for]."[66] But the lack of preparation also arose from larger factors, including the newness of undocumented activism and the challenges of organizing without status. Elena added:

> [Underpreparation] also is a reflection of what's happening in real life. If you go to DC or if you look at the legislature, nobody is going to train you how to be undocumented or how to confront what's going on with anti-immigrant legislation. You're put in that environment and you have to deal with it.[67]

The result, she acknowledged, was not simply discomfort but also burnout: some people became overwhelmed by the ongoing, daily challenges of their activism.[68] However, as organizers became more knowledgeable about "how to be undocumented" or "how to confront what's going on with anti-immigrant legislation," and as more funding and more staffing gave organizations the bandwidth to offer more intentional and specialized training, they began to change their practice. As a result, more intentional, fully elaborated forms of political education and leadership instruction—like those recently implemented by LUCHA, Puente, and Aliento—have begun to reduce the need for strategies of emotional reinterpretation.

Some organizers have also questioned features of emotion cultures that nudge activists toward emotions that fuel mobilization—not just solidarity but hope, awe, or the various registers of anger—rather than encouraging them to recognize and respond to whatever emotions they are, in fact, feeling.[69] In the arts workshops at Aliento, for example, emotions are not addressed tactically, or as the focus of performative strategies, but as indicia of the injury or well-being of activists and community members. One goal, Montoya explained, is to "normalize" a range of emotions by demonstrating that undocumented people have different emotional reactions to the circumstances in which they find themselves. She offered a four-square diagram, with anger and fear in one vertical column and happiness and sadness in another. We want to demonstrate, she emphasized, that "all of these emotions are ok."[70]

Through questions like these, a movement that formed its practices in the heat of exigency, propelling its activists into a sense of purpose and transformative activity, has begun to revise those practices for the longer term. Performative practices have often worked in crucial ways, conferring the knowledge and instilling the self-confidence in participants that have brought change to Arizona and built visibility throughout the country. But with that success, some of these practices became less necessary, others could be supplanted through the knowledge gained, and still others have revealed themselves to have painful, unanticipated costs. As in the period of "attrition through enforcement," a hostile climate has become the setting for a generative surge of thinking about organizing. With a longer time horizon and a fuller understanding of the consequences of performative organizing, organizers are increasingly prioritizing the support and preparation of activists as they continue to negotiate the expectations of their prospective audiences.

LEARNING FROM THE UNDOCUMENTED IMMIGRANTS' MOVEMENT: DE FACTO CITIZENSHIP, SELF-PRODUCED RESOURCES, AND "STRATEGIC CAPACITY"

The movement that answered state hostility in Arizona and bolstered a nationwide upsurge in undocumented resistance offers lessons to legal actors, to those who organize immigrant and other "challenger" movements, and to those who study them. Although the most enduring solution to the precarity of undocumented communities—federal legislative reform—has remained out of reach, this movement can claim a number of uncanny victories. Its voter engagement campaigns dramatically expanded the state's Latino electorate, bringing new officeholders throughout Maricopa County and placing the state in the Democratic column in the 2020 presidential election. Its political, electoral, and litigation-based campaigns against "attrition through enforcement" unseated its most visible leaders—State Senator Russell Pearce and Sheriff Joe Arpaio— and led to the policy's gradual attenuation.[71] Its innovative tactics fueled a wave of protest efforts that gave rise to DACA and the short-lived DAPA. It won driver's licenses for DACA recipients and helped place in-state tuition for undocumented students on the 2022 ballot. But the greatest accomplishments of the movement may lie in its unlikely trajectory: its surprising emergence; its persistence through a series of obstacles, including the election of a president who recapitulated and amplified the conditions of the original threat; and its transformation of participants who once lived below the radar of public visibility into highly effective change makers.

For legal actors, and those they represent, this experience offers lessons that are both humbling and challenging. Most Americans understand, correctly, that legal status is vital to the aspirations of undocumented migrants. Legal status creates opportunities for secure employment, limits the possibility of family separation through detention and deportation, allows people to plan long-term futures, and offers a first step toward formal citizenship. But legal actors often assume that legal status, indeed formal citizenship, is the sine qua non of full engagement in the polity and of a sense of belonging in social and political communities. The experience of undocumented activists suggests, however, that law is not the exclusive route to these forms of de facto membership.

Robust political participation—whether or not it culminates in the casting of a vote—may fuel an understanding of, affinity for, and sense of investment in political institutions. For undocumented activists, this sense of affinity and investment may accrue with ongoing political engagement, even without the grant of formal membership. Many activists develop a sense of political voice and an appreciation of the accountability of public officials through activities like marching, lobbying legislators, and mobilizing Latino voters. They form a sense of social belonging in their neighborhoods and their city through face-to-face canvassing or organizing for local improvements. Through protest activity, including direct action and civil disobedience, they develop feelings of agency and of connection to past movements that have struggled for a more just and inclusive United States. None of these experiences of de facto membership mitigate the responsibility of legal actors for granting the formal rights for which this movement has so resourcefully advocated. But they suggest that political voice, agency, and integration are not solely a product of formal status. Those who mobilize for their political rights make their road to political belonging, in part, by walking it.

The experience of immigrant activists in Arizona and elsewhere also offers a challenge to the modest understandings of civic responsibility that have become characteristic of American citizens. Many activists I encountered in Arizona expressed the view that their extended—and sometimes adversarial—engagement with political institutions actually demonstrates a commitment that *should* be associated with citizenship. Some expressed frustration that many, if not most, of those who enjoy the privilege of citizenship do not share this sense of responsibility. Their ongoing activity has the potential not only to energize the local and national political communities of which they are a part but also to offer those who may take their formal citizenship for granted a motivating example of engaged and responsible membership.[72]

The unlikely path of this movement also yields insights that may guide future movements and those scholars who seek to understand them. The first is a new turn on a familiar precept: that externally provided, material resources may not be the primary or dispositive factor in the emergence of a "challenger" movement.[73] A key lesson of the Phoenix movement is that even newer, community-based movements can self-produce resources, of types that have sometimes evaded analysts' attention. In its initial resistance to "attrition through enforcement," the Phoenix movement generated a surprisingly rich array of cultural resources: tactics, symbols, and intragroup practices. Some were borrowed from other movements: participants with intersectional identities—such as Chicano or LGBT activists—brought tactics they had used in those efforts; others leaned on culturally familiar repertoires of the civil rights movement. Some tactical resources were the discoveries of early organizers: Lydia Guzman's Respect/Respeto Hotline, Tonatierra and Puente's barrio defense committees, and the capitol vigil by undocumented women of faith. Others—such as storytelling within organizations or the solidaristic practices of the "open hand"—arose from exigent efforts to support and empower an embattled population unaccustomed to public visibility. Still others emerged when ongoing

practices of national nonprofits—such as outreach to prospective Latino voters—were turned to local uses, for example, removing officials
like Joe Arpaio, by utilizing the energies and stories of undocumented
canvassers.

These "cultural" resources did more than fuel the tactical repertoire
of pro-immigrant protesters. They also fortified other kinds of resources
that enabled the movement to emerge. The hotline and barrio defense
strategy forged the skeletal networks of the movement and created participants who were more alert to threat and knowledgeable about how
to defend themselves. The practices of the "open hand"—Puente's community meetings or ADAC and LUCHA's exchange of stories—built
organizational and human resources, by extending the reach of the
movement and enabling participants to bolster each other for action.
These synergies among conceptually distinct categories of resources
often exist, yet their mutually reinforcing effects sometimes fly below
the radar of observers.

Two practices served particularly well to foster these varied resources
in the nascent movement. The practice of performative citizenship—the
enactment of political membership exemplified by voter engagement campaigns such as Adios Arpaio—fortified the human resources of the movement, enhancing the political understanding, political confidence, and
sense of belonging of canvassers and extending the movement through
the creation of citizen-allies. As importantly, performative citizenship
built the "moral resources" or legitimacy of the movement through its
evocation of paradigmatic citizenship roles and its concrete contributions
to the electoral process. Although the moral resources of a newer movement are often thought of as externally produced—through the endorsement of celebrities or the support of established politicians—they may
be internally fostered as well. The civil rights movement mastered this
strategy, although it hasn't always been analyzed in these terms.[74] The
Birmingham campaign built "moral resources" by exposing its nonviolent protesters to the brutal excesses of Bull Connor's dogs and hoses; its
Mississippi Freedom Democratic Party built legitimacy by training disenfranchised Black citizens in electoral practices and sending a delegation to
the 1964 Democratic Convention. The performative citizenship of the undocumented immigrants' movement extended this legitimating practice
from participants whose de jure citizenship was denied to participants
whose de facto citizenship had yet to be formally recognized.

Fostering the emotion of solidarity is another distinctive, resource-
building practice of this movement. Though the role of emotions in social

movement activity has captured growing attention in recent years,[75] emotions are not always understood as a resource whose cultivation can be vital to the emergence or persistence of social movements.[76] Organizers in the Phoenix movement—and other movements of undocumented immigrants—have grasped this insight as they have sought to mobilize members of a community that shares a deep history of past struggle and present danger. Solidarity connects emotions of empathy, fellow feeling, or love, with an action tendency toward individual sacrifice to right collective injustice; in so doing, it activates shared experience and directs it toward mutual defense.[77] "Open hand" practices that foster mutual recognition and trust among those who confront similar challenges, and examples of the power of organized communities to protect loved ones, friends, and neighbors, foster feelings that turn the distinctive vulnerability of undocumented participants into a distinctive strength.

Yet as the movement negotiated a changing policy and enforcement landscape, another attribute enabled it to persist over time. That strength is captured by Marshall Ganz's term "strategic capacity."[78] Drawing on a qualitative study of the California farmworker movement, Ganz described strategic capacity as the ability to devise strategies that turn environmental challenges to organizers' purpose. It requires a keen understanding of the most salient facts about a movement's surrounding environment and the ability to "devise novel solutions by recontextualizing their understanding of the data." This capacity, Ganz emphasizes, is not an inherent talent of particular organizers; it arises from specific features of organizations and of the leadership teams that guide them. Organizations must be broad enough in their outreach to discern the range of salient facts that are shaping the environment and inclusive enough in their decisional structure to enable different voices to contribute to solutions. Leadership teams must encompass a range of experiences, perspectives, and networks and include "borderlands" figures who can move within plural communities or environments. They must command a broad repertoire of tactics and frames, and they must be able to combine them in original ways, recognizing the "focal" moments that demand larger reorientations. In the midst it all, they must sustain a high level of motivation for their work.

This description captures many strengths of the Phoenix movement, that might serve as a model for future movements. Organizations there have retained a varied outreach, drawing information from organizers in Washington, D.C.; participation in local Tables,; and intimate, ongoing connections to immigrant communities. Their decisional structures, even as they have grown more specialized, have relied on input from participants, gleaned from one-on-one mentoring and from brainstorming built into membership meetings. While organizations have privileged the perspectives of those most affected, they have encompassed adults and youth, longtime residents and recent arrivals, and even some participants who enjoy forms of legal status. Leaders have included figures like Carlos Garcia, Erika Andiola, or Reyna Montoya, who have a foot in different worlds, combining detailed understanding of institutional functioning with painful familial experience with detention or deportation. Both leaders and activists have had exceptional motivation: their deep connections—to loved ones, friends, and neighbors threatened by immigration enforcement—have been transformed by the practices of the "open hand" into animating, activating solidarity. Finally, as leaders have contemplated strategic choices, they have been able to draw on a broad repertoire—tactics, stances, symbols, and frames—often self-produced from within the movement.

Some of these resources have had particular value because they have functioned both as vehicles for socializing new members to activism within organizations and as tactics for addressing decision makers and the public when activists turned outward. Experiential storytelling and the management and projection of emotion have been resources of this kind. Performative citizenship, another central practice, has been distinctively valuable because it permits activists to do the work of the movement—be it registering voters or contesting deportations—while enacting the political membership to which they aspire. The durability of this movement arises not simply from the utility of these practices but from the dexterity and creativity with which organizers and leaders have managed them. They have grasped that some changes in the external environment require pragmatic adjustments. These may be the modest changes that shifted narratives from the stories of individual triumph utilized in Congress to the collaborative stories of partnering to stop Joe Arpaio told on doorsteps. Or they may be the more dramatic changes that transformed hopeful petitioners for CIR into engaged adversaries assailing continuing family separation and using direct action and civil disobedience to highlight the "apprehension to deportation pipeline."

Ignited by the Trump administration, another important transition may be underway, this one internal and of uncertain scope. Facing a period of renewed hostility, in which local change remains possible but the federal action that could create paths to citizenship or suspend deportations has moved further out of reach, leaders have begun to think about the sustainability of the movement over time. This reflection has framed performativity—the embrace of aspirational stances that wield external influence as they are internalized over time—as a double-edged sword. Tactics of performative citizenship have remained vital assets of the movement because they build the institutional knowledge, tactical facility, and political confidence of activists, even as they challenge the assumptions of officials. Yet other performative strategies have been questioned, because their aspirational stances may deplete rather than fortify activists as they persuade officials or the public. The exhausting, serial storytelling that risks the self-conception of the teller to aid the understanding of the listener falls into this category, as do the emotion cultures that use affective scripting to bolster activists when more intentional training may offer greater benefit. The recognition that human beings, however provident, solidaristic, and resilient, cannot always will themselves or inspire each other to be everything that a movement requires reflects the strategic capacity of this movement. Whether this recognition will spur modest adaptations or more transformative changes remains to be seen. Yet the ability to perceive, reflect, and adapt, in response to new information or changing circumstances, exemplifies the strength that undocumented activists will carry with them as they move into an uncertain future.

Methodological Appendix

A methodological appendix, as I understand it, serves two functions. It explains how the author has performed her research, and it situates and legitimates the major features of that research in relation to conventional norms of social science or explains specific innovations in or departures from those norms.

I am not a social scientist, although I have been mentored in this research by some generous and distinguished scholars in that field. Nor is this a conventional work of qualitative social science, although it relies heavily on interviewing and ethnographic observation. This work, as I note in the introduction, aims to tell a story: a story that is strongly informed by qualitative empirical research and that gives rise to theoretical observations that engage a number of literatures, but whose more systematic empirical exploration will require further efforts. Consequently, this appendix leans more toward explanation than legitimation, although I aim to be transparent about the ways in which the research raised issues, from the perspective of social science practice.

The research, as I explain in the introduction, consisted of ethnographic observation of the meetings, trainings, and actions of three primary and two secondary organizations, as well as roughly one hundred semistructured, recorded interviews with undocumented activists and documented allies. I used a snowball sampling method, which generally connected me from one activist to other activists but occasionally connected me with public or Democratic Party officials or members of the media. (With Puente, as I note later, I was sometimes introduced to activists by other activists, rather than simply referred to them.) Many of those I interviewed were undocumented. Although I never questioned interviewees about their immigration status, most people volunteered the information, frequently as part of the answer to my first question, which was about their path into pro-immigrant activism.

With a few exceptions (explained later), those who are undocumented are designated by pseudonyms in the book. It has been a long and circuitous path to this outcome. When I initially sought institutional review board (IRB) approval for the research, I did so under a protocol that required me to anonymize interviewees in any work that came from the research, in order to protect those who might be undocumented. Shortly after I began my work in Phoenix, self-identified undocumented interviewees began to object to anonymization.[1] Several remarked that they were undocumented and unafraid and would prefer to be named in the research; one told me that my protocol went against the self-revelatory impetus of the movement. I returned to the IRB and asked if I might implement a hybrid protocol, through which I give each interviewee a choice about whether they will appear by name or be anonymized in the research. To my surprise, the IRB agreed.[2] During the primary research, I gave all interviewees this choice; a majority opted to be identified by name in the research. After the election of Donald Trump, however, I was concerned that this choice, made under a different administration, could expose undocumented activists to untenable risk. After consulting with other researchers and one organizational leader in Phoenix, I decided that I would anonymize anyone who had identified themselves in their interview as undocumented, unless they initially requested to be identified by name and 1) I was still in touch with them and they had confirmed, after the election of Donald Trump, that they would still prefer to be identified by name, or 2) they were people with sufficiently high public profiles that quoting them in this book would not affect their visibility. This was not an easy decision: viewed in one light, it seemed paradoxical and wrong, in a study of immigrant agency, to contravene the decisions of interview subjects in this way. But given the changed circumstances, the difficulties of contacting those I had interviewed several years earlier, and the enormous stakes for them of a decision to disclose, I decided presumptive anonymization was the best course. I had the opportunity to revisit this decision again, because the last draft of the book was written after Joe Biden was elected president in November 2020. After some amount of thought, I decided to preserve the mostly anonymized protocol that I had established during the Trump years. Although the climate for undocumented immigrants is now less facially hostile—albeit characterized by some of the kinds of inconsistencies that plagued the Obama administration—I had been seriously rattled by how quickly things had changed after Trump was elected, and, given the divided state of the country, how quickly they might change again in the future. And while I appreciated my interviewees' observations about the tensions between an anonymizing protocol and the self-consciously revelatory spirit of the movement, I also came to think that there was a difference between an undocumented protester revealing her status at a specific political moment at which she could at least make a calculated estimate of its consequences, and a white citizen, who experienced none of the same stakes, making that revelation once and for all, without knowledge of the circumstances in which future readers might come upon it. Although the combination of actual names (for some activists, for organizations) and pseudonyms at first struck me as strange, I have come to think that it serves the dual goals of telling the story of actual people in an actual place and protecting the identities of those who might be at risk.

Beyond questions of immigration status, two other features of my data merit consideration. The first is gender. Approximately two-thirds of my interviewees were female-identified; one-third were male identified (there were not, according to the demographic information I asked interview subjects to provide, any gender nonbinary people in my sample). This gender ratio among my interviewees corresponded roughly with the proportions of men and women I observed within organizations during the ethnographic portions of my research. In both cases, this representation of women is, of course, disproportionate to their numbers in the general population. Similar gender disparities existed within the leadership of the organizations I followed. During the research period, in the five organizations that were the foci of my observation, there were six women and three men who served as executive directors. As a theorist of gender, I was interested in this disproportion (as I began to perceive it, in the early stages of the research), and I asked interview subjects about it at two junctures in the research. The first was at the beginning, as I was first observing it. And the second was when organizers at ADAC and LUCHA began to comment on the growing presence of "moms" within their organizations. In relation to the "moms," the question(s) (Why do you think they are coming? Why moms and not dads?) tended to prompt more reflection and analysis, and the answers were consistent with lines of analyses I have seen in the literature on gender and immigrant populations more generally. First, many parents join the movement because their children are involved in it; moms, because of the gendered distribution of familial labor (generally and in Latino immigrant homes more specifically), are likely to be more directly involved with their children and more focused on their activities. Second, dads are likely to be spending more of their available time on market labor, making it difficult for them to participate in activism. I encountered more difficulty when I asked younger women about the disproportion of women participants or leaders in their organization. Some shrugged off the question, others viewed it with perplexity. Most simply accepted these indicia of female leadership as the state of the world in the 2010s. Older women were more willing to consider the question; for example, it prompted an interesting discussion with a Latina ally who had grown up with parents in the Chicano movement, and who saw the representation of women in the undocumented immigrants' movement as a positive development. But in general this feature of the research did not prompt the level of discussion that I, as a gender scholar, had anticipated. I also looked briefly at the differences in answers to an initial question that I asked interview subjects, about their paths to activism, to see if there were any gender-specific differences I could observe in their narratives. The primary differences that I noted were that (1) when describing the turning points that had encouraged them toward activism, male youth participants were more likely to cite frustrations in employment, while female youth participants were more likely to cite frustrations in accessing higher education (consistent with data in the literature suggesting young men are more likely to be early entrants into the labor market, a factor that may itself affect the ratio of female to male participants); and (2) female youth participants sometimes cited the influence of a mother who wanted more for them than she had been able to achieve because of gender constraints (although male youth participants often described being supported by mothers, albeit for different reasons).

The second demographic feature of the data worthy of discussion is age. In my interview sample, youths predominate. Roughly 60 percent of my interview subjects were in the youth cohort (ages eighteen to thirty). The rest ranged between thirty and eighty years of age, with gradually diminishing cohorts in thirty to forty, forty to fifty-five, and fifty-five plus groups. There are several reasons for this pattern. First, I interviewed a disproportionate number of youths during the voter engagement campaigns of summer–fall 2012. These campaigns brought together large numbers of youths in discrete locations (e.g., at the offices of Promise-Arizona, for the Adios Arpaio campaign), making it possible for me to interview many participants in a short period. Second, for reasons I explain later, youths were happy to talk with me throughout the period of the research, whereas adults at Puente, for example, needed to become more familiar with me over time, or to be introduced by mutual acquaintances, before they were willing to interview. This pattern meant that proportionately more of my research with Puente was observation based, and it reduced the proportion of adult interviewees in my sample, particularly those who identified themselves as undocumented. In addition, more of the organizations with which I worked (two of the three organizations I focused on in the primary phase of my research, for example) were youth focused, reflecting the predominance of youth in the undocumented immigrants' movement nationwide.

THE TIME FRAME OF THE RESEARCH AND ITS CONSEQUENCES

The primary research was conducted between 2012 and 2016, with additional observation and interviews conducted during the first year of the Trump administration in 2017, and limited, intermittent follow-ups between 2017 and 2020. The extended time frame of the research was a product of several factors. The first was the fact that my research was sited far from where I lived and worked. I completed all of my research in Phoenix, while I was living and working in Berkeley, California (and for one year in Princeton, New Jersey). Consequently, the observation and interviews were conducted on biweekly trips during 2012–13, which became monthly trips in 2014–15, and in the summer of 2016, when I did follow-up interviews. Making sure I fully understood the practices I was witnessing and interviewing enough activists to achieve theoretical saturation took considerably longer because I was not constantly present. Because I was in the field for an extended period, I observed changes in the practices I was studying, which led me to frame additional research questions, which in turn required more time in the field.

A second reason for the extended time frame was the challenges I experienced gaining entrée in the early stages of the research. Because I was working outside my usual substantive fields and had not done empirical work with social movement organizations before, I entered the field with few contacts among Phoenix organizations. I was also, as I explain in the introduction, a thoroughgoing outsider to the communities I hoped to study. I was white, a citizen by birth, a non-Spanish speaker, a Californian, older (often considerably), and separated by income and education from most of the people I aimed to observe and interview. This experiential distance produced different kinds of obstacles with different (primary) organizations. The two predominantly youth-based organizations, ADAC and LUCHA, agreed and adapted readily to my presence, and participants and organizers were happy to speak with me in recorded interviews. The fact that all the youths I met at these organizations were fluent English speakers, that most meetings—at the outset of my research—were conducted in English (and personal communication among participants tended to be flexibly bilingual) made conversations easier and made me less conspicuous during the time I spent with the organizations. However, because these organizations prioritized storytelling as a tactical tool, and tended to have strong, normative emotion cultures modeled by experienced activists and organizers, the challenge was figuring out whether these activists were responding to my questions with reflection specific to the occasion of the interview or were sharing, perhaps reflexively, some version of the stories and emotions that they had learned to share with the general public. (I explore this challenge at more length later.)

Activists at Puente, on the other hand, responded to me with understandable reserve. This was a community-based organization, with many monolingual Spanish speakers; meetings and conversations were also conducted in Spanish. This meant that I stood out not simply by virtue of my appearance—there were only a few white allies who worked regularly with Puente—but also because virtually every time I spoke I was violating the linguistic norms of the place. Its "open hand" events—designed to provide community members with experiences of enjoyment and solidarity—also featured strong elements of Mexican and Mexican American cultures, in the food, music, and arts influences they incorporated. Moreover, older participants—who did not have the integrative experience of the public schools or university campuses, and whose workplaces were populated predominantly by immigrants—were not accustomed to extended conversations with white, middle-aged, female academics. After a few awkward attempts to gather information or arrange interviews—during which activists tended to refer me to Carlos Garcia—I decided to change my approach. While I began interviewing simultaneously with my observation at ADAC and LUCHA, I spent the first approximately two years at Puente simply observing. I attended their actions, of which Puente had many (these were generally held in both Spanish and English); I participated in events like marches, rallies, or vigils outside jails or detention centers. I attended their convenings, which was a valuable way to learn about Puente's relationship to organizing on a national level. I lent a hand, painting banners for marches or driving activists to events, when it was needed. As I acquired a modest level of Spanish, I attended some community meetings. My hope was that as people saw me with some regularity, they might feel a little less wary. I began to have short, casual conversations, particularly with younger participants or those adults who had some English proficiency. Ileana Salinas, a youth activist who sometimes worked with me as an interpreter, and Sandy Weir, a member of the Unitarian Universalist Congregation of Phoenix, who worked with Puente on the Unitarians' 2012 General Assembly in Phoenix, introduced me to some of the adults they knew at Puente. I gradually found a group of adults (particularly those who had been on the Undocubus) who were willing to talk with me in an interview setting, and Ileana provided simultaneous interpretation in most cases. In late 2014, I asked Carlos Garcia, with whom I had had casual conversations but had not yet been able to schedule an interview, whether he would like to speak to a class I was teaching on the Immigrant Rights movement at Berkeley Law School. He was interested in the idea of talking with young lawyers about the work of social movements. He spoke with them on several occasions over the course of two years, sometimes by himself and sometimes with Annie Lai, the former ACLU-AZ lawyer with whom he had collaborated on *Puente v. Arpaio*. After brief expositions from Carlos or Annie, these sessions consisted primarily of questions and answers (from myself and from members of the class), so they had roughly the format of interviews. Later, I interviewed Carlos in Phoenix as well. The more gradual start at Puente also extended the time frame of the research.

A final factor that protracted the period of the research was the election of 2016. By the time November arrived, I had completed the preliminary research, as well as several months of follow-up research in the summer of 2016. I had a fellowship year in which to analyze my interview data and begin to frame the book. With the election of Donald Trump, however, it seemed vital to return to Phoenix. I wondered how the organizations there would withstand a federal administration whose anti-immigrant stance recalled "attrition through enforcement," and how their strategies and tactics might differ when the federal government was not simply ambivalent or dysfunctional in responding to immigrants but unequivocally hostile. Intensive interviewing with a small number of organization leaders in 2017, and more intermittent follow-ups as I began to write the book, also extended the time frame of the research.

As I explain in the introduction, the temporally extended time frame had important implications for the way that I conceived the work. It persuaded me that it would not be fully satisfying to depict the practices that fostered immigrant agency at one point in time or as practices or processes abstracted from the dimension of change over time. So I decided to embed my more conventional sociolegal inquiries into organizational practices and their effects on immigrant agency or activist consciousness in a broader story about the movement in Arizona, defined by a temporal beginning, middle, and end, as well as by thematic features. The extended time frame of the research and my decision to tell a story that had the feature of temporal progression had two more concrete consequences for my research.

First, not all of my interviews with activists focused on the same phenomena or the same questions. The world of activism looked different in 2014 than in 2012, and consequently I asked different questions about it. This created challenges in analyzing the interviews, because while there were some questions that were answered by virtually all subjects (e.g., a question about how they came to activism or a question about what qualities or activities should define citizenship or create a presumptive entitlement to citizenship), many more (which focused on narratives, emotions, or tactics) tended to be tailored to the period during which the interview was conducted.[3] This means that some of the analytic conclusions I offer do not have the strength of one hundred, or even fifty, interviews behind them.[4] I see two features of the research as mitigating—although not eliminating—this problem. First, those portions of the book that tend to "pause" the temporal progression of the narrative to take a closer look at what was happening within organizations, or at the emerging political consciousness of activists (chapters 2, 3, and 6), tend to be grounded in larger numbers of interviews, as well as in observation. But in general, after the voter engagement campaigns of 2012 (during which I interviewed a larger number of youths) my interviews tended to be distributed fairy regularly over time. So each temporal period yielded substantial numbers of interviews, and the temporally specific observations I offer reflect readily perceptible patterns among those interviews.

Second, to offer a more complete narrative with a roughly chronological structure, I needed to discuss an early period during which I was not yet in the field. Consequently, the material in chapter 1 (on the movement between 2008 and 2010) and first part of chapter 4 (on the campaign for the 2010 DREAM Act and DACA) draws heavily on a database of conventional and social media sources, as well as a body of scholarly research on the movement of undocumented immigrants. In addition, I interviewed both Chicano or Latino leaders who played a role in the early movement in Phoenix, as well as youth activists who mobilized for the DREAM Act or DACA, about their experiences. However, these interviews, unlike many of those I conducted, were retrospective in character—that is, they were not contemporaneous with that activist experience.

INTERVIEWING STORYTELLERS AND PERFORMATIVE CITIZENS

A final challenge in my research was an issue easier to state than resolve: I was interviewing a group of people who not only were accomplished storytellers, who believed that the fate of their movement could hang on their ability to present a compelling narrative, but were also eager performative citizens, accustomed to embracing stances—be they emotional or tactical—that might begin as a combination of hope and assertion and only gradually come to be understood and internalized. In other words, the very practices I was studying meant that this group of activists were acculturated both to sharing a particular kind of story and to projecting a degree of agency that they might not yet have come entirely to inhabit. I wondered constantly about how this dynamic was affecting the interviews I conducted. To be clear: the point is not that anyone aimed to mislead me. It is that advancing a particular kind of narrative or projecting a degree of agency became second nature to those socialized to activism within undocumented organizations, particularly those serving youth (which tended to have a more performative emphasis). This tendency emerged with particular strength when activists engaged those who were less experientially proximate, and whom they hoped to engage as allies. My identity—as an experientially distant, white upper-middle class citizen, and as a presumptive white progressive—put me squarely in that camp.[5] Not only was I a member of one of their "target" audiences, but I lacked any of the shared attributes that might have made them more likely to confide in me about their lives.[6]

This identitarian issue was likely also complicated by my particular persona: I tend to be a receptive rather than a skeptical, or even dispassionate, listener; I am quick to appreciate effort and—given my theoretical predilections—to glimpse agency, even in the interstices of a highly constraining situation. I was concerned, throughout the research, that all of these factors would intersect to make activists less likely to share troubles or doubts—in their own lives or about organizational norms—and more likely to offer an account intuitively tailored for public consumption. At some level, this risk simply inhered in my particular engagement with these particular activists; it was not possible to eliminate it. But as I suggest briefly in my introduction, I used two kinds of strategies to mitigate or manage it.

One was to embrace my subject position and see what I could learn as a target of performative citizenship. I recall one occasion on which I was preparing to begin an interview with a young activist, when she was stopped by an older organizer who said, "Before you do that, let me give you your talking points!" My first reaction was frustration: I was now going to spend an hour with someone who was far less likely to share her individual perspectives than to serve as a mouthpiece for her colleague's talking points. But then I thought, if I'm not simply studying individual activists, but organizations and the way they shape individual activists, I'd like to know what those "talking points" are. Some useful parts of my analysis—for example, my discussion of "metanarratives" in chapter 2—arose from analyzing viewpoints so consistently and similarly articulated that I became aware of them as the "talking points" of the organizations I was studying. But discerning the difference between organizational "talking points" (or practices) and individual consciousness—and understanding the relation between the former and the latter—would be possible only if there were some activists who were not giving me (explicitly or more intuitively) their organization's "talking points." So I also employed strategies that aimed to encourage activists to feel comfortable speaking candidly with me, despite my experiential difference.

A more extended time frame, as I note in the introduction, was one of these strategies. I assumed that the more familiar activists were with me—the more they became accustomed to seeing me, observing and participating in the work of the organization—the more likely they were to feel comfortable sharing individualized stories and perspectives, notwithstanding my experiential distance. But what I hoped would be even more effective was interviewing a smaller group of activists multiple times. Consequently, I interviewed roughly ten activists more than once and four as many as six or eight times. (These four also became my primary informants for the final, Trump-era period of the research.) I did find that, among these activists, I was more likely to hear expressions of frustration, demoralization, or doubt, or qualms about organizing practices or their own roles as activists. Because I was more familiar with them and with how they tended to express themselves, I was also more likely to pick up on moments of hesitation or ambivalence or to press them slightly harder for a full explanation than I tended to do with activists I had just met. It was activists in this latter group who first began to raise questions about the emotional costs of central organizing practices, which I had begun to wonder about over the course of the research. So I believe this strategy succeeded to some degree, although, of course, what a more experientially proximate interviewer might have learned from these activists—or what any interviewer might have learned from activists less socialized to a performative stance—is a question about which I can only speculate.

Notes

INTRODUCTION

1. William Gamson argued that organizers often appeal to anger to create the "fire in the belly and iron in the soul" of social movement activists. Gamson, *Talking Politics*, 32.

2. McAdam, "Framing Function of Movement Tactics," 338–56.

3. Hochschild, *Managed Heart* (introducing concept of emotion work).

4. This increase was spurred substantially by Operation Gatekeeper, a Clinton-era initiative that sought to deter undocumented migration by reinforcing the border in the San Diego sector and shifting the path of migration eastward, where migrants would confront the obstacle of the brutal Sonora desert. The strategy did not deter migration but rather led to an increase of deaths in the Sonoran passage.

5. The *Huffington Post* reported in 2012 that "between 2001 and 2010, Arizona's non-Latino population grew by 17.3%. The state's Latino growth rate was 46.3%, they now comprise nearly one third of the state's population and about 47% of its children under 19." Ramos, "What Arizona's Ethnic Studies Ban Says about America." Whites who had enjoyed uncontested control over the state's government began to glimpse a future in which political and cultural dominance would slip from their hands.

6. Kobach, "Reinforcing the Rule of Law."

7. Proposition 200 (2004) (undocumented immigrants not eligible for public benefits) passed by 56 percent ("Key Ballot Measures"). Proposition 100 (2006) (undocumented immigrants not eligible for bail for "serious felonies") passed by 77 percent ("Arizona Bailable Offenses, Proposition 100"). Proposition 102

(2006) (undocumented immigrants not eligible to receive punitive damages in state lawsuits filed in Arizona) passed by 74 percent ("Arizona Standing in Civil Actions, Proposition 102"). Proposition 103 (2006) (English as official state language) passed by 74 percent ("Key Ballot Measures"). Proposition 300 (2006) (undocumented students not eligible for in-state tuition or public scholarships) passed by 71.4 percent ("Arizona Public Program Eligibility, Proposition 300"). Although the initiative process is subject to many species of manipulation, it may send a message more powerful than that reflected in ordinary legislation: initiatives that prevail have the imprimatur of law, and they also directly reflect popular opinion.

8. Sinema, "No Surprises."

9. Sinema, "No Surprises," 67. Here, too, proponents aimed at curtailing the state's population of immigrants: "Denying the in-state tuition, besides being fair to residents, also deters illegal immigrants from coming here." McKinley, "Arizona Law Takes a Toll on Nonresident Students" (quoting Rep. John Kavanagh).

10. McKinley, "Arizona Law Takes a Toll on Nonresident Students."

11. Carlos Garcia and Annie Lai, interview with author, March 2016.

12. Beard, "Arizona Is Now in Recession."

13. This law went into effect in 2008 and was upheld by the Supreme Court in *Chamber of Commerce v. Whiting*, 563 U.S. 582 (2011).

14. National Conference of State Legislatures, "Analysis of Arizona's Immigrant Enforcement Laws." At the peak of this legislative activity, the state also passed HB 2281, a measure directed to the public schools. Ramos, "What Arizona's Ethnic Studies Ban Says about America." This law, which prohibited courses that "promote resentment toward a group or class of people," aimed to dismantle Tucson Unified School District's Ethnic Studies Program. This program was created to encourage academic engagement and increase graduation rates among Latino youth. Its correlation with improvements in graduation rates had fueled pride and hope among Latino communities and their allies. The legislative attack on this program, as the state enacted SB 1070, prompted fears that the legislature was targeting not only undocumented residents, who were predominantly Latino, but all Latino residents.

15. This was the only challenged provision of the law upheld in *Arizona v. United States*, 567 U.S. 387 (2012).

16. Arizona Senate, HB 2162 (amending SB 1070), final reading no. 1, April 19, 2010 (Sen. Pearce).

17. Arizona Senate Subcommittee on Public Safety and Human Services, SB 1070, hearing, January 20, 2010 (Sen. Melvin).

18. Flag, "Is There a Connection Between Undocumented Immigrants and Crime?" (concluding, based on a new study from Pew Research and the Marshall Project and earlier research, that increases in undocumented migration in urban areas studied do not lead to increases in rates of crime, over five different categories).

19. Arizona Senate, HB 2162 (amending SB 1070), final reading no. 1, April 19, 2010 (Sen. Cheuvront); and Arizona House of Representatives, SB 1070, third reading, April 13, 2010 (Rep. Miranda).

20. This strategy reached its apogee when Rob Krentz, a well-known border rancher, was murdered on his land in March 2010. Although the murder was

never solved, allegations that footprints had been found pointing from Krentz's ranch toward the border allowed Pearce and his allies to allege that Krentz had been murdered by undocumented immigrants, enabling a final, effective push for passage. Archibold, "Ranchers Alarmed by Killing Near Border."

21. *Arizona v. United States*, 567 U.S. 387 (2012).

22. Kathryn Abrams, fieldnotes, April 2012.

23. Kathryn Abrams, fieldnotes, April 2012.

24. Voss and Bloemraad, eds., *Rallying for Immigrant Rights*.

25. Examples of this juxtaposition of structural constraint and individual agency in the legal field are discussed (and perpetuated) in Abrams, "Sex Wars Redux." A notable exception to this pattern in legal scholarship is critical race or Black feminism, in which agency is frequently analyzed in collective terms. See, for example, Harris, "Race and Essentialism in Feminist Legal Theory."

26. Abril Gallardo, interview with author, September 2012.

27. This turned out to be a pattern that some—though by no means all—participants cited in their trajectory to activism. See, for example, Marisol, interview with author, April 2013; Verónica, interview with author, April 2013; Reyna Montoya, interview with author, August 2012; and Matías, interview with author, May 2014.

28. During the summer of 2012, I worked similarly in the city of Tucson. I ultimately decided that the proximity of the border, and the humanitarian work it necessitated, made immigration-related activism in Tucson sufficiently distinct that comparisons would not be straightforward. Thereafter I focused exclusively on Phoenix and Maricopa County.

29. The activists who populated and ultimately led such organizations seemed not only the most affected by state hostility but also the most likely to be shaped and fortified by collective, organizational forms of empowerment. Because of their focus on undocumented activists, I refer to these organizations at some points in the text as "undocumented organizations," although not all of their members were undocumented, immigrants, or even Latinos.

30. There are many ways to define and distinguish organizers and activists. In these organizations, the same people often played both roles or progressed from activist to organizer. In general, I use *activist* to refer to someone who takes part in outward-facing social movement actions aimed at influencing the public or securing some form of political or legal change. I use *organizer* to refer to someone who trains or supervises groups of activists, and/or does outreach to the broader community to inform, educate, or encourage organizational (ie, social movement) participation. Some organizers with greater experience also engage in more strategic decision-making about how to execute campaigns, or select among possible tactical options, or revise existing organizing practices. In some parts of the book, I refer to these organizers as *leaders*.

31. Carlos Garcia, interview with author, March 2015.

32. When PAZ's executive director, Petra Falcon, became the leader of the Comprehensive Immigration Reform (CIR) Table—an umbrella organization aimed at coordinating the efforts of local organizations during the push for CIR in Congress—I attended those meetings regularly as well.

33. During the primary period of my research, I also attended meetings of an umbrella organization, Somos America (We Are America), whose president

I observed on my initial visit to Phoenix. Somos had been an early site committed to giving voice to undocumented communities, and coordinating the work of nascent organizations in the early years of "attrition through enforcement." Although its role in amplifying undocumented voice appeared to decline as dedicated organizations by and for undocumented immigrants gained strength, Somos meetings remained a useful place to hear about the work being done by a range of organizations. I found some of its past leaders to be valuable sources of information about the early years of "attrition through enforcement."

34. During my time in Phoenix, I also attended educational or cultural events related to immigrant activism in the greater Phoenix area. Playwright and activist James Garcia, whom I interviewed early in the research, connected me with the New Carpa Theater Company, which he founded. I attended screenings of some of the films made about Phoenix activists, and panels on DREAMer and immigrant politics at ASU.

35. As I explain in chapter 3, following the success of several voter engagement campaigns staffed by immigrant canvassers, the Arizona legislature passed a statute making it a felony to deliver the ballot of someone who was not a family member.

36. I also helped out at the organizations in which I observed: counting or folding leaflets, picking up meals, and driving activists who lacked cars to meetings or actions.

37. It is noteworthy, however, that despite this view of California, virtually no one over the course of the research expressed any interest in California as a place to live. And only one interview subject had left for California after the passage of SB 1070, but returned within a year. These facts are supportive of the views expressed to me explicitly in some interviews, that activists viewed Arizona as their home or their place, regardless of the hostility with which it confronted them.

38. Abril Gallardo, interview with author, June 2016.

39. See, for example, Zepeda-Millan, *Latino Mass Mobilization*; and Voss and Bloemraad, *Rallying for Immigrant Rights*.

40. See, for example, Prieto, *Immigrants under Threat*; Escudero, *Organizing While Undocumented*; and Nicholls, *Dreamers*.

41. Mansbridge and Morris, *Oppositional Consciousness*.

42. See, for example, Hildebrandt et al., *Performing Citizenship*; Isin and Nielsen, *Acts of Citizenship*; Meyer and Fine, "Grassroots Citizenship at Multiple Scales"; and Coll, "Citizenship Acts and Immigrant Voting Rights Movements."

43. Cf. Taylor and Crossley, "Abeyance."

CHAPTER 1. CONFRONTING "ATTRITION THROUGH ENFORCEMENT"

1. Although it would be preferable to be able to pinpoint more precisely the time of the movement's emergence, the facts that the empirical portion of my research began in spring 2012, and that my research into the early period of resistance to "attrition through enforcement" did not include direct observation

or contemporaneous interviews (but was based on an archive of media and secondary materials and retrospective interviews with participants), make this more difficult. What I am able to state with empirical confidence is that the movement had emerged—with dedicated organizations, coordinated actions, broad tactical repertoires, and confident outward-turned activists—by the time I entered the field in 2012.

2. This third focus comprehends a range of elements that are sometimes described as the "cultural turn" in social movement analysis; they focus broadly on how human beings involved in social movement activity understand and make meaning in the world. Jasper, "Cultural Approaches in the Sociology of Social Movements." Proponents of the cultural turn place less emphasis on objective factors such as resources or political structures and more emphasis on subjective or interpretive factors such as the strength of collective identity, or the presence of particular emotional states among social movement participants, or the extent to which a movement's central messages resonate with its prospective audiences. Of these elements, the last—which is described as 'framing" theory, or attention to the resonance of social movement frames—is sometimes extracted from this broader array and described as the third focus of social movement scholars. Benford and Snow, "Framing Processes and Social Movements." Although I believe that utilizing frames that resonate with the public and with decision makers is vital for the adaptation and persistence of social movements, and I argue below that storytelling, emotions, and tactics of performative citizenship are all used to introduce and shift the frames of the movement, I find that in explaining emergence, particularly for a movement composed of undocumented noncitizens, participants' ability to perceive themselves as agents and changemakers—a quality comprehended by Doug McAdam's term "cognitive liberation"—is more important. In focusing on this quality as a third determinant of social movement emergence, I follow McAdam's "political process" theory, which combines these three elements. McAdam and Tarrow, "Political Context of Social Movements"; and McAdam, *Political Process*.

3. A Rasmussen poll taken several days after SB 1070 was signed into law found that 64 percent of Arizonans polled supported it. "Arizona Voters Favor Welcoming Immigration Policy."

4. Tilly, *From Mobilization to Revolution*; McAdam, *Political Process and the Development of Black Insurgency*; and Meyer, "Protest and Political Opportunities," 125–45. These theorists have also argued that political opportunity can shape the tactical repertoires utilized by social movements and the outcomes of their efforts.

5. McAdam and Tarrow, "Political Context of Social Movements."

6. Meyer, "Protest and Political Opportunities," 125–45.

7. Almeida, "Role of Threat in Collective Action," 43–62.

8. Almeida, "Role of Threat in Collective Action," 43–62.

9. Zepeda-Millán, "Weapons of the (Not So) Weak," 269–87; and Zepeda-Millán, *Latino Mass Mobilization*.

10. The first significant federal judicial response occurred in 2010, when a district court, adjudicating a preemption challenge by the Obama administration,

issued a preliminary injunction against several features of SB 1070. *United States v. Arizona*, 703 F. Supp. 2d 980 (D. Ariz. 2010). All but one of these features were struck down by the Supreme Court in 2012, yet the most important of these, the "show me your papers" provision, was allowed to stand. *Arizona v. United States*, 567 U.S. 387 (2012).

11. Matías, interview with author, May 2014.

12. Alfredo Gutierrez, interview with author, September 2013.

13. Sandoval and Tambini, "State of Arizona."

14. Daniel Ortega, interview with author, July 2014.

15. Ximena, interview with author, April 2015.

16. Martín, interview with author, July 2016.

17. Daniel Ortega, interview with author, July 2014.

18. Almeida, "Role of Threat in Collective Action," 43–62.

19. McCarthy and Zald, "Resource Mobilization," 1212–41.

20. McAdam, *Political Process and the Development of Black Insurgency*.

21. Edwards and McCarthy, "Resources and Social Movement Mobilization," 116–52.

22. Ganz, *Why David Sometimes Wins*.

23. Edwards and McCarthy, "Resources and Social Movement Mobilization," 116–52.

24. Edwards and McCarthy, "Resources and Social Movement Mobilization," 116–52.

25. For a highly informative account of the struggle of immigrant groups against Joe Arpaio by two Phoenix-area journalists that foregrounds the role of Lydia Guzman, see Sterling and Joffe-Block, *Driving While Brown*.

26. Lydia Guzman, interview with author, April 2014.

27. Lydia Guzman, interview with author, April 2014.

28. Lydia Guzman, interview with author, April 2014. (explaining that approximately 50% of the hotline calls focused on law enforcement while others reported health and human service issues).

29. Lydia Guzman, interview with author, April 2014.

30. *Melendres v. Arpaio*, 989 F. Supp. 2d 822 (D. Ariz. 2013) (findings of fact and conclusion of law).

31. See *Arizona v. United States*, 567 U.S. 387 (2012).

32. Lydia Guzman, interview with author, April 2014.

33. Carlos Garcia, interview with author, July 2017.

34. See *United States v. Arizona*, 703 F. Supp. 2d 980 (D. Ariz. 2010). The Supreme Court affirmed the district court decision about three provisions of SB 1070, but reversed as to Section 2(b), the "show me your papers" provision.

35. Alexander, *Vigil* (those who have had "know your rights" training relate to activists their success in resisting ICE pressure to sign "voluntary departures").

36. Alfredo Gutierrez, interview with author, September 2013.

37. Lydia Guzman, interview with author, April 2014.

38. Lydia Guzman, interview with author, April 2014.

39. Abrego, "Legal Consciousness of Undocumented Latinos," 337–69.

40. Gonzales, *Lives in Limbo*.

41. Elena, interview with author, July 2014; Camila, interview with author, May 2014; Matías, interview with author, May 2014; and Luis, interview with author, May 2014.

42. The first reaction to Prop 300 of many of those I interviewed was that, through hard work, they would be able to figure out a way to attend a four-year college. As one young man put it, "Where there's a will, there's a way." Matías, interview with author, May 2014.

43. Elena, interview with author, July 2014; and Matías, interview with author, May 2014.

44. Elena, interview with author, July 2014.

45. Matías, interview with author, May 2014.

46. Elena, interview with author, July 2014.

47. Among my interviewees, some give credit for the initial idea to Congressman Raul Grijalva, while others claim the idea first came from Carlos Garcia of Puente. It is likely that both elected officials and early movement leaders were involved.

48. Roberto Reveles, interview with author, July 2014.

49. Sandoval and Tambini, "State of Arizona."

50. Daniel Ortega, interview with author, February 2013.

51. Daniel Ortega, interview with author, February 2013.

52. Reuters staff, "Immigration Law Boycott."

53. Robert Reveles, interview with author, January 2014.

54. Sandra Weir, interview with author, April 2013.

55. James Garcia, interview with author, April 2013.

56. James Garcia, interview with author, April 2013.

57. Oppel, "Arizona, Bowing to Business."

58. Alexander, *Vigil*. The Virgin of Guadalupe is an image of the Virgin Mary as she appeared to a poor indigenous man who became St. Juan Diego, in Mexico City in 1531. The Virgin is regarded as a patron saint of Mexico and symbolizes God's love for and identification with the poor (www.franciscanmedia.org/our-lady-of-guadalupe/). Small statues of the Virgin are often carried or pulled in portable shrines in pro-immigrant protests in Phoenix.

59. Mercedes, interview with author, February 2013.

60. Mercedes, interview with author, February 2013.

61. Mercedes, interview with author, February 2013.

62. Civic engagement is discussed, as a paradigmatic form of "performative citizenship," in chapter 3.

63. The Center for Community Change, now known as Community Change, is a movement-mentoring organization that seeks to "empower low-income people to bring about positive change in the community" (https://communitychange.org).

64. Although the organization's focus shifted to undocumented youth and Latino voters, the "vigil ladies" remained active in the new organization, appearing at rallies and marches with a portable shrine to the Virgin. The vigil was also briefly reinstated at the capitol, as the community awaited the Supreme Court's decision on SB 1070 in *Arizona v. United States*.

65. Attention to the political consciousness of movement participants may be described as a feature of the "cultural turn" in social movement scholarship

(although McAdams's work on "cognitive liberation" predates a good deal of this scholarship). This heterogeneous body of work focuses on subjective or interpretive factors affecting movement participants or their publics, including analysis of framing, identity, and emotions in their relation to the emergence and/or persistence of social movements. Goodwin, Jasper, and Polletta, *Passionate Politics*.

66. McAdam and Tarrow, "Political Context of Social Movements."

67. McAdam, *Political Process*, 49–50, 1930–70.

68. Mansbridge, "Making of Oppositional Consciousness," 1.

69. An emergent literature on "urban citizenship" or "non-citizen citizenship" or "grass-roots citizenship" describes the participation of people with "irregular status" in political actions conventionally populated by citizens as challenging the ways theorists and laypersons conceive citizenship. This literature is discussed in chapter 3.

70. For example, attempts to register Black voters in the Mississippi Delta and other deep South regions in the early 1960s, close to a century after the Fifteenth Amendment conferred an equal right to vote but before the passage of the Voting Rights Act of 1965, was an example of this kind of strategy.

71. An even more ambivalent federal policy, such as that pursued by the Obama administration, may produce similar effects when it separates families, multiplies the grounds of deportation, or contracts the procedural rights of immigrants facing removal.

72. Menjivar and Abrego, "Legal Violence," 1380–1421.

73. Prieto, *Immigrants under Threat*, 8–16, 107–30. Prieto argues that immigrants who have accommodated themselves to "the shell" are more likely to engage in activism when they confront an immediate threat, or what Prieto calls a "close call" with immigration enforcement. It may be that legal strategies such as "attrition through enforcement" create ongoing "close calls" that are more widespread throughout the undocumented population. He also argues that immigrants who do become active are likely to have a more instrumental view of their participation: they are defending the conditions of life that they have worked hard to create, rather than seeking social transformation. Although I did not conceive the question in these terms when I was conducting my research, I would say that I saw this orientation among some of the adult activists with whom I worked but also witnessed aspirations to broader social transformation, particularly among the most active, veteran participants.

74. Gonzales, *Lives in Limbo*.

75. Bloemraad and Voss, "Movement or Moment?," 683–704.

76. Bloemraad and Voss, "Movement or Moment?," 683–704.

CHAPTER 2. STORYTELLING AND EMOTION CULTURES IN UNDOCUMENTED ORGANIZATIONS

1. Nancy Fraser describes this function as enabling "oppositional interpretations" of participants' identities, interests, and needs. Fraser "Rethinking the Public Sphere," 67 (describing the role of feminist organizations in the 1960s and 1970s). Fraser and Michael Warner refer to such group contexts as

"counterpublics." See generally Warner, *Publics and Counterpublics*, 90, 56. Warner defines a "public" as "a social space created by the reflexive circulation of discourse," where "discourse" encompasses the kinds of practices, idioms, affects, and modes of expression that help to form and transform its members identities. Counterpublics are publics defined by their subordinate status, their distinct forms of discourse, and their critical relation to power.

2. Fraser, "Rethinking the Public Sphere," 56–80.

3. Zimmerman, "Transmedia Testimonio," 1892–93.

4. Polletta, *It Was Like a Fever*, 1–32.

5. The understanding of "stories" framed here synthesizes a number of works of narrative theory and the sociology of narrative. See, for example, Meyers, *Victims' Stories*; Polletta, *It Was Like a Fever*; Ganz, "Why Stories Matter"; and Ewick and Silbey, "Subversive Stories and Hegemonic Tales." My understanding of storytelling as a socially structured practice draws on the particularly helpful framing of Ewick and Silbey.

6. Polletta, *It Was Like a Fever*, 20.

7. Ewick and Silbey, "Subversive Stories and Hegemonic Tales," 197–226.

8. Abrams, field notes, January 2013.

9. Abrams, field notes, Spring 2014. The ceremonial or celebratory aspect of the storytelling was made clear by the fact that he had already offered the story in the course of a general meeting only a few months earlier.

10. Abrams, field notes, September 2013.

11. Abrams, field notes, June 2013. Although organizers referred to this as a "house meeting"—referencing tradition in immigrant organizing of reaching out to community members by organizing a meeting in the familiar setting of a volunteer's home—this particular meeting was held at LUCHA's Phoenix office.

12. Ganz, *Why David Sometimes Wins*. The model has been distilled for immigrant activists by the Center for Community Change and its sister organization, the New Organizing Institute. NOI, *Campaign for Arizona's Future*. The NOI materials, which were used by PAZ in the Adios Arpaio campaign, cite Ganz explicitly. LUCHA uses a less formal but conceptually similar version of this model.

13. Verónica, interview with author, April 2013.

14. Marisol, interview with author, April 2013.

15. Ewick and Silbey, "Subversive Stories and Hegemonic Tales," 213.

16. See NOI, *Campaign for Arizona's Future*. This training guide was used in the Adios Arpaio civic engagement campaign led by PAZ, discussed in chapter 3.

17. Snow and Benford, "Ideology, Frame Resonance," 197–218. (frames are means of "simplifying and condensing aspects of the 'world out there' . . . in ways that are intended to mobilize potential adherents and constituents, to garner bystander support, and to demoralize antagonists"). See also Benford and Snow, "Framing Processes and Social Movements."

18. These views of the strengths of storytelling held by activists are also shared, in large degree, by scholars. Polletta, *It Was Like a Fever*; and Meyers, *Victims' Stories*. But narrative theorists also point to other qualities that contribute to the persuasiveness of stories in protest, politics, and policy making.

Polletta, *It Was Like a Fever* (pointing to ellipsis as a vehicle for engaging listeners and arguing that literary devices such as irony, unexpected reversals, and changes in verb tense may render "victim" stories more credible and persuasive).

19. Marisol, interview with author, March 2013.

20. Marisol, interview with author, March 2013.

21. Luis, interview with author, May 2014.

22. Polletta, *It Was Like a* Fever, 20. Francesca Polletta, an astute analyst of storytelling in social movements, highlights these literary virtues as potential strengths of "victim" narratives.

23. See NOI, *Campaign for Arizona's Future*, 17 ("each of us has a compelling story to tell"). A small number of interview responses trace this metanarrative to training.

24. Patricia, interview with author, August 2012.

25. White, *Content of the Form*. As described by Hayden White, annals are simply a list (without temporality or unifying theme), and a chronicle is a temporally organized account without thematic closure.

26. Polletta, *It Was Like a Fever* (arguing that unexplained features of narrative draw readers in).

27. Ileana Salinas and Reyna Montoya, interview with author, August 2016.

28. Marisol, interview with author, March 2013.

29. Verónica, interview with author, April 2013; and Marisol, interview with author, March 2013.

30. Ileana Salinas and Reyna Montoya, interview with author, August 2016.

31. Ileana Salinas and Reyna Montoya, interview with author, August 2016.

32. Ileana Salinas and Reyna Montoya, interview with author, August 2016.

33. Ileana Salinas and Reyna Montoya, interview with author, August 2016.

34. Ileana has dealt with this ambivalence by participating in a new organization that promotes healing from experiences of detention and deportation through participation in the arts. She finds communicating her experience through music and teaching others to approach their experiences through artistic expression allows for greater creativity and eases the feeling that she is compromising herself. See chapters 6–7.

35. Natalia, interview with author, December 2012.

36. I take the term "emotion culture" from Chua, *Politics of Love in Myanmar*. The culture(s) I identify respond to different challenges than the emotion culture Chua describes among emerging LGBT activists in Myanmar. Yet both work to prepare an unlikely set of participants for activism, foster deep solidarity among them, and cultivate in them the commitment, tenacity, and resilience to remain in the political field.

37. Goodwin and Pfaff, "Emotion Work in High-Risk Social Movements."

38. Goodwin and Pfaff, "Emotion Work in High-Risk Social Movements," 282.

39. Unlike storytelling, in which practices of modeling or eliciting stories may be deliberate and self-aware, it is not always clear that the emotion cultures that develop within these organizations are as explicit or operate within this same degree of intentionality. Though it is difficult to say with any kind of empirical confidence, my observation suggests that emotion cultures emerge through a

combination of intentionality and intuition. Organizers sometimes describe the cultivation of certain emotions in intentional or strategic terms. When Monica Sandschafer, the founding director of LUCHA, spoke about the importance of "celebrating small victories" (interview with author, November 2012), or when Carlos Garcia, the director and lead organizer at Puente, described giving people a sense of connection to each other that reduced the impulse to "self-deport" (interview with author, March 2015), they were describing practices that reflected deliberation on the part of organizers. But at other times the features of shared emotional life that helped to orient and socialize activists seemed to arise from spontaneous expressions of feeling or from intuitions about how new participants can be motivated in doing their work. For example, when ADAC members teared up while sharing their stories at organizational meetings, they may have had a sense that allowing their emotions to come to the surface could help new participants see the human connection that can flow from the sharing of emotion, or they may simply have been letting their guard down with a group of people with whom they felt powerful kinship, or they may have been doing some combination of the two. This mix of intentionality and intuition with which organizations cultivate emotions varies in different contexts, and for different organizers, but both play a role in this essential practice of undocumented organizations.

40. Puente attracted a number of youth activists through its leadership in the Not1More Deportation campaign, described in chapter 5. In the years since the primary period of my research ended, Puente has added more youth projects and activities, some of which have an arts focus.

41. Prieto, *Immigrants under Threat.*

42. Petra Falcon, interview with author, June 2012.

43. Ileana Salinas, interview with author, June 2016.

44. Carlos Garcia, interview with author, March 2015.

45. Carlos Garcia, interview with author, March 2015.

46. Carlos Garcia, interview with author, March 2015.

47. Carlos Garcia and Annie Lai, interview with author, March 2016.

48. Carlos Garcia and Annie Lai, interview with author, March 2016.

49. This theme emerged regularly in my interviews with activists. See, for example, Ileana Salinas and Reyna Montoya, interview with author, August 2016; Erika Andiola, interview with author, April 2015; Luis, interview with author, May 2014; and Camila, interview with author, May 2014.

50. As Roberto Gonzales explains, youth can be empowered through childhood by their immersion in the enabling, integrative environment of public education, yet may become confused and demoralized when, approaching adulthood, they encounter barriers created by their status. See Gonzales, *Lives in Limbo.* Storytelling, and the emotion cultures of youth organizations, I have observed, can help young activists recover some of that early sense of empowerment or potential.

51. Storytelling may be the first vehicle for cultivating solidarity among activists. But its message—that *you are not alone: you are seen and understood, by others who have shared your* experience—is echoed in many facets of organizational emotion culture. Solidarity is conveyed symbolically in the rituals of group meetings: the icebreakers, the friendly competition that infuses ADAC

meetings, the "cafecitos," the unity clap that brings meetings to a close, the practice of forming circles or holding hands, at difficult times for the movement or for individual families or members.

52. Dolores, interview with author, August 2012.

53. Roberto, interview with author, February 2013; and, Sofia interview with author, January 2015.

54. Abrams, field notes, June 2013.

55. Marisol, interview with author, April 2013; and Natalia, interview with author, December 2012. Although I heard this aphorism frequently in my interviewing, organizations may take different approaches to challenging new activists in this way. Organizations of adults, like Puente, tend to pay closer attention to what any given participant feels capable of at any juncture. Even youth organizations that believe in pushing young activists out of their comfort zone may support them with individualized debriefs and mentoring when they have taken on unfamiliar and challenging tasks. This is particularly true at LUCHA, which engages in a self-conscious practice of one-on-one mentoring.

56. Reddy, "Emotional Liberty, Politics and History," 256–88. Reddy argues that emotives are neither strictly constative (descriptive) nor strictly performative, but they have "1) a descriptive appearance; 2) a relational intent; 3) a self-exploratory or self-altering effect." William Reddy, "Against Constructionism," 268.

57. These emotives surfaced not only in collective settings but also in interviews that I did with individual organizers.

58. Chua, *Politics of Love in Myanmar.* Chua also finds that connecting particular emotions with new and valued identities can be an effective form of emotional pedagogy.

59. This is a recurrent theme at Puente's general meetings and in their communications, both with community members and with the public.

60. Garcia, "Arizona, Arpaio and SB1070" ("The safest place for anyone targeted by these laws is out, proud, and part of an organized community.").

61. Martín, interview with author, August 2016; and Ileana Salinas, interview with author, February 2015.

62. This emotive was first deployed by undocumented youth and later taken up by adults. See chapter 4. In that chapter, I discuss the implications of this posture for tactics and for the political consciousness of activists. Here my focus is on the "emotive" force of the descriptive claim itself.

63. Roberto, interview with author, March 2013; and Marisol, interview with author, April 2012.

64. Marisol, interview with author, April 2013.

65. Marisol, interview with author, April 2013.

66. Alejandra, interview with author, July 2013

67. The role of performative strategies—in particular, performative citizenship—in this movement is discussed in chapter 3.

68. Goodwin and Pfaff, "Emotion Work in High-Risk Social Movements," 282.

69. Monica Sandschafer, interview with author, November 2012. LUCHA's founding director, Monica Sandschafer was the first to describe this approach to me.

70. This campaign is discussed in chapter 4.

71. Abrams, field notes, November 2012.

72. This campaign is discussed in chapter 5.

73. Several days before the strike, ICE agents in Tucson had been surprised by a mass civil disobedience action in which protesters chained themselves to busses transporting migrants for Operation Streamline court proceedings. Because the Phoenix action came at the end of a major conference organized by Puente to introduce the next phase of Not1More Deportation, leaders speculated that the Phoenix ICE office may have been trying to avoid a similar confrontation.

74. Abrams, field notes, October 2013.

CHAPTER 3. PERFORMATIVE CITIZENSHIP
AND THE ADIOS ARPAIO CAMPAIGN

1. Roberto, interview with author, March 2013 (all quotes from Roberto come from this interview).

2. The I Am a DREAM Voter campaign, which was run by ADAC in the summer and fall of 2012, had a slightly different focus than Adios Arpaio: it sought to enlist the participation of voters who would support the rights of DREAMers. Yet it served the same broad goal of registering, and increasing the electoral participation of, Latino voters and other prospective allies of immigrants.

3. Because my research focuses on the practices of organizations and the political consciousness of activists, my analysis of performative citizenship centers its effects on activists themselves. The anecdotal examples of its influence on public perceptions that I have encountered through my research enable me to raise questions about prospective audience response, but not to answer them.

4. Coll, "Citizenship Acts and Immigrant Voting Rights Movements," 993–1009.

5. McThomas, *Performing Citizenship*; and Meyer and Fine, "Grassroots Citizenship at Multiple Scales" 323–48 (describing campaigns for citizen-like rights such as drivers' licenses or voting in local school board elections).

6. Meyer and Fine, "Grassroots Citizenship at Multiple Scales," 323–48 (discussing Justice for Janitors campaign).

7. Meyer and Fine, "Grassroots Citizenship at Multiple Scales," 4.

8. McNevin, "Doing What Citizens Do," 67–77.

9. The notion of the performative, or performativity, may have originated in Austin's notion of "performative utterances," words that produce effects in the world when uttered by particular actors in specified contexts, according to recognized protocols. See Austin, *How to Do Things with Words*. But it has (varied) iterations in a range of fields including gender studies (see Butler, *Gender Trouble*; and Sedgwick, *Touching Feeling*); sociology (see Tilly, *Contentious Performances*; and Goffman, *Presentation of Self in Everyday Life*); theories of enactment in philosophy (see Ware "Acts and Action"); and the humanities-based field of performance studies (see Schechner, *Performance Studies*). Its trajectory through the literature on citizenship and immigration, which is more recent, is the focus of my upcoming discussion.

10. Austin, *How to Do Things with Words*.

11. Hildebrant and Peters, "Performing Citizenship: Testing New Forms of Togetherness," 1–13; and Isin, "How to Do Rights with Things," 45–56. Both Hildenbrant and Isin invoke the Austinian performative (although Isin offers a broad analogy, and Hildebrant both references the Austinian performative and notes that those lacking citizenship may effect an "unhappy" performative because they lack the requisite authority to bring the belonging asserted into being.). Isin, in particular, may favor the Austinian account because he is interested in a kind of rupture that is accomplished rapidly and abruptly through this kind of assertion.

12. Butler, *Gender Trouble*; and Butler, "Performative Acts and Gender Constitution," 519–31. I tend to draw more on the Butlerian analogy, because its challenge to the "given-ness" of the binary in question (in this case citizenship/noncitizenship, ostensibly established by the state, rather than male/female or masculine/feminine, ostensibly established by nature) and its ongoing, recursive process of making and remaking the spectrum that displaces the binary better suit my longer-term vision of how undocumented activism produces change.

13. Isin and Nielsen, "Introduction: Acts of Citizenship," 1–12. Isin and Nielsen refer to these disorienting interventions as "acts of citizenship," which they contrast with "citizenship actions," which involve more familiar tasks such as serving on juries or voting in elections.

14. Beltrán, "Going Public," 595–622. Beltrán uses the "performative vocabulary" of Hannah Arendt, who describes the political as the creation of "spaces of freedom and common appearance where none existed before." Beltrán, "Going Public," 597.

15. Nyers, "No One Is Illegal between City and Nation," 162.

16. Nyers, "No One Is Illegal between City and Nation," 165.

17. "Today we march, tomorrow we vote," was one of the signature chants of the 2006 marches.

18. Hildebrant and Peters, "Performing Citizenship," 1–13.

19. As I describe later, even undocumented immigrants receive constitutional protections that are guaranteed to "persons" or are the product of simple prohibitions on state action. And while undocumented immigrants—in the vast majority of contexts—cannot vote, there is no legal restriction on their ability to speak to legislators or register voters, save that their visibility in such roles creates a greater risk of apprehension, detention, and deportation.

20. Isin, "How to Do Rights with Things," 38–39 ("acts of citizenship," a category with significant overlap with what I call performative citizenship, "can be enacted without subjects being able to articulate reasons").

21. Abrams, field notes, April 2013 (LUCHA membership meeting); María José, interview with author, July 2013 ("[Some people think] we're just here to take advantage of people. And the day of service was just so they can see that we care about the state").

22. The voyage of the Undocubus, explored in chapter 4, may be an exception to this observation with its explicit borrowing of legacy tactics of the civil rights movement and its broad hortatory agenda.

23. Typically, organizations staff civic engagement campaigns with a smaller group of organizers, who receive stipends, and a larger group of volunteers, who may receive midday meals and supplies, such as water or clipboards, that assist in canvassing, but are unpaid.

24. Elena, interview with author, July 2014.

25. Luz, interview with author, July 2012.

26. Daniel Valenzuela, interview with author, September 2013.

27. Daniel Valenzuela, interview with author, September 2013.

28. Browne, "Young Activists Who Can't Vote Influence Those Who Can."

29. Browne, "Young Activists Who Can't Vote Influence Those Who Can."

30. ADAC initiated this campaign as an affiliate of UWD, which coordinated a nationwide effort.

31. Leticia de la Vara, interview with author, August 2012.

32. Brendan Walsh (political director of Phoenix local of Unite Here), interview with author, July 2013.

33. Brendan Walsh, interview with author, July 2013.

34. ADAC also sought volunteers at high-volume engagement sites such as supermarkets; ADAC and LUCHA recruited canvassers at their DACA information sessions.

35. In all campaigns, these included Latino residents. In later campaigns this group was extended to include other low-income voters of color and even single, white women.

36. Élias, interview with author, September 2012.

37. Petra Falcon, interview with author, December 2012.

38. Patricia, interview with author, August 2012. As I discuss in the appendix, the findings in this section are based on intensive interviewing during the voter engagement campaigns of 2012 and continuing interviews about voter engagement canvassing across the time period of the research; therefore they involve larger numbers of interviews than those, for example, that addressed the Undocubus trip or the Not1More Deportation campaign. Consequently the interviews that I cite in this section, in support of particular propositions, are representative rather than comprehensive.

39. Abril Gallardo, interview with author, September 2012.

40. Francisco, interview with author, July 2013.

41. Monica Sandschafer, interview with author, November 2012. Sandschafer explained, "We want[ed] to make sure that the frame . . . through which we [we]re approaching the community isn't about victimhood. And isn't about. . . . 'Hey, we got screwed in this electoral cycle' . . . [instead] putting our work and the results—the sheer numbers of volunteers and hours and new registrants and folks from the PEVL [permanent early voting list] and all of that—in the context of Latino power was really important."

42. Dolores, interview with author, August 2012.

43. Patricia, interview with author, August 2012.

44. Natalia, interview with author, December 2012.

45. Natalia, interview with author, December 2012.

46. Reyna Montoya interview with author, August 2012.

47. Natalia, interview with author, December 2012.

48. For example, it is undocumented canvassers who describe to citizens the means by which they can cast their ballots, how the vote can shape policy making, or how it enables voters to hold elected officials accountable.

49. Although undocumented immigrants are not permitted, in the vast majority of jurisdictions, to exercise the vote, there is no prohibition on their involvement

in the electoral process. However, many members of the public—including those who understand that many undocumented people aspire to formal membership—assume that undocumented people are not involved in the electoral process, either because they fail to consider all the nonvoting roles that are required to support the vote, or because they assume that, being unable to vote, undocumented immigrants would not be interested in these supporting roles.

50. The weather in the Phoenix area makes canvassing in the months preceding November elections the political equivalent of an extreme sport. Canvassers reported that prospective voters often acknowledged this, sometimes inviting them into their homes for a drink.

51. Eduardo, interview with author, August 2013.

52. Daniel Valenzuela, interview with author, September 2013; and Monica Alonzo, "SB 1070 Fuels a Movement of New Voters" (describing assessments of City Council member Valenzuela, Rep. Gallego, and candidate Richard Carmona).

53. Adam Liptak, "Arizona Can Ban 'Ballot Harvesting.'" The law, HB 2023, was temporarily enjoined by the Ninth Circuit Court of Appeals immediately before the election; that injunction was then stayed by the Supreme Court.

54. Hector Tobar, "Letter from Maricopa County."

55. Hector Tobar, "Letter from Maricopa County."

56. This law was struck down by an en banc panel of the Ninth Circuit Court of Appeals, which found that it had the intent and effect of discriminating against minority voters, in violation of Section 2 of the Voting Rights Act. *Democratic National Committee v. Hobbs*, 948 F.3d 989 (9th Cir. 2020). The Supreme Court reversed in *Brnovich v. Democratic National Committee*, 594 U.S. __ (2021), holding in a 6–3 decision that the law did not violate Section 2 of the Voting Rights Act.

57. Ariel Fuchs, interview with author, October 2017; Anayeli, interview with author, August 2012; and Eduardo, interview with author, July 2013.

58. Mercedes, interview with author, February 2013.

59. Abril Gallardo, interview with author, October 2012.

60. Julieta, interview with author, January 2013.

61. Reyna Montoya, interview with author, August 2012.

62. Élias, interview with author, October 2012.

63. Eduardo, interview with author, August 2013.

64. Élias, interview with author, October 2012. A member of Team Awesome had offered a similar view, following the election of Daniel Valenzuela: "We elect people and we give them our power. But just as we give it, we can take it away." Sabat, "Team Awesome Is Giving Latinos a New Reason to Vote."

65. Élias, interview with author, October 2012.

66. Abril Gallardo, interview with author, October 2012.

67. In her discussion of immigrant activists' campaign for the right to vote in Cambridge, Massachusetts, Kathleen Coll also emphasizes that activists treated the vote not simply as a right that should be associated with de facto membership, but as a responsibility that they were eager to carry out. Coll, "Immigrant Voting Rights Movements," 1006 (immigrants claim "the right to participate fully in democratic politics" as "a shared responsibility of the governed").

68. Meyer and Fine, "Grassroots Citizenship at Multiple Scales," 323–48. As Meyer and Fine observe, however, many citizens fail to demonstrate this kind of affirmative commitment or responsibility to their polities.

69. Patricia, interview with author, August 2012; and Abril Gallardo, interview with author, October 2012 ("It's like you start to own your city, own your state").

70. Chapter 6 describes interviewees' answers to the question of what should make a person entitled to citizenship.

71. I explore this dimension of the movement in chapter 5.

72. A rider on the Undocubus, for example, described a sense of powerful connection to the civil rights movement. Ramirez Jimenez, "In Admiration." See generally Abrams, "Performative Citizenship," 1–28.

73. Engin Isin, for example, describes that habitus as including acts such as voting, jury service, and (where applicable) military service. Isin, "Theorizing Acts of Citizenship." This may reinforce the point made by Meyer and Fine ("Grassroots Citizenship at Multiple Scales," 217) that the repertoire of most formal citizens is quite restricted—or impoverished—when compared with the activities of immigrant activists.

74. This ambivalent response is discussed in more detail in chapter 6.

75. Polletta, "Structural Context of Novel Rights Claims," 367–406. The same claim could—theoretically—be made about anti-immigrant state officials, particularly when undocumented immigrants themselves are the plaintiffs.

CHAPTER 4. THE OPPOSITIONAL AWAKENING OF THE "UNDOCUMENTED AND UNAFRAID"

1. *Melendres v. Arpaio*, 989 F. Supp. 2d 822 (D. Ariz. 2013).

2. Goodman, "'No Papers, No Fear.'"

3. I use the term *long campaign* in this chapter to indicate the fact that I am considering an effort that began with the campaign for a stand-alone DREAM Act in 2010, and when that failed, shifted to a demand directed at President Obama for relief from deportation for undocumented youth. Analyzing this longer period allows me to document changes in narratives, emotions, tactics of performative citizenship, and particularly an underlying political consciousness, that would not be as easy to demonstrate were the chapter to focus solely on the campaign for the DREAM Act or the effort that culminated in the announcement of DACA. The journey of the Undocubus, in contrast, is more of a discrete campaign with a beginning, end, and set of unifying narratives, emotional stances, and tactics.

4. NDLON played a central coordinating role in the Undocubus campaign. UWD was one of several national organizations coordinating the campaign for the DREAM Act and the push for DACA. I focus on it because of its relationship to organizations in Phoenix, and because it was itself an organization led by and for undocumented immigrants.

5. By 2012, "copycat" laws patterned on SB 1070 had been adopted in Alabama, Georgia, Indiana, South Carolina, and Utah. Wang, "What's Next for Arizona's SB 1070 and Other Copycat Laws?"

6. Mansbridge, "Making of Oppositional Consciousness," 1.

7. Nicholls, *Dreamers*, 74–98. Nicholls argues that youth gained an upper hand as the movement's emphasis shifted from CIR to the DREAM Act and they achieved greater ability to advocate on their own behalf, set their own priorities, and control their own narratives.

8. The DREAM Act, which would have provided a path to citizenship for (some) undocumented youth brought to the United States as children, had been introduced in varying forms since 2001. The 2010 DREAM Act was the version that came closest to becoming law. It passed the House of Representatives and failed by five votes in the Senate.

9. See chapter 2.

10. Beltrán, "'Undocumented, Unafraid, and Unapologetic,'" 80–104.

11. Warner, *Trouble with Normal*.

12. Nyers, "No One Is Illegal between City and Nation," 160–81.

13. Reichard, "Why This Undocumented Latina Launched." "Regardless of his activism and work around immigrants' rights and justice," IYJL activist Tania Unzueta explained, "some turned their back on him because there was something negative in his record. We wanted to challenge this. We wanted to share our own stories."

14. Unzueta glimpsed traces of the "good immigrant" story even in the activists' disruptive narratives. "We were not as solid as we are today," she mused, "in many ways we were still talking about how 'good' we were. But the talks and conversations were powerful. . . . [I]t was a key moment for how we understand undocumented people." Reichard, "Why This Undocumented Latina Launched."

15. Holderness, "Immigrant Youth Justice League."

16. Holderness, "Immigrant Youth Justice League."

17. Montgomery, "Trail of Dream Students."

18. Montgomery, "Trail of Dream Students."

19. ADAC members also organized their own forms of direct action to influence McCain. In the late fall, several members mounted a nine-day hunger strike: each day of fasting marked a year that Congress had failed to pass the DREAM Act. Garcia, "Students Fast."

20. Of the five participants in the DREAM 5 action, only one (the sole legal permanent resident involved in the action) was from Arizona. But organizers saw the siting of the action, at "ground zero" of anti-immigrant state activity, as significant, and ADAC assisted with the action.

21. Erika Andiola, interview with author, April 2015.

22. Cruz, "Daniel Rodriguez Speaks."

23. The measure passed the House and fell five votes short in an effort to attain cloture in the Senate.

24. Elena, interview with author, July 2014.

25. This recognition was particularly sobering to activists in Arizona, where attrition through enforcement had been associated primarily with Republican politicians.

26. Dreamers Adrift, Dreamers Adrift Community Organization Facebook page.

27. CultureStr/ke, Tumblr.

28. Dreamers Adrift, Dreamers Adrift Community Organization Facebook page. In many of the videos on the Dreamers Adrift site, the "story" is not a simple narrative offered by one individual or group; it emerges through poly-vocality, from a set of interactions among different characters.

29. See Dreamers Adrift, "Undocumented and Awkward, Episode 3"; and Dreamers Adrift, "Undocumented and Awkward, Episode 5."

30. See Dreamers Adrift, "Undocumented and Awkward, Episode 8."

31. See Dreamers Adrift, "'I Am a Crime"; and Dreamers Adrift, "'Undocu-media Workshop' Announcement."

32. Undocunation, Facebook.

33. Antonio, interview with author, February 2013.

34. Alejandra, interview with author, July 2013.

35. Funds from the sale of these photographs were used to support scholar-ships for undocumented youth. Alejandra, interview with author, July 2013.

36. Elena, interview with author, July 2014.

37. Elena, interview with author, July 2014.

38. By late 2013, ADAC moved to Spanish-only meetings.

39. UWD is the largest national organization led and populated by undoc-umented youth. It offers funding, training, and programmatic and logistical support to state and local DREAMer organizations, such as ADAC, who may establish relationships as affiliates.

40. Office of the Director, U.S. Immigration and and Customs Enforcement, "Exercising Prosecutorial Discretion."

41. thedreamiscoming2011, "Georgina Perez, Georgia Dreamers."

42. Lozano, "Young Latinos Keeping Their Eyes on the Prize."

43. See Dreamers Adrift, "Obama, Don't Deport My Mama."

44. Other activists used more conventional appeals. DREAMers sought the assistance of immigration law professors, who used an open letter to Obama to explain their conclusion that deferred action had been and could be legally implemented by the executive. Motomura et al. to the President.

45. Ileana Salinas, interview with author, February 2015.

46. Elena, interview with author, July 2014. Members of ADAC also orga-nized direct action events, such as a rally outside the local office of Intel, when President Obama came there to speak.

47. Khan, "Campaign for an American DREAM Walkers Hold Protest"; and Behar, "DREAMers End Sit-In at Obama Offices."

48. Hing, "DREAMers Stage Sit-Ins."

49. Khan, "Campaign for an American DREAM Walkers Hold Protest."

50. Hing, "DREAMers Stage Sit-Ins."

51. Monica Sandschafer, interview with author, June 2012.

52. Although "Undocubus" was the most often-used name for the cam-paign, the website for the campaign refers to it as Sin Papeles, Sin Miedo: Ride for Justice. Sin Papeles, Sin Miedo (literally, "without papers, without fear") is the most common Spanish translation of "undocumented and unafraid"; its use here symbolizes the fact that a group of community members whose primary language was Spanish chose to utilize the tactics of youth protesters.

53. Franco, "How a Bus Full of Undocumented Families Could Change."

54. Carlos Garcia, interview with author, March 2015 (describing organizing currents that culminated in Undocubus ride).

55. This approach, which supports members with solidaristic social and cultural activities while it prepares them to take part in resistance actions, is discussed in chapter 3.

56. In a tribute to the queer cultural focus of the trip, riders nicknamed the bus "Priscilla," after the 1994 Australian road film, *The Adventures of Priscilla, Queen of the Desert*. This film follows a group of drag queens and trans performers as they mount a series of performances across the Australian desert.

57. Ximena, interview with author, April 2015.

58. For example, Gloria Esteva, from the San Francisco area, made the trip with her daughter Kitzia; Chicago organizers Rosi Carrasco and Martin Unzueta traveled with their daughters, undocuqueer activists Tania and Ireri Unzueta Carrasco.

59. Despite the ways in which the stories of the "undocumented and unafraid" diverged from the early DREAMer narratives, political officials, including President Obama as he announced the DACA program, continued to showcase academic standouts who were here "through no fault of their own."

60. Terriquez, "Intersectional Mobilization," 343–62. One recent sociological study found that close to 20 percent of the undocumented activists surveyed identified as LGBT.

61. Torres, "Fearless and Speaking for Ourselves."

62. Flores, "Letter to My Mother."

63. Wong and Munoz, "Don't Miss the Bus," 61–66; and Sziarto and Leitner, "Immigrants Riding for Justice," 1–3. This campaign was conceived by the union HERE (Hotel Employees and Restaurant Employees International Union) and shaped both by the growing inclination of mainstream unions such as the AFL-CIO to reach out to immigrant workers and by the anti-immigrant sentiment aroused by 9/11. Interestingly, riders on the Undocubus rarely cited this campaign in their public statements or blog posts, while they often referenced the Civil Rights Freedom Rides and other tactics of that movement. The reasons for this choice, if indeed it was a choice, are unclear, although they may have involved the desire to associate their campaign with a movement of US citizens widely celebrated in the political culture. They may also have felt less connection to the Immigrant Workers Freedom Rides because that campaign was centrally an effort to build solidarity between immigrant workers and their allies, who rode together on the buses (Sziarto and Leitner, "Immigrants Riding for Justice"), whereas the Undocubus was primarily an effort to organize and foster community among those who were undocumented.

64. Abrams, "Performative Citizenship," 1–28.

65. Ramirez Jimenez, "In Admiration."

66. Ximena, interview with author, April 2015.

67. Flores, "Letter to My Mother."

68. Salgado, "An Undocubus Sketchbook."

69. "Meaning of the Mariposa (Butterfly)."

70. "Sharing Stories with the People of Knoxville."

71. NDLONvideos, "Si No Nos Invitan, Nos Invitamos Solos."

72. NDLONvideos, "Si No Nos Invitan, Nos Invitamos Solos."

73. This feature of movement building within organizations is explored in chapter 2.

74. The Not1More Deportation campaign is the focus of chapter 5.

75. Hendley, "Puente's 'Undocubus' Riders Arrested."

76. Eastman, "UndocuBus Represents Pure and Simple Lawlessness."

77. Olivas, "Advice to Immigrants." Although nominally a commentary on the Undocubus, Professor Olivas focused primarily on whether young immigrants eligible for DACA should reveal themselves to federal authorities.

78. Villazor and Glazer, "First Step to Understanding the Challenges."

79. Vargas, "Coming Out Adds a Voice to the Chorus."

80. Cruz, "We Dream at All Ages."

81. Ximena, interview with author, April 2015.

82. It may be that canvassers, as youth socialized within educational institutions, are more likely to see themselves as comparable to their citizen peers. The Undocubus riders, who took direction from the sensibilities of adult activists, may not have been socialized to this strong sense of comparability.

83. They did not view the exclusion from the franchise as unique, either. Riders saw parallels to black voters in the early civil rights struggle, for example, whose voices had been silenced or diluted through unjust manipulations of the political process. Abrams, "Performative Citizenship," 1–28.

84. Bogado, "Dignity beyond Voting."

85. Bogado, "Dignity beyond Voting."

86. Torres, "Fearless and Speaking for Ourselves."

87. Coming out as undocumented as an act of "political subjectification" is discussed in Nyers, "No One Is Illegal between City and Nation" and in chapter 3.

88. Reichard, "Why This Undocumented Latina Launched" (quoting Tania Unzueta).

89. Martín, interview with author, August 2016.

90. Roberto, interview with author, March 2013.

91. Reichard, "Why This Undocumented Latina Launched" (quoting Tania Unzueta).

92. Bedau, *Civil Disobedience in Focus.*

93. The ambivalent effects of Not1More Deportation, a campaign of sustained disruption and civil disobedience, are discussed in chapter 5.

94. Elena, interview with author, July 2014.

95. Elena, interview with author, July 2014.

96. Hing, "How Undocumented Youth Nearly Made Their DREAMS Real" (quoting Mohamed Abdollahi).

97. Martín, interview with author, August 2016.

98. Martín, interview with author, August 2016.

99. Martín, interview with author, August 2016.

100. Erika Andiola, interview with author, April 2015.

101. Consuelo, interview with author, August 2016.

102. Ximena, interview with author, April 2015.

103. Meyer and Fine, "Grassroots Citizenship at Multiple Scales," 323–48. Both of these attributes are identified in the literature on "grassroots citizenship."

104. As I describe in chapter 6, these attributes are not simply part of the common, cultural understanding of citizenship; they are part of the way that undocumented activists understand normative citizenship as well.

105. Elena, interview with author, July 2014.

106. Landau, "Out of the Shadows, into the Spotlight."

107. Jones, "Coming Out Illegal."

108. Ramirez Jimenez, "In Admiration."

109. Ximena, interview with author, April 2015.

CHAPTER 5. THE OPPOSITIONAL CITIZENSHIP OF THE NOT1MORE DEPORTATION CAMPAIGN

1. Dinan, "Illegal Immigrants Arrested in Phoenix Deportation Protest."

2. Reyna Montoya, interview with author, August 2014.

3. "History of the #Not1More Campaign."

4. *Puente v. Arpaio*, 2:14-cv-1356-DGC (D. Ariz. filed June 18, 2014).

5. For a discussion of the early development of this strategy see chapter 3.

6. Latino Voices, "Immigrants Reunite with Deported Parents at Border."

7. Camila, interview with author, May 2014.

8. DreamActivistdotOrg, "Arizona Activist Erika Andiola's Home Was Raided."

9. Bring Them Home was initiated by the National Immigrant Youth Alliance. However, Puente did a Bring Them Home action in spring 2014, involving two young men who had been deported as a result of alcohol-related offenses. It was the focus of the "Walk to End Deportations" and the vigil outside the Florence detention center discussed in the last part of this chapter.

10. The Undocubus campaign is described in chapter 4.

11. Mateo, "Fight to Keep Families Together."

12. Matías, interview with author, May 2014.

13. Reyna Montoya, interview with author, January 2014.

14. Abrams, field notes, August 2013.

15. Abrams, field notes, August 2013.

16. Abrams, field notes, August 2013.

17. Carlos Garcia, interview with author, March 2015.

18. Office of the Director, "Exercising Prosecutorial Discretion."

19. Puente Arizona, "Norma, cuando vas a volver?"

20. Carlos Garcia, interview with author, March 2015.

21. Carlos Garcia, interview with author, March 2015.

22. Carlos Garcia, interview with author, March 2015.

23. Camila, interview with author, May 2014.

24. Carlos Garcia, interview with author, March 2015.

25. *Melendres v. Arpaio*, 989 F. Supp. 2d 822 (D. Ariz. 2013) (findings of fact and conclusion of law).

26. Preemption is a doctrine grounded in the supremacy of federal law (U.S. Const. art. VI) and the federal congressional power to make a "uniform rule

of naturalization" (U.S. Const. art. I, § 8), which invalidates state laws that are explicitly or operationally inconsistent with the exercise of federal power in this area.

27. Sandoval and Tambini, "State of Arizona."

28. Carlos Garcia, interview with author, March 2015.

29. Cruz, "We Dream at All Ages."

30. Section 287(g) of the US Immigration and National Act authorizes DHS to enter into agreements with state and local law enforcement officials that enable these officials to assume some of the responsibilities of federal immigration enforcement. Undocubus riders visited several cities where law enforcement officials had entered into 287(g) agreements with the federal government, much as Joe Arpaio had in Phoenix.

31. Goodman, "Undocumented Immigrants Push Obama."

32. Erika Andiola, interview with author, April 2015.

33. Reyna Montoya, interview with author, January 2014.

34. Reyna Montoya, interview with author, January 2014.

35. Latino Rebels, "Open Letter to the Immigrant Rights Movement."

36. *Plyler v. Doe*, 457 U.S. 202 (1982).

37. Gonzales views this phenomenon somewhat more skeptically than I describe it here. In his book *Lives in Limbo*, he describes the activism of undocumented youth, which he associates primarily with the experience of attending college, as a respite from or "buffer against the condition of illegality," during which youth enjoy a sense of "cultural membership" and empowerment, despite their lack of formal status (164–75). However, the financial challenges they encounter as they navigate higher education; their continuing connection to struggling, stigmatized communities; and the uncertain prospects their status produces following graduation make this a partial and usually temporary respite. Gonzales, *Lives in Limbo*, 170–74. However, in work focusing on youth who have received DACA, Gonzales suggests that DACA may subtly alter this picture. Because it enables youth to surmount some obstacles (inability to work, for example) that prompted the transition to illegality, DACA may provide a more durable sense of cultural integration, although the ability to leverage the potential gains of DACA may depend on recipients' level of education and access to community resources. Gonzales, Terriquez, and Ruzcyzk, "Becoming DACA-mented," 1852–72.

38. This experience, as I explain later, also created space in this campaign for citizens with undocumented parents, who experienced a similar precarity by virtue of their familial ties.

39. Reyna Montoya, interview with author, January 2014.

40. Camila, interview with author, May 2014.

41. Carlos Garcia, interview with author, March 2015.

42. Obama, "Remarks by the President . . . on Immigration"

43. Carlos Garcia, interview with author, March 2015.

44. Because of the burden it places on the listener, the response to unmitigated suffering can also slide unpredictably from empathy or interest to pity or resistance, producing a reaction against the narrator, or seeing her as less than fully human. This danger is discussed in chapter 2.

45. The distinction that I make here largely tracks the distinction made by Charles Tilly and Sidney Tarrow between "contained" and "transgressive" forms of contention. *Contentious Politics*, 62.

46. The total number of undocumented immigrants who leave the country during any given presidential administration is a function of two different numbers: those who are "removed" (i.e., have been ordered by a court or border official to leave the country) and those who are "returned" (i.e., released back across the border without receiving a formal order of removal). See Editorial Board, "All Presidents Are Deporters in Chief." See also Department of Homeland Security, *Table 39*. President Obama had the highest number of removals of any president up to 2017, when his administration removed 432,448 immigrants in 2013. This figure was sometimes utilized by activists and media sources in claiming that Obama had deported more immigrants than any president in history. Marshall, "Obama Has Deported More People." However, because the Obama administration prioritized removals, and because several factors (e.g., decreased migration and community education that curtailed "voluntary" departures) reduced the number of returns during his administration, the total number of immigrants deported under Obama, while notably high (over 500,000 per year until the final two years of his presidency), particularly for a professed supporter of immigrants, did not reach the totals deported by President George W. Bush or President Clinton. Department of Homeland Security, *Table 39*. The highest total number of deportations occurred in 2000, when President Clinton deported a total of 1,864,343 immigrants, including 1,675,876 returns. Editorial Board, "All Presidents Are Deporters in Chief."

47. "Our Hunger Strike Makes Public the Heartache."

48. Carlos Garcia, interview with author, March 2015.

49. Carlos Garcia, interview with author, March 2015.

50. This tension between undocumented activists' perceived need to demonstrate vulnerability to win public support and their resistance to manifesting it in a way that might suggest helplessness or incite pity is addressed in chapter 2.

51. Ramirez Jimenez, "In Admiration: Learning about the Civil Rights Movement,"

52. NDLONvideos, "Most Passionate Speech You Have Ever Heard."

53. Gamson, *Talking Politics*, at 32.

54. Reyna Montoya, interview with author, August 2014.

55. NDLONvideos, "Si No Nos Invitan, Nos Invitamos Solos."

56. Arendt, "Rights of Man," 24–37.

57. In the following discussion, I use the term "the state" to indicate the institutions of government and the officials who do the work of those institutions, at both state and federal levels. In this context the term "state" does not refer solely to the state of Arizona.

58. Mansbridge and Morris, *Oppositional Consciousness*.

59. Mansbridge, "Making of Oppositional Consciousness, 1–19.

60. Erika Andiola, interview with author, April 2015.

61. "Undocumented Immigrant Leaders Form Blue Ribbon Commission."

62. Latino Rebels, "NDLON Publishes Blue Ribbon Immigration Recommendations."

63. "How Many DACA Recipients Are There in the United States?"

64. Obama, "Remarks by the President . . . on Immigration."

65. Cantor, "Who Would Benefit from DAPA?"

66. Latino Rebels, "NDLON Publishes Blue Ribbon Immigration Recommendations."

67. Carlos Garcia, interview with author, March 2015.

68. Latino Rebels, "NDLON Publishes Blue Ribbon Immigration Recommendations."

69. "Blue Ribbon Commission to the President."

70. Mora, "Blue Ribbon Commission Response."

71. Brown, "Undocumented Immigrants Call for White House Boycott."

72. Akbar, "Toward a Radical Imagination of Law," 405–79.

73. Latino Rebels, "NDLON Publishes Blue Ribbon Immigration Recommendations."

74. Latino Rebels, "NDLON Publishes Blue Ribbon Immigration Recommendations."

75. Carlos Garcia, interview with author, March 2015.

76. Latino Rebels, "NDLON Publishes Blue Ribbon Immigration Recommendations."

77. Obama, "Remarks by the President . . . on Immigration."

78. Carlos Garcia, interview with author, March 2015.

79. Paulos, "People with Criminal Records . . . Are Our Friends and Family."

80. *Texas v. United States*, 86 F. Supp. 3d 591, 677 (S.D. Tex. 2015), *aff'd __ F.3d __ (5th Cir. 2015), aff'd by an equally divided Court* 579 U. S. __ (June 23, 2016).

81. Reyna Montoya, interview with author, August 2014.

82. Ileana Salinas, interview with author, June 2016.

83. Abrams, field notes, February 2014.

84. This vigil is analyzed at greater length in Abrams, "Vigil at the End of the World," 247–57.

85. Abrams, field notes, April 2014.

86. Fernanda's struggle was echoed in a slightly different register by Ileana Salinas, a youth activist who reported feeling not only enervated but compromised by the experience of sharing her narratives with certain kinds of audiences. See chapter 2.

87. Carlos Garcia, interview with author, March 2015.

88. Latino Voices, "DREAM 9 Pushed It Too Far."

89. Navarette, "A DREAMer's Nightmare."

90. The trajectory of oppositional immigrant activism, curtailed by the injunction against DAPA, and then more decisively by the Trump presidency, does not permit the empirical assessment of this more modest claim.

91. Ileana Salinas, interview with author, January 2017.

92. ADAC collaborated with ACLU-AZ to mount a successful constitutional challenge to Governor Brewer's executive order barring drivers' licenses for DACA recipients. See *ADAC v Brewer*, 757 F.3d 1053 (9th Cir. 2014). ADAC's public campaign ultimately persuaded MCCC to grant in-state tuition for DACA recipients, a decision later replicated by the regents of the state university system.

But a challenge by the state attorney general ultimately reversed these gains. See *State of Arizona v. Maricopa County Community College District Board*, No. CV-17-0215-PR (April 9, 2018), *aff'g State ex rel. Brnovich v. Maricopa Cty. Cmty. Coll. Dist. Bd.*, 242 Ariz. 325 (App. 2017). This campaign is discussed in chapter 7.

CHAPTER 6. THE ASSET MAP OF THE MOVEMENT

1. Exec. Order No. 13768; and Exec. Order No. 13767. Exec. Order No. 13780, frequently described as the first "Muslim ban," was also announced during this period.

2. As I explain in the methodological appendix, I had assumed that my research would be complete after the summer of 2016. As I recognized the magnitude of change that was likely to follow from the election of Trump, I decided it was important to do additional, leadership-level interviews and a modest amount of observation to gain some perspective on how organizations and communities were responding to the enhanced enforcement and shift in discourse on immigration introduced by the new administration. The trip in January 2017 was my first effort to gather this information.

3. Ileana Salinas interview with author, January 2017.

4. Ileana Salinas, interview with author, January 2017.

5. Carlos Garcia, interview with author, July 2017.

6. Carlos Garcia, interview with author, January 2017.

7. Carlos Garcia, interview with author, January 2017.

8. Carlos Garcia, interview with author, January 2017.

9. Reyna Montoya, interview with author, January 2017.

10. Reyna Montoya, interview with author, January 2017.

11. Abril Gallardo, interview with author, January 2017.

12. Abril Gallardo, interview with author, January 2017.

13. UCLA Center for Health Policy Research, "Section I: Asset Mapping."

14. Abril Gallardo, interview with author, January 2017.

15. I had heard this theme—that withstanding what one fears brings a sense of strength—from activists describing everything from storytelling to civil disobedience. Marisol, interview with author, April 2013 (reflecting on storytelling); Elena, interview with author, September 2014 (reflecting on civil disobedience); and Martín, interview with author, August 2016 (reflecting on civil disobedience).

16. Ileana Salinas, interview with author, July 2017 (using the term to describe an organizer she admired). When I asked her what she meant by this term, Ileana replied that it refers to many things: emotional resilience, the capacity to create and draw on vast networks, and the experience of having organized and mobilized with many different groups.

17. Chapter 1, relying on a typology expounded by Edwards and McCarthy in "Resources and Social Movement Mobilization," identified five kinds of resources: socio-organizational, moral, cultural, human, and material. I consider the first four here. The inflow of material resources to Phoenix organizations is discussed briefly in chapter 7.

18. Carlos Garcia, interview with author, January 2017.

19. Abril Gallardo, interview with author, January 2017.

20. Reyna Montoya, interview with author, January 2017.

21. Lena, interview with author, September 2013.

22. Ileana Salinas and Reyna Montoya, interview with author, August 2016. "It's part of the stigma of mental health. That is very big in our community," noted Ileana Salinas, who had worked as a mental health advocate. "In the Latino community it's like I don't want help. . . . [Focusing on healing is] a sign of weakness—a lot of people see it as that."

23. Ileana Salinas and Reyna Montoya, interview with author, August 2016.

24. Reyna Montoya, interview with author, June 2016.

25. Reyna Montoya, interview with author, June 2016. Marco Flores, an "artivist" who traveled briefly with the Undocubus, made a similar point in chapter 4.

26. Bosniak, *Citizen and the Alien*, 19–20. Interestingly, these indicia or dimensions of de facto membership track the salient dimensions of citizenship as defined by scholars such as Linda Bosniak (defining "domains" of citizenship including political participation, rights bearing, and social-cultural membership). As I discuss in the appendix, the findings in this section, which are based on an analysis of my interviews across the time period of the research. involve larger numbers of interviews than those, for example, that applied to the Undocubus trip or the Not1More Deportation campaign. Consequently, the interviews that I cite in the notes as supporting particular propositions in this section are representative but not comprehensive.

27. Williams, *Alchemy of Race and Rights*. As critical race theorists and scholars of the civil rights movement have observed, not all citizens enjoy the same sense of belonging or—if practice is the measure of entitlement—the same rights.

28. Coll, "Citizenship Acts and Immigrant Voting Rights Movements," 993–1009 (describing local contexts in which noncitizens have sought or won the right to vote).

29. Alejandra, interview with author, June 2016; and Martín, interview with author, August 2016.

30. Consuelo, interview with author, August 2016.

31. Martín, interview with author, August 2016.

32. Ileana Salinas, interview with author, June 2016.

33. NDLONvideos, "Si No Nos Invitan, Nos Invitamos Solos." The intervention in a hearing of the US Civil Rights Commission at which a Phoenix activist made this statement is discussed in chapter 4.

34. Martín, interview with author, August 2016 ("I pay taxes. Every time I buy, I consume."); and Consuelo, interview with author, August 2016 ("If my taxes are legal, why am I illegal?").

35. Consuelo, interview with author, May 2015.

36. Victoria, interview with author, December 2012.

37. Natalia, interview with author, December 2012.

38. Roberto, interview with author, March 2013.

39. Araceli, interview with author, June 2013; and Natalia, interview with author, December 2012 ("It is what you love.").

40. Valeria, interview with author, August 2013; Ileana Salinas, interview with author, August 2013; and Mariana, interview with author, September 2013.

41. Verónica, interview with author, April 2013.

42. Marisol, interview with author, April 2013; and Natalia, interview with author, December 2012 ("That should be enough for us to be able to vote. Because a lot of the times, we're more invested than other people in our country.").

43. Ximena, interview with author, April 2015; and Ileana Salinas, interview with author, February 2015 (describing a statement to detention officer: "I have proof through my grades, through the community service that I do, I have proof that I am a good citizen.").

44. Quoted in Bogado, "Dignity beyond Voting."

45. For a thoughtful and well-elaborated discussion of the limits of legal rights for immigrants, in Arizona as elsewhere, see Venkatesh, "Mobilizing under 'Illegality.'"

46. Araceli, interview with author, June 2013.

47. Verónica, interview with author, April 2013.

48. Araceli, interview with author, June 2013 (marching "gives you this boost of confidence, of I can do this").

49. Ximena, interview with author, April 2015.

50. Julieta, interview with author, January 2013.

51. Julieta, interview with author, January 2013 (describing Latin American migrants as "not wanting to question authority but wanting to comply with the law").

52. KYR and marches are distinctive among the activities of performative citizenship I have examined because both activists and nonactivists may engage in them. Because my research focused almost exclusively on activists, my data do not enable me to speak to the question of whether KYR trainings affect immigrant activists and nonactivist immigrants differently. However, virtually all of the activists I questioned about it experienced a positive, empowering response to the trainings themselves. It is not implausible that those inclined toward activism are more likely to draw a more positive set of messages from KYR training because they feel less deferent toward state actors or feel more comfortable challenging authority.

53. Mariana interview with author, September 2013.

54. Martín, interview with author, August 2016.

55. Ileana Salinas, interview with author, February 2015.

56. Ximena, interview with author, April 2015.

57. *Arizona v. United States*, 567 U.S. 387 (2012).

58. *Melendres v. Arpaio*, 989 F. Supp. 2d 822 (D. Ariz. 2013) (findings of fact and conclusion of law).

59. *ADAC v. Brewer*, 2:12-cv-02546 (D. Ariz. filed November 29, 2012).

60. *Puente v. Arpaio*, 2:14-cv-1356-DGC (D. Ariz. filed June 18, 2014).

61. Polletta, "Structural Context of Novel Rights Claims," 367–406.

62. This was an unexpected insight that arose from a number of interviews with activists from ADAC and Puente, who had been involved in federal court litigation against Arizona officials. As a law professor and a student of the civil rights movement, I had expected that activists would embrace both the practical

benefit and the symbolic legitimation of legal victories. Their actual responses were far more complicated.

63. David, interview with author, September 2014.

64. Erika Andiola, interview with author, April 2015.

65. Erika Andiola, interview with author, April 2015; and Reyna Montoya, interview with author, June 2016.

66. Erika Andiola, interview with author, April 2015.

67. Elena, interview with author, July 2014.

68. Elena, interview with author, July 2014.

69. Alejandra, interview with author, June 2016.

70. Sofia, interview with author, January 2015.

71. *Plyler v. Doe*, 457 U.S. 202 (1982).

72. Abrego, "Legal Consciousness of Undocumented Latinos," 336–69.

73. Erika Andiola in chapter 5 ("We have to stop pretending that we're living normal lives. This could happen to any of us at any time.").

74. Gonzales, "Learning to Be Illegal," 602–19. Gonzales's work on the consciousness of undocumented youth on the cusp of adulthood is discussed in chapter 3.

75. Gonzales, Terriquez, and Ruzczyk, "Becoming DACA-mented," 1852–72.

76. Abrego, "Legal Consciousness of Undocumented Latinos," 336–69.

77. Puente's "open hand, closed fist" organizing approach is described in chapters 1 and 2.

78. Élias, interview with author, September 2012.

79. Abril Gallardo, interview with author, September 2012.

80. Emilia, interview with author, June 2016.

81. Emilia, interview with author, June 2016.

82. Emilia, interview with author, June 2016.

CHAPTER 7. *LA LUCHA SIGUE:* SHIFTING STRATEGIES AND BUILDING FOR A POST-TRUMP FUTURE

Literally translated as "the struggle continues," *la lucha sigue*, common among activists in Phoenix, is used in a variety of different ways, from a shout of determination at marches or rallies, to a resolute statement of purpose when taking the next step in a plan or process, to a shrug of resignation about the long time horizon of the movement.

1. Kate's Law, H.R. 3004 (2017–18), was passed by the Republican-led House of Representatives. It was supported by the White House but was not passed by the Senate.

2. Abril Gallardo, interview with author, July 2017.

3. Taylor and Crossley, "Abeyance," 1–3; and Taylor, "Social Movement Continuity," 761–75.

4. Carlos Garcia, interviews with author, January and July 2017; Abril Gallardo, interviews with author, January and July 2017; and Reyna Montoya, interviews with author, January and July 2017.

5. Carlos Garcia, interview with author, July 2017.

6. Carlos Garcia, interview with author, July 2017.

7. See also Chacón, "Immigration and the Bully Pulpit," 249. Chacón describes important differences between Obama's and Trump's approaches to immigration enforcement but also characterizes Obama as having perpetuated high levels of deportation, as having legitimated a "crime and security" frame for viewing immigration.

8. Carlos Garcia, interview with author, July 2017.

9. For a discussion of *Puente v. Arpaio*, see chapter 6.

10. Valdes, "Is It Possible to Resist Deportation in Trump's America?"

11. Valdes, "Is It Possible to Resist Deportation in Trump's America?" (emphasis added).

12. US Immigration and Customs Enforcement, "Criminal Alien Program."

13. Eagly, "Criminal Justice for Noncitizens," 1184 (discussing operation of the Criminal Alien Program, which places ICE agents in local jails in Maricopa County).

14. Carlos Garcia, interview with author, July 2017.

15. Carlos Garcia, interview with author, July 2017.

16. Carlos Garcia, interview with author, July 2017.

17. See Reyna Montoya, interview with author, January 2017, and discussion in chapter 6.

18. Abril Gallardo, interview with author, July 2017.

19. Abril Gallardo, interview with author, July 2017.

20. Abril Gallardo, interview with author, July 2017.

21. Abril Gallardo, interview with author, July 2017.

22. Abril Gallardo, interview with author, July 2017.

23. Gomez and Robles, "How to Turn Fear and Anger into Political Power." Alejandra Gomez and Tomás Robles Jr. are the coexecutive directors of LUCHA.

24. Abril Gallardo, interviews with author, June and July 2016.

25. Abril Gallardo, interview with author, July 2017,

26. Abril Gallardo, interview with author, July 2017.

27. Santos, "Joe Arpaio's Surprising Legacy in Arizona." The deportation of five family members and the detention of a sixth left Garcia, as he put it, "with no options. And that's what has pushed someone like me to actually run for office."

28. Hsieh, "'Die Soon Traitor.'"

29. Gomez, "New Phoenix Council Members 'Unapologetic.'"

30. Gomez, "New Phoenix Council Members 'Unapologetic.'" After a period during which he held the role of coexecutive director, Carlos Garcia left the leadership of Puente in October 2021.

31. This case ultimately reached the Supreme Court, which concluded in June 2020 that the Trump administration had not articulated a rationale sufficient to justify the rescission of DACA. See *Department of Homeland Security v. Regents of University of California*, 591 U.S. __, 140 S. Ct. 1891 (2020).

32. Reyna Montoya, interview with author, June 2020.

33. Reyna Montoya, interview with author, June 2020.

34. "Maricopa Community College Sued for Granting In-State Tuition to DREAMers."

35. *State of Arizona v. Maricopa County Community College District, Abel Badillo, and Bibiana Vazquez*, No. CV2013-009093 (Maricopa County Superior Court, 2015).

36. Jung, "Arizona Board of Regents Grants In-State Tuition."

37. *State ex rel. Brnovich v. Maricopa County Community College District Board*, 242 Ariz. 325 (App. 2017). The court of appeals was ultimately upheld in a unanimous decision by the Arizona Supreme Court, denying in-state tuition to DACA recipients. *State of Arizona v. Maricopa County Community College District Board*, et al., No. CV-17-0215-PR (AZ April 9, 2018). However, some DACA recipients attending four Arizona universities may be eligible for reduced tuition as a result of a Regents decision that establishes a tuition rate of 150 percent of in-state tuition for all graduates of Arizona high schools. See Romo, "Arizona Supreme Court Denies In-State Tuition."

38. Reyna Montoya, interview with author, July 2017.

39. Reyna Montoya, interview with author, July 2017.

40. Christie, "In-State Tuition . . . on 2022 Ballot Measure."

41. Carlos Garcia, interview with author, March 2015.

42. Reyna Montoya, interview with author, June 2020.

43. Abril Gallardo, interview with author, June 2016.

44. Abril Gallardo, interview with author, July 2017.

45. Abril Gallardo, interview with author, July 2017.

46. This program, created by the Bush administration and sited in border jurisdictions including Tucson, has been notorious for its en masse plea hearings. Lydgate, "Assembly Line Justice."

47. Further information on these newer campaigns may be found on Puente's website, puenteaz.org.

48. Taylor and Crossley, "Abeyance," 1–3.

49. Abril Gallardo, interview with author, January 2017.

50. For a classic discussion of the effects of professionalization on formerly grassroots organizations, see Staggenborg, "Consequences of Professionalization," 585–605.

51. This term is taken from Edwards and McCarthy, "Resources and Social Movement Mobilization," 122.

52. In some accounts of the immigrant rights movement (see Nicholls, *Dreamers*), such guidance has been described as formative for many organizational practices, such as storytelling. While it is possible that this more top-down influence was constitutive in the Phoenix movement, that is not the way that participants tend to describe it. Although they reference, and in my work I witnessed, intermittent trainings and convenings organized by movement mentoring groups, they ascribe more of the influence they experienced to their peers and to the dynamics of the local organizations. Some leaders also reported that mentoring organizations gave unusually wide berth to Arizona organizations because they assumed that local groups were the best judges of the distinctively hostile circumstances they were encountering. Elena, interview with author, July 2014. See Abrams, field notes, October 2012 (during a panel discussion at ASU, the UWD leader described her trepidation at entering the state of Arizona and deep respect for the work of organizers there).

53. Aliento may have a distinctive trajectory in this respect. It was initially funded by two prestigious foundation fellowships to Reyna Montoya, from the Soros Foundation and the Echoing Green Foundation. Montoya was one of the first undocumented recipients of either fellowship. Exposure to the work of fellow grantees and to the goals, processes, and metrics of these foundations may have engendered new ideas about specialization, training, assessing outcomes, and other features of organizing.

54. As discussed in chapters 4 and 5, this practice may also be conducted in a more oppositional vein, through disruptive direct action and civil disobedience. This oppositional mode of performative citizenship was utilized more intermittently during the Trump period, perhaps a recognition of the diminished prospects of engaging an anti-immigrant executive or Congress through efforts aimed at producing a moral reckoning. Ileana Salinas, interview with author, January 2017 (noting the difficulty of shaming Trump, who is acting on his campaign promises).

55. For a discussion of how these attitudes were engendered in youth canvassers, see chapter 3.

56. As I explain in chapter 2, "emotives" are ostensible descriptions of emotional stances that may function not simply as descriptive but also as normative. A good example is the familiar declaration "we are undocumented and unafraid."

57. This perception is articulated most clearly in chapter 2, where I describe Ileana's experience of sharing stories that underscore emotional vulnerability, and in chapter 5, where I note Fernanda's painful emotional depletion in the midst of the Not1More Deportation campaign.

58. Natalia, interview with author, December 2012.

59. German Cadenas, interview with author, January 2017. See also Erika Andiola, interview with author, April 2015 ("People started seeing [what] I did that with my mom, and so my Facebook, my Twitter, and even my cell phone somehow became the hotline for people. . . . I was so burned out just to hear so many stories. . . . I wanted to help everybody, but I couldn't.").

60. Ileana Salinas and Reyna Montoya, interview with author, August 2016.

61. Ileana Salinas and Reyna Montoya, interview with author, August 2016.

62. Ileana Salinas and Reyna Montoya, interview with author, August 2016.

63. Ileana Salinas and Reyna Montoya, interview with author, August 2016.

64. German Cadenas, email to author, September 20, 2021.

65. Elena, interview with author, July 2014.

66. Elena, interview with author, July 2014.

67. Elena, interview with author, July 2014.

68. Elena, interview with author, July 2014.

69. For a full discussion of these features of organizational "emotion cultures," see chapter 2.

70. Ileana Salinas and Reyna Montoya, interview with author, August 2016.

71. After court actions invalidated many of the laws that implemented the policy of "attrition through enforcement" (see "Arizona's Once-Feared Anti-Immigrant Law" and Kiefer, "Another Arizona Immigration Law Shot Down") and movement-led campaigns ousted SB 1070 sponsor Russell Pearce and Sheriff Joe Arpaio from office, some commentators argued that the most important

legacy of "enforcement by attrition" may be the movement of undocumented immigrants and allies that it created. See, for example, Valeria Fernandez, "Arizona"; and Brocious, "Looking Back at SB 1070 a Decade Later."

72. Meyer and Fine, "Grassroots Citizenship at Multiple Scales," makes a similar point.

73. A discussion of indigenous or community-based resources may be found in chapter 1.

74. For example, in an original and illuminating essay on the Birmingham campaign, Doug McAdam describes this tactic as creating a resonant new frame for the movement (albeit a moral one), rather than as generating moral, or legitimating, resources ("Framing Function of Movement Tactics," 338–56).

75. Van Ness and Summers-Effler, "Emotions in Social Movements," 411–28; Jasper, *Emotions of Protest*; Flam and King, *Emotions and Social Movements*; and Goodwin, Jasper, and Polletta, *Passionate Politics*.

76. One exception is the understanding of anger as the emotional fuel that can drive social movement emergence. Gamson, *Talking Politics*, 32.

77. DeBlasio and Selva, "Emotions in the Public Sphere," 13–44. See also Ahmed, *Cultural Politics of Emotions*; and Jasper, "Emotions and the Microfoundations of Politics," 14–30.

78. Ganz, "Resources and Resourcefulness," 1011–18. See also Ganz, *Why David Sometimes Wins*.

METHODOLOGICAL APPENDIX

1. This requirement was included on the written consent form that interviewees signed as the interview began.

2. Some scholars have reported that IRB processes were requiring anonymization when undocumented activists (as interview subjects, and as a collective political stance) wanted to be named in the research. See, for example, Unzueta Carrasco and Seif, "Disrupting the Dream," n2 (describing IRB policy that prevented authors from using the names of undocumented activists who wanted their names published).

3. For this reason, while I began by using Dedoose and trying to create a coding scheme for all of the interviews as a group, I ultimately felt more comfortable separating the interviews into subgroups according to the questions or themes they addressed, coding these smaller groups of interviews by hand, and then comparing any themes that could provide the basis for intergroup comparisons, when I was thinking about the longitudinal aspects of the research.

4. This—as well as the changing conception of the narrative elaborated below—helps to explain why I describe the book as a story-forward account with theoretical implications, rather than a standard work of empirical social science.

5. This was a guess on their part, but my employment at a university associated with the state of California, student activism, and the free speech movement—associations that were mentioned by a surprising number of activists with whom I spoke—surely helped.

6. I glimpsed the possible consequences of this difference when, during the course of my Arizona research, I did a series of interviews with "undocuqueer"

activists with the help of a Berkeley student who was himself undocuqueer. Subjects in many of these interviews revealed a level of pain and struggle that I was not accustomed to hearing in my interviews in Arizona. There are many ways to parse this difference: it could be that undocuqueer activists encounter forms of struggle within and outside the movement that straight, cisgender undocumented people do not (only a few of my Arizona interviewees identified themselves as undocuqueer), or it could be that the adversity in Arizona requires a kind of emotional stiff upper lip—or, in my terms, a kind of emotional performativity—on the part of activists that the California environment does not. But it seemed possible that the presence of my colleague, who was experientially proximate to the people we were interviewing, elicited a level of candid disclosure that I was unable to elicit as a solo interviewer.

Bibliography

Abrams, Kathryn. "Performative Citizenship in the Civil Rights and Immigrant Rights Movements." In *A Nation of Widening Opportunities: The Civil Rights Act at 50*, edited by Ellen Katz and Samuel Bagenstos, 1–28. Ann Arbor: Michigan Publishing, 2015.

——. "Sex Wars Redux: Agency and Coercion in Feminist Legal Theory." *Columbia Law Review* 95, no. 2 (1995): 304–76.

——. "A Vigil at the End of the World." In *Looking for Law in All the Wrong Places: Justice Beyond and Between*, edited by Marianne Constable, Leti Volpp, and Bryan Wagner, 247–57. New York: Fordham University Press, 2019.

Abrego, Leisy. "Legal Consciousness of Undocumented Latinos: Fear and Stigma as Barriers to Claims Making for First Generation and 1.5 Generation Immigrants." *Law and Society Review* 45, no. 2 (2011): 337–69.

——. "Legitimacy, Social Identity, and the Mobilization of Law: The Effects of Assembly Bill 540 on Undocumented Students." *Law & Social Inquiry* 33, no. 3 (2009): 709–34.

ADAC v Brewer, 757 F.3d 1053 (9th Cir. 2014).

ADAC v. Brewer, 2:12-cv-02546 (D. Ariz., filed November 29, 2012).

Ahmed, Sara. *The Cultural Politics of Emotions*. 2nd ed. Edinburgh: Edinburgh University Press, 2014.

Akbar, Amna A. "Toward a Radical Imagination of Law." *New York University Law Review* 93, no. 3 (2018): 405–79.

Alexander, Jenny, dir. *The Vigil*. Arizona: Activevista Media, 2014. Film.

Almeida, Paul. "The Role of Threat in Collective Action." In *Wiley-Blackwell Companion to Social Movements*, 2nd ed., edited by David A. Snow, Sara A.

Soule, Hanspeter Kriesi, and Holly McCammon, 43–62. Oxford: John Wiley & Sons, 2019.

Alonzo, Monica. "SB 1070 Fuels a Movement of New Voters." *Phoenix New Times*, July 5, 2012. www.phoenixnewtimes.com/news/sb-1070-fuels-a -movement-of-new-voters-6454767.

Archibold, Randal. "Ranchers Alarmed by Killing Near Border." *New York Times*, April 4, 2010. www.nytimes.com/2010/04/05/us/05arizona.html.

Arendt, Hannah. *The Origins of Totalitarianism*. New York: Harcourt, Brace, 1951.

———. "The Rights of Man; What Are They?" *Modern Review* 3 (1949): 24–37.

"Arizona Bailable Offenses, Proposition 100." Ballotpedia. November 7 2006. https://ballotpedia.org/Arizona_Bailable_Offenses,_Proposition_100_ (2006).

"Arizona Public Program Eligibility, Proposition 300." Ballotpedia. November 7, 2006. https://ballotpedia.org/Arizona_Public_Program_Eligibility, _Proposition_300_(2006).

"Arizona Standing in Civil Actions, Proposition 102." Ballotpedia. November, 7 2006. https://ballotpedia.org/Arizona_Bailable_Offenses,_Proposition _100_(2006).

Arizona v. United States, 567 U.S. 387 (2012).

"Arizona Voters Favor Welcoming Immigration Policy, 64% Support New Immigration Law." Rasmussen Reports. April 28, 2010. www.rasmussenreports .com/public_content/politics/general_state_surveys/arizona/arizona_voters _favor_welcoming_immigration_policy_64_support_new_immigration_law ?popup=false.

"Arizona's Once-Feared Anti-Immigrant Law, SB 1070, Loses Most of Its Teeth in Settlement." *LA Times*, September 15, 2016. www.latimes.com/nation/la -na-arizona-law-20160915-snap-story.htm.

Austin, J. L. *How to Do Things with Words*. Oxford: Clarendon Press, 1962.

"Ballot Measures." *CNN*, November 2, 2004. www.cnn.com/ELECTION /2004/pages/results/ballot.measures/.

Beard, Betty. "Arizona Is Now in Recession." *Arizona Republic*, May 9, 2008. www.azcentral.com/news/articles/2008/05/09/20080509biz-recession0509 .html.

Bedau, Hugo Adam, ed. *Civil Disobedience in Focus*. London: Routledge, 1991.

Behar, Saadia. "DREAMers End Sit-In at Obama Offices." *People's World*, June 13, 2012. www.peoplesworld.org/article/dreamers-end-sit-in-at-obama -office/.

Beltrán, Cristina. "Going Public: Hannah Arendt, Immigrant Action, and the Sphere of Appearance." *Political Theory* 37, no. 5 (2009): 595–622.

———. "'Undocumented, Unafraid, and Unapologetic': DREAM Activists, Immigrant Politics and the Queering of Democracy." In *From Voice to Influence: Understanding Citizenship in a Digital Age*, edited by Danielle Allen and Jennifer Light, 80–104. Chicago: University of Chicago Press, 2015.

Benford, Robert, and David Snow. "Framing Processes and Social Movements: An Overview and Assessment." *Annual Review of Sociology* 26 (2000): 611–39.

Bloemraad, Irene, and Kim Voss. "Movement or Moment? Lessons from the Pro-Immigrant Movement in the United States and Contemporary Challenges." *Journal of Ethnic and Migration Studies* 46, no. 4 (2020): 683–704.

"Blue Ribbon Commission to the President: No More Meetings about Us without Us." #Not1More. July 28, 2014. www.notonemoredeportation.com /2014/07/28/blue-ribbon-commission-to-the-president-no-more-meetings -about-us-without-us/.

Bogado, Aura. "Dignity beyond Voting: Undocumented Immigrants Cast Their Hopes." *Colorlines*. October 25, 2012. www.colorlines.com/articles/dignity -beyond-voting-undocumented-immigrants-cast-their-hopes.

Border Protection, Antiterrorism, and Illegal Immigration Control Act of 2005. H.R. Res. 4437, 10th Cong. (2005). https://www.congress.gov/bill/109th -congress/house-bill/4437/text.

Bosniak, Linda. *The Citizen and the Alien: Dilemmas of Contemporary Membership*. Princeton, NJ: Princeton University Press, 2006.

Brocious, Ariana. "Looking Back at SB 1070 a Decade Later." Arizona Public Media. August 7, 2020. https://news.azpm.org/p/news-articles/2020/8/7 /178119-looking-back-at-sb-1070-a-decade-later/.

Brown, Carrie Budoff. "Undocumented Immigrants Call for White House Boycott." *Politico*, July 29, 2014. www.politico.com/story/2014/07/undocumented -immigrants-white-house-immigration-109450.

Browne, Devin. "Young Activists Who Can't Vote Influence Those Who Can." *Fronteras*, May 15, 2012. www.fronterasdesk.org/content/young-immigrant -activists-who-cant-vote-influence-those-who-can.

Butler, Judith. *Gender Trouble: Feminism and the Subversion of Identity*. New York: Routledge, 1990.

———. "Performative Acts and Gender Constitution: An Essay in Phenomenology and Feminist Theory." *Theater Journal* 40, no. 4 (1988): 519–31.

Cantor, Guillermo. "Who Would Benefit from DAPA?" *Immigration Impact*, March 4, 2016. https://immigrationimpact.com/2016/03/04/who-benefits-from -dapa/#.YNoybBNKhQJ.

Chacón, Jennifer M. "Immigration and the Bully Pulpit." *Harvard Law Review Forum* 130, no. 7 (2017): 243–68.

Chamber of Commerce v. Whiting, 563 U.S. 582 (2011).

Christie, Bob. "In-State Tuition for Immigrants to Be on 2022 Ballot Measure." *AP News*, May 10, 2021. https://apnews.com/article/immigration -government-and-politics-8a56eaf98133dc8f9776326479f8bd3b.

Chua, Lynette. *The Politics of Love in Myanmar: LGBT Mobilization and Human Rights as a Way of Life*. Stanford, CA: Stanford University Press, 2018

Coll, Kathleen. "Citizenship Acts and Immigrant Voting Rights Movements in the US." *Citizenship Studies* 15, no. 8 (2011): 993–1009.

Cruz, Daniela. "We Dream at All Ages." *No Papers, No Fear: Ride for Justice Blog*, August 7, 2012. http://nopapersnofear.org/blog/post.php?s=2012-08 -07-we-dream-at-all-ages.

Cruz, Gabriel. "Daniel Rodriguez Speaks about 'Dream Act 5' outside McCain's Phoenix Office." May 18, 2010. YouTube video, 2:44. www.youtube.com /watch?v=fviT-u7DMSQ.

Culturestr/ke. "CultureStrike's Tumblr Page." Tumblr, April 11, 2018. https://
culturestrike.tumblr.com/.
———. "#Undocumented #Immigration #immigrantart (at San Francisco, Cali-
fornia)." Tumblr, April 11, 2018. https://culturestrike.tumblr.com/.
DeBlasio, Emiliana, and Donatella Selva. "Emotions in the Public Sphere: Net-
worked Solidarity, Technology and Social Ties." In *Emotions and Loneliness
in a Networked Society*, edited by Bianca Fox, 13–44. Cham, Switzerland:
Palgrave Macmillan, 2019.
Democratic National Committee v. Hobbs, __ F.3d __ (9th Cir. January 27, 2020).
Department of Homeland Security. *Table 39, Aliens Removed or Returned:
Fiscal Years 1892–2017*. April 9, 2019. www.dhs.gov/immigration-statistics
/yearbook/2017/table39.
Department of Homeland Security v. Regents of University of California, 591
U.S. __, 140 S. Ct. 1891 (2020).
Dinan, Stephen. "Illegal Immigrants Arrested in Phoenix Deportation Protest."
Washington Times, August 22, 2013. www.washingtontimes.com/news/2013
/aug/22/illegal-immigrants-arrested-in-phoenix-deportation/.
DreamActivistdotOrg. "Arizona Activist Erika Andiola's Home Was Raided;
Her Mother and Her Brother Taken!" January 11, 2013. YouTube video,
1:58. www.youtube.com/watch?v=nMPWhn8HEJk.
Dreamers Adrift. Dreamers Adrift Community Organization Facebook page.
Facebook, March 5, 2021. https://www.facebook.com/DreamersAdrift/.
———. "'I Am a Crime: A Video Workshop' Announcement." Facebook,
March 27, 2012. www.facebook.com/DreamersAdrift.
———"Obama, Don't Deport My Mama." Facebook, May 16, 2011. www
.facebook.com/DreamersAdrift/.
———. "'Undocumedia Workshop' Announcement." Facebook, December 6,
2011. www.facebook.com/DreamersAdrift.
———. "Undocumented and Awkward." Facebook, November 8, 2011. www
.facebook.com/DreamersAdrift.
———. "Undocumented and Awkward, Episode 3." Facebook, November 27,
2011. www.facebook.com/DreamersAdrift.
———. "Undocumented and Awkward, Episode 5: 'First Date Awkward-
ness.'" Facebook, December 7, 2011. www.facebook.com/DreamersAdrift.
———. "Undocumented and Awkward, Episode 8: 'Problem Addicts; We
run into them ALL the time. Sometimes they're allies. Sometimes they're
DREAMers as well.'" Facebook, January 4, 2012. www.facebook.com
/DreamersAdrift.
———. "Video #3: Día de los Sueños." Facebook, November 18, 2010. https://
www.facebook.com/DreamersAdrift/posts/119278141467771.
Duara, Nigel. "Arizona's Once-Feared Immigration Law, SB1070, Loses More
of Its Power in Settlement." *LA Times*, September 15, 2016. www.latimes
.com/nation/la-na-arizona-law-20160915-snap-story.html.
Eagly, Ingrid. "Criminal Justice for Noncitizens: An Analysis of Variation in
Local Enforcement." *NYU Law Review* 88, no 4 (2013): 1126–1223.
Eastman, John. "The UndocuBus Represents Pure and Simple Lawlessness."
New York Times, September 5, 2012. www.nytimes.com/roomfordebate

/2012/08/01/is-getting-on-the-undocubus-a-good-idea/undocubus-represents-pure-and-simple-lawlessness.

Editorial Board. "All Presidents Are Deporters in Chief." *New York Times*, July 13, 2019. www.nytimes.com/2019/07/13/opinion/sunday/trump-deportations-immigration.html.

Edwards, Bob, and John D. McCarthy. "Resources and Social Movement Mobilization." In *The Blackwell Companion to Social Movements*, edited by David A. Snow, Sarah A. Soule, and Hanspeter Kriesi, 116–52. Malden, MA: Blackwell Publishing, 2004.

Escudero, Kevin. *Organizing While Undocumented: Immigrant Youth's Political Activism under the Law*. New York: New York University Press, 2020.

Ewick, Patricia, and Susan Silbey. "Subversive Stories and Hegemonic Tales: Toward a Sociology of Narrative." *Law & Society Review* 29, no. 2 (1995): 197–226.

Exec. Order. No. 13767, 82 Fed. Reg. 8793 (January 25, 2017). www.whitehouse.gov/presidential-actions/executive-order-border-security-immigration-enforcement-improvements/.

Exec. Order. No. 13768, 82 Fed. Reg. 8799 (January 27, 2017). www.whitehouse.gov/presidential-actions/executive-order-enhancing-public-safety-interior-united-states/.

Exec. Order. No. 13769, 82 Fed. Reg. 8977 (January 27, 2017). www.whitehouse.gov/presidential-actions/executive-order-protecting-nation-foreign-terrorist-entry-united-states/.

Exec. Order. No. 13780, 82 Fed. Reg. 13209 (March 6, 2017). https://trumpwhitehouse.archives.gov/presidential-actions/executive-order-protecting-nation-foreign-terrorist-entry-united-states-2/?utm_source=link.

Fernandez, Valeria. "Arizona: A Hotbed of Pro-Immigrant Change?" *Al Jazeera America*, November 20, 2014. http://america.aljazeera.com/articles/2014/11/20/arizona-a-hotbedofproimmigrantchange.html

Flag, Anna. "Is There a Connection between Undocumented Immigrants and Crime?" *The Upshot* (blog), *New York Times*, May 13, 2019. www.nytimes.com/2019/05/13/upshot/illegal-immigration-crime-rates-research.html.

Flam, Helena, and Debra King. *Emotions and Social Movements*. London: Routledge, 2005.

Flores, Marco. 2012. "Letter to My Mother." Tumblr, September 18, 2012. http://undocubus.org/blog/post.php?s=2012-09-18-letter-to-my-mother.

Franco, Marisa. "How a Bus Full of Undocumented Families Could Change the Immigration Debate." *Yes! Magazine*, November 30, 2012. www.organizingupgrade.com/archive-how-a-bus-full-of-undocumented-families-could-change-the-immigration-debate/.

Fraser, Nancy. "Rethinking the Public Sphere: A Contribution to the Critique of Actually Existing Democracy." *Social Text* 25/26 (1990): 56–80.

Gamson, William. *Talking Politics*. Cambridge: Cambridge University Press. 1992.

Ganz, Marshall. *Why David Sometimes Wins: Leadership, Organization, and Strategy in the California Farmworkers Union*. Oxford: Oxford University Press, 2009.

———. "Resources and Resourcefulness: Strategic Capacity in the Unionization of California Agriculture, 1959–1966." *American Journal of Sociology* 105, no. 4: 1003–62.

———. "Why Stories Matter: The Art and Craft of Social Change." *Sojourner*, March 2009. https://sojo.net/magazine/march-2009/why-stories-matter?action =magazine.article&issue=sojo903&article=why-stories-matter.

Garcia, Carlos. "Arizona, Arpaio, and SB1070 Spur Crusade for Immigrant Rights." Politic365. June 20, 2012.

———. "Not1More Means Not One More." *Puente Movement Blog*, November 27, 2014. http://puenteaz.org/blog/not1more-means-not-one-more/.

Garcia, Uriel J. "Students Fast to Pressure McCain for DREAM Act Support." *State Press*, November 29, 2010. www.statepress.com/article/2010/11/students -fast-to-pressure-mccain-for-dream-act-support.

Goffman, Erving. *The Presentation of Self in Everyday Life*. New York: Doubleday, 1959.

Gomez, Alejandra, and Tomás Robles Jr. "How to Turn Fear and Anger into Political Power." *New York Times*, December 21, 2019. www.nytimes.com /2019/12/21/opinion/sunday/latinos-arizona-battleground.html.

Gomez, Laura. "New Phoenix Council Members 'Unapologetic' about Who They Are." *Arizona Mirror*, June 11, 2019. www.azmirror.com/2019/06/11 /new-phoenix-council-members-unapologetic-about-who-they-are/.

Gonzales, Roberto. "Learning to Be Illegal: Undocumented Youth and Shifting Legal Contexts in the Transition to Adulthood." *American Sociological Review* 76, no. 4 (2011): 602–19.

———. *Lives in Limbo: Undocumented and Coming of Age in America*. Oakland: University of California Press, 2015.

Gonzales, Roberto, Veronica Terriquez, and Stephen Ruszczyk. "Becoming DACA-mented: Assessing the Short-Term Benefits of Deferred Action for Childhood Arrivals (DACA)." *American Behavioral Scientist* 58, no. 14 (2014): 1852–72.

Goodman, Amy. "'No Papers, No Fear': As Arpaio Fights Suit, 4 Undocumented Immigrants Reveal Their Status." *Democracy Now*, July 26, 2012. www.democracynow.org/2012/7/26/no_papers_no_fear_as_arpaio.

———. "Undocumented Immigrants Push Obama to Realise Their American Dream." *No Paper No Fear: Ride for Justice Blog*, September 6, 2012. http://nopapersnofear.org/blog/archive.php?cat=riders.

Goodwin, Jeff, James Jasper, and Francesca Polletta, eds. *Passionate Politics: Emotions and Social Movements*. Chicago: University of Chicago Press. 2001.

Goodwin, Jeff, and Steven Pfaff. "Emotion Work in High-Risk Social Movements: Managing Fear in the U.S. and East German Civil Rights Movements." In *Passionate Politics: Emotions and Social Movements*, edited by Jeff Goodwin, James Jasper, and Francesca Polletta, 282–302. Chicago, University of Chicago Press, 2001.

Harris, Angela. "Race and Essentialism in Feminist Legal Theory." *Stanford Law Review* 42, no. 3 (1990): 581–616.

Hendley, Matthew. "Puente's 'Undocubus' Riders Arrested Outside Democratic National Convention." *Phoenix New Times*, September 5, 2012. www

.phoenixnewtimes.com/news/puentes-undocubus-riders-arrested-outside
-democratic-national-convention-6653292.

Hildebrandt, Paula, Kerstin Evert, Sybille Peters, Mirjam Schaub, Kathrin Wildner, and Gesa Ziemer, eds. *Performing Citizenship: Bodies, Agencies, Limitations.* London: Palgrave Macmillan, 2019.

Hildebrant, Paula, and Sibylle Peters. "Performing Citizenship: Testing New Forms of Togetherness." In *Performing Citizenship: Bodies, Agencies, Limitations,* edited by Paula Hildebrant, Kerstin Evert, Sybille Peters, Mirjam Schaub, Kathrin Wildner, and Gesa Ziemer, 1–13. London: Palgrave Macmillan, 2019.

Hing, Julianne. "DREAMers Stage Sit-Ins at Obama Offices to Force Deportation Standoff." Colorlines, June 13, 2012. www.colorlines.com/articles/dreamers-stage-sit-ins-obama-office-force-deportation-standoff.

———. "How Undocumented Youth Nearly Made Their DREAMS Real in 2010." *Colorlines,* December 20, 2010. www.colorlines.com/articles/how-undocumented-youth-nearly-made-their-dreams-real-2010.

"The History of the #Not1More Campaign." National Day Laborers Organizing Network. N.d. www.notonemoredeportation.com/the-history-of-the-not1more-campaign/.

Hochschild, Arlie. *The Managed Heart: Commercialization of Human Feeling.* Berkeley: University of California Press, 1983.

Holderness, Peter. "Immigrant Youth Justice League—2010 Coming Out." April 12, 2016. YouTube video, 5:39. www.youtube.com/watch?v=Sv6d7 TEeCGY.

"How Many DACA Recipients Are There in the United States?" *USAFACTS,* September 23, 2020. https://usafacts.org/articles/how-many-daca-recipients-are-there-united-states/.

Hsieh, Steven. "'Die Soon Traitor': Hate Targets City Council Candidate Carlos Garcia." *Phoenix New Times,* April 29, 2019. www.phoenixnewtimes.com/news/hate-phoenix-city-council-district-8-candidate-carlos-garcia-mike-johnson-11277001.

Isin, Engin. "How to Do Rights with Things: The Art of Becoming Citizens." In *Performing Citizenship: Bodies, Agencies, Limitations,* edited by Paula Hildebrant, Kerstin Evert, Sybille Peters, Mirjam Schaub, Kathrin Wildner, and Gesa Ziemer, 45–56. London: Palgrave Macmillan, 2019.

———. "Theorizing Acts of Citizenship." In *Acts of Citizenship,* edited by Engin F. Isin and Greg M. Nielsen, 15–43. London: Palgrave Macmillan, 2008.

Isin, Engin, and Greg Nielsen. , eds. *Acts of Citizenship.* London: Palgrave Macmillan, 2008.

———. "Introduction: Acts of Citizenship." In *Acts of Citizenship,* edited by Engin F. Isin and Greg M. Nielsen, 1–12. London: Palgrave Macmillan, 2008.

Jasper, James. "Cultural Approaches in the Sociology of Social Movements." In *Handbook of Social Movements across Disciplines,* edited by Conny Roggeband and Bert Klandermans, 59–109. New York: Springer Publishing, 2010.

———. "Emotions and the Microfoundations of Politics: Rethinking Ends and Means." In *Emotions, Politics, and Society*, edited by Simon Clark, Paul Hoggett, and Simon Thompson, 59–109. Basingstoke, UK: Palgrave Macmillan, 2006.

———. *The Emotions of Protest*. Chicago: University of Chicago Press, 2008.

Jasper, James, and Francesca Polletta. "The Cultural Context of Social Movements." In *Wiley-Blackwell Companion to Social Movements*, edited by David A. Snow, Sarah A. Soule, Hanspeter Kriesi, and Holly J. McCammon, 63–78. Oxford: John Wiley & Sons, 2019.

Jasper, James, and Jane Poulsen. "Recruiting Strangers and Friends: Moral Shocks and Social Networks in Animal Rights and Anti-Nuclear Protests." *Social Problems* 42, no. 4 (1995): 493–512.

Jones, Maggie. "Coming Out Illegal." *New York Times Magazine*, October 21, 2010. www.nytimes.com/2010/10/24/magazine/24DreamTeam-t.html.

Jung, Carrie. "Arizona Board of Regents Grants In-State Tuition to Certain Immigrants." KJZZ, May 5, 2017. https://kjzz.org/content/136510/arizona -board-regents-grants-state-tuition-certain-immigrants.

Kate's Law. H.R. 3004, 115th Cong. (2017–18).

"Key Ballot Measures." *CNN*, November 7, 2006. www.cnn.com/ELECTION /2006/pages/results/ballot.measures/.

Khan, Mahwish. "Campaign for an American DREAM Walkers Hold Protest at Obama Campaign HQ in Denver." *America's Voice* (blog), June 7, 2012. https://americasvoice.org/blog/cad-walkers-holding-protest-at-obama -campaign-hq-in-denver.

Kiefer, Michael. "Another Arizona Immigration Law Shot Down by 9th Circuit." *Arizona Republic*, October 15, 2014. www.azcentral.com/story /news/politics/immigration/2014/10/15/immigration-prop100-aclu-arizona -unconstitutional/17310919.

Kobach, Kris. "Reinforcing the Rule of Law: What States Can and Should Do to Reduce Illegal immigration." *Georgetown Immigration Law Journal* 22 (2008): 459–83.

Landau, Marie. "Out of the Shadows, into the Spotlight." *In These Times*, July 5, 2010. https://inthesetimes.com/article/out-of-the-shadows-into-the -spotlight.

Latino Rebels. "NDLON Publishes Blue Ribbon Immigration Recommendations for President." *Latino Rebels* (blog), April 10, 2014. www.latinorebels.com /2014/04/10/ndlon-publishes-blue-ribbon-immigration-recommendations -for-president/.

———. "Open Letter to the Immigrant Rights Movement: Our Families Can't Wait." *Latino Rebels* (blog), January 18, 2014. www.latinorebels.com/2014 /01/18/open-letter-to-the-immigrant-rights-movement-our-families-cant-wait/.

Latino Voices. "DREAM 9 Pushed It Too Far, According to Immigration Lawyer." *HuffPost*, July 27, 2013. www.huffpost.com/entry/dream-9-imigration -lawyer_n_3663516.

———. "Immigrants Reunite with Deported Parents at Border, DREAMers Call for Immigration Reform." *HuffPost*, June 12, 2013. www.huffpost .com/entry/immigrants-reunite-with-deported-parents_n_3430399.

Liptak, Adam. "Arizona Can Ban 'Ballot Harvesting,' Supreme Court Says." *New York Times*, November 5, 2016. www.nytimes.com/2016/11/06/us /politics/arizona-supreme-court-absentee-ballots.html.

Lozano, Pepe. "Young Latinos Keeping Their Eyes on the Prize for Immigration Reform." *People's World*, October 12, 2011. https://peoplesworld .org/article/young-latinos-keeping-their-eyes-on-the-prize-for-immigration -reform/.

Lydgate, Joanna. "Assembly Line Justice: A Review of Operation Streamline." Warren Institute, University of California-Berkeley School of Law, January 2010.

Mansbridge, Jane. "The Making of Oppositional Consciousness." In *Oppositional Consciousness: The Subjective Roots of Social Protest*, edited by Jane Mansbridge and Aldon Morris, 1–19. Chicago: University of Chicago Press, 2001.

Mansbridge, Jane, and Aldon Morris, eds. *Oppositional Consciousness: The Subjective Roots of Social Protest*. Chicago: University of Chicago Press, 2001.

"Maricopa Community College Sued for Granting In-State Tuition to DREAMers." *Arizona Daily Independent News Network*, June 28, 2013. https:// arizonadailyindependent.com/2013/06/28/maricopa-community-college -sued-for-granting-in-state-tuition-to-daca-students/.

Marshall, Serena. "Obama Has Deported More People Than Any Other President." *ABC News*, August 29, 2016. https://abcnews.go.com/Politics /obamas-deportation-policy-numbers/story?id=41715661.

Mateo, Lizbeth. "The Fight to Keep Families Together Does Not End at Deportation." *HuffPost*, July 22, 2013. www.huffingtonpost.com/lizbeth-mateo /the-fight-to-keep-familie_b_3634915.html.

McAdam, Doug. "The Framing Function of Movement Tactics: Strategic Dramaturgy in the Civil Rights Movement." In *Comparative Perspectives on Social Movement: Political Opportunities, Mobilizing Structures, and Cultural Framings*, edited by Doug McAdam, John McCarthy, and Mayer Zald, 338–56. Cambridge: Cambridge University Press, 1996.

———. *Political Process and the Development of Black Insurgency*. 2nd ed. Chicago: University of Chicago Press, 1999.

McAdam, Doug, and Sidney Tarrow. "The Political Context of Social Movements." In *Wiley-Blackwell Companion to Social Movements*, edited by David A. Snow, Sarah A. Soule, Hanspeter Kriesi, and Holly J. McCammon, 19–42. Oxford: John Wiley & Sons, 2019.

McCarthy, John, and Mayer Zald. "Resource Mobilization and Social Movements: A Partial Theory." *American Journal of Sociology* 82, no. 6 (1977): 1212–41.

McKinley, Jesse. "Arizona Law Takes a Toll on Nonresident Students." *New York Times*, January 27, 2008. www.nytimes.com/2008/01/27/us/27tuition .html.

McNevin, Anne. "Doing What Citizens Do: Migrant Struggles at the Edge of Political Belonging," *Local-Global: Identity, Security, Community* 6 (2009): 67–77.

McThomas, Mary. *Performing Citizenship: Undocumented Migrants in the United States*. New York: Routledge, 2016.

"The Meaning of the Mariposa (Butterfly): A Symbol for All." *No Papers No Fear: Ride for Justice Blog*, September 20, 2012. http://nopapersnofear .org/blog/post.php?s=2012-09-20-the-meaning-of-the-mariposa-butterfly-a -symbol-for-all.

Melendres v. Arpaio, 989 F. Supp. 2d 822 (D. Ariz., 2013) (findings of fact and conclusion of law).

Menjivar, Cecilia, and Leisy Abrego. "Legal Violence: Immigration Law and the Lives of Central American Immigrants." *American Journal of Sociology* 117, no. 5 (2012): 1380–1421.

Meyer, David. "Protest and Political Opportunities." *Annual Review of Sociology* 30 (2004): 125–45.

Meyer, Rachel, and Janice Fine. "Grassroots Citizenship at Multiple Scales: Rethinking Immigrant Civic Participation." *International Journal of Politics, Culture, and Society* 30, no. 4 (2017): 323–48.

Meyers, Diana Tietjens. *Victims' Stories and the Advancement of Human Rights*. Oxford: Oxford University Press, 2016.

Montgomery, David. "Trail of Dream Students Walk 1,500 Miles to Bring Immigration Message to Washington." *Washington Post*, May 1, 2010. www.washingtonpost.com/wp-dyn/content/article/2010/04/30/AR2010043 001384_3.html.

Mora, Maria de Jesus, Rodolfo Rodriguez, Alejandro Zermeño, and Paul Almeida. "Immigrant Rights and Social Movements." *Sociology Compass* 12, no. 8 (2018): 1–7.

Mora, Maru. "Blue Ribbon Commission Response: President Must Meet with Undocumented People." NDLON, September 5, 2014. https://ndlon.org /president-must-meet-with-undocumented-people/.

Motomura, Hiroshi, et al. to the President, May 28, 2012. University of Houston Law Center. www.law.uh.edu/ihelg/documents/ExecutiveAuthorityFor DREAMRelief28May2012withSignatures.pdf.

National Conference of State Legislatures. "Analysis of Arizona's Immigrant Enforcement Laws." July 28, 2011. www.ncsl.org/research/immigration /analysis-of-arizonas-immigration-law.aspx.

Navarette, Rub, Jr. "A DREAMers Nightmare." *San Jose Mercury News*, January 15, 2013. www.mercurynews.com/2013/01/15/ruben-navarrette-a -dreamers-nightmare/.

NDLONvideos. "The Most Passionate Speech You Have Ever Heard." April 17, 2014. YouTube video, 3:07. www.youtube.com/watch?v=lSStVYqxcno.

———. "Si No Nos Invitan, Nos Invitamos Solos: No Papers No Fear Protest in Alabama." August 18, 2012. YouTube video, 2:35. www.youtube.com /watch?v=Iaj95A8ac8U&ab_channel=NDLONvideos.

New Organizing Institute (NOI). *Campaign for Arizona's Future: Where Real Power Begins*. Training Guide, June 2012 (adapting the work of Marshall Ganz of Harvard University).

Nicholls, Walter. *The Dreamers*. Stanford, CA: Stanford University Press, 2013.

———. "Making Undocumented Immigrants into a Legitimate Political Subject: Theoretical Observations from the United States and France." *Theory, Culture & Society* 30, no. 3 (2013): 82–107.

Nyers, Peter. "No One Is Illegal between City and Nation," In *Acts of Citizenship*, edited by Engin F. Isin and Greg M. Nielsen, 160–81. London: Palgrave Macmillan, 2008.

Obama, President Barack. "Remarks by the President in Address to Nation on Immigration." November 20, 2014. Obama White House Archives. https://obamawhitehouse.archives.gov/the-press-office/2014/11/20/remarks -President-address-nation-immigration.

———. "Remarks by the President on Immigration." June 15, 2012. Obama White House Archives. https://obamawhitehouse.archives.gov/the-press-office /2012/06/15/remarks-president-immigration.

Office of the Director, U.S. Immigration and Customs Enforcement. "Exercising Prosecutorial Discretion." US Immigration and Customs Enforcement Files, Washington, DC. June 17, 2011. www.ice.gov/doclib/secure-communities /pdf/prosecutorial-discretion-memo.pdf.

Olivas, Michael. "Advice to Immigrants: Don't Get on the Undocubus." *New York Times*, September 5, 2012. www.nytimes.com/roomfordebate/2012/08 /01/is-getting-on-the-undocubus-a-good-idea/advice-to-immigrants-dont-get -on-the-undocubus.

Oppel, Richard, Jr. "Arizona, Bowing to Business, Softens Stand on Immigration." *New York Times*, March 18, 2011. www.nytimes.com/2011/03/19/us /19immigration.html.

"Our Hunger Strike Makes Public the Heartache We Endure in Private Every Single Day." #Not1More. February 23, 2014. www.notonemoredeportation .com/2014/02/23/our-hunger-strike-makes-public-the-heartache-we-endure -in-private-every-single-day.

Paulos, Abraham. "People with Felonies, Criminal Records and Gang Affiliation Are Our Friends and Family." *Huffington Post*, November 30, 2014. www.huffingtonpost.com/abraham-paulos/people-with-felonies-crim_b _6228310.html.

Plyler v. Doe, 457 U.S. 202 (1982).

Polletta, Francesca. *It Was Like a Fever: Storytelling in Politics and Protest.* Chicago: University of Chicago Press, 2006.

———. "The Structural Context of Novel Rights Claims: Southern Civil Rights Organizing 1961–66." *Law & Society Review* 34, no. 2 (2000): 367–406.

Prieto, Greg. *Immigrants under Threat: Risk and Resistance in Deportation Nation.* New York: New York University Press, 2018.

Puente Arizona. "Norma, cuando vas a volver?" April 20, 2014. YouTube video, 2:45. https://www.youtube.com/watch?v=Ep9eeQTJqqc&feature= youtu.be.

Ramirez Jimenez, Mari Cruz. "In Admiration: Learning About the Civil Rights Movement." *No Papers, No Fear: Ride for Justice* (blog), August 16, 2012. http://nopapersnofear.org/blog/post.php?s=2012-08-16-in-admiration -learning-about-the-civil-rights-movement.

Puente v. Arpaio, 2:14-cv—1356-DGC (D. Ariz., filed June 18, 2014).

Ramos, Kristian. "What Arizona's Ethnic Studies Ban Says about America." *Huffington Post*, June 1. 2012. www.huffingtonpost.com/kristian-ramos /what-arizonas-ban-on-ethn_b_1557422.html.

Reddy, William. "Against Constructionism: The Historical Ethnography of Emotions." *Current Anthropology* 38, no. 3 (1997): 327–51.

———. "Emotional Liberty, Politics and History in the Anthropology of Emotions." *Cultural Anthropology* 14, no. 2 (1999): 256–88.

Reichard, Raquel. "Why This Undocumented Latina Launched 'Coming out of the Shadows Month.'" *Latina*, March 7, 2016. www.latina.com/lifestyle /our-issues/latina-launches-coming-out-shadows-month.

Reuters Staff. "Immigration Law Boycott Cost Arizona $140 Mln: Study." *Reuters*, November 18, 2010. www.reuters.com/article/us-arizona-boycott /immigration-law-boycott-cost-ariz-140-mln-study-idUSTRE6AH55W 20101118.

Romo, Vanessa. "Arizona Supreme Court Denies DACA Students In-State Tuition." *NPR*, April 10, 2018. www.npr.org/sections/thetwo-way/2018 /04/10/601247684/arizona-supreme-court-denies-daca-students-in-state -tuition.

Sabat, Albert. "Team Awesome Is Giving Latinos a New Reason to Vote." *ABC News*, October 25, 2012. http://abcnews.go.com/ABC_Univision/News /team-awesome-undocumented-activists-arizona-latino-voter-turnout/story ?id=17563331.

Salgado, Julio. "An Undocubus Sketchbook." *No Papers, No Fear: Ride for Justice* (blog), September 14, 2012. http://nopapersnofear.org/blog/post.php ?s=2012-09-14-an-undocubus-sketchbook.

Sandoval, Carlos, and Catherine Tambini. "The State of Arizona." *PBS/Independent Lens*, January 27, 2014. www.pbs.org/independentlens/films/state -of-arizona/.

Santos, Fernanda. "Joe Arpaio's Surprising Legacy in Arizona." *Politico*, November 10, 2019. www.politico.com/magazine/story/2019/11/10/joe -arpaio-arizona-latino-activists-elected-office-229906/.

Schechner, Richard. *Performance Studies: An Introduction*. New York: Routledge, 2002.

Sedgwick, Eve. *Touching Feeling: Affect, Pedagogy, Performativity*. Durham, NC: Duke University Press, 2003.

"Sharing Stories with the People of Knoxville." *No Papers, No Fear Ride for Justice* (blog), September 1, 2012. http://nopapersnofear.org/blog/post.php ?s=2012-09-01-sharing-stories-with-the-people-of-knoxville.

Sinema, Kyrsten. "No Surprises: The Evolution of Anti-Immigrant Legislation in Arizona." In *Punishing Immigrants: Policy, Politics, and Injustice*, edited by Charis Kubrin, Marjorie Zatz, and Ramiro Martinez, 62–90. New York: New York University Press, 2012.

Snow, David A., and Robert Benford. "Ideology, Frame Resonance and Participation Mobilization." In *International Social Movement Research*, edited by Bert Klandermans, Hanspeter Kriesl, and Sidney Tarrow, 1:197–217. Stamford, CT: JAI Press, 1988.

Snow, David A., Donatella Della Porta, Bert Klandermans, and Doug McAdam, eds. *The Wiley-Blackwell Encyclopedia of Political and Social Movements*. 2nd ed. Malden, MA: Blackwell Publishing, 2013.

Staggenborg, Suzanne. "The Consequences of Professionalization and Formalization in the Pro-Choice Movement." *American Sociological Review* 53, no. 4 (1988): 585–605.

State of Arizona v. Maricopa County Community College District, Abel Badillo, and Bibiana Vazquez, No. CV2013-009093 (Maricopa County Superior Court, 2015).

State of Ariziona v. Maricopa County Community College District Board, et al., No. CV-17-0215-PR (AZ April 9, 2018), *aff'g* State ex rel. Brnovich v. Maricopa Cty. Cmty. Coll. Dist. Bd., 242 Ariz. 325 (App. 2017).

Sterling, Terry Greene, and Jude Joffe-Block. *Driving While Brown: Sheriff Joe Arpaio versus the Latino Resistance*. Oakland: University of California Press, 2021.

Sziarto, Kristin, and Helga Leitner. "Immigrants Riding for Justice: Space-Time and Emotions in the Construction of a Counter-Public." *Political Geography* 29 (2010): 381–91.

Taylor, Verta. "Social Movement Continuity: The Women's Movement in Abeyance." *American Sociology Review* 54, no. 5 (1989): 761–75.

Taylor, Verta, and Allison Crossley. "Abeyance." In *Wiley-Blackwell Encyclopedia of Social and Political Movements*, 2nd ed., edited by David A. Snow, Donatella Della Porta, Bert Klandermans, and Doug McAdam, 1–3. Malden, MA: Blackwell Publishing. 2013.

Terriquez, Veronica. "Intersectional Mobilization, Social Movement Spillover, and Queer Youth Leadership in the Immigrant Rights Movement." *Social Problems* 62, no. 3 (2015): 343–62.

Texas v. United States, 86 F. Supp. 3d 591, 677 (S.D. Tex. 2015), *aff'd* __ F.3d __ (5th cir. 2015), *aff'd by an equally divided Court* 579 U. S. __ (June 23, 2016).

thedreamiscoming2011. "Georgina Perez, Georgia Dreamers." April 5, 2011. YouTube video, 3:31. www.youtube.com/watch?v=mTeh1moqiEU.

Tilly, Charles. *Contentious Performances*. New York: Cambridge University Press, 2008.

———. *From Mobilization to Revolution*. New York: McGraw-Hill, 1978.

Tilly, Charles, and Sidney Tarrow. *Contentious Politics*. 2nd ed. Oxford: Oxford University Press, 2015.

Tobar, Hector. "Letter from Maricopa County: Can Latinos Swing Arizona?' *New Yorker*, August 1, 2016. www.newyorker.com/magazine/2016/08/01/promise-arizona-and-the-power-of-the-latino-vote.

Torres, Gerardo. "Fearless and Speaking for Ourselves." *No Papers No Fear: Ride for Justice* (blog), August 18, 2012. http://nopapersnofear.org/blog/post.php?s=2012-08-18-fearless-and-speaking-for-ourselves.

UCLA Center for Health Policy Research. "Section 1: Asset Mapping." N.d. https://healthpolicy.ucla.edu/programs/health-data/trainings/Documents/tw_cba20.pdf.

"Undocumented Immigrant Leaders Form Blue Ribbon Commission for Independent Deportation Review." #Not1More. March 14, 2014. www.notonemore

deportation.com/2014/03/14/undocumented-immigrant-leaders-form-blue
-ribbon-commission-for-independent-deportation-review/.

Undocunation. Facebook, December 21, 2012. www.facebook.com/pages
/Undocunation/233268960140317.

United States v. Arizona, 703 F. Supp. 2d 980 (D. Az. 2010).

Unzueta Carrasco, Tania, and Hinda Seif. "Disrupting the Dream: Undocumented Youth Reframe Citizenship and Deportability Through Anti-
Deportation Activism." *Latino Studies* 12 (2014): 279–99.

US Immigration and Customs Enforcement. "Criminal Alien Program." www
.ice.gov/criminal-alien-program.

Valdes, Marcela. "Is It Possible to Resist Deportation in Trump's America?"
New York Times, May 23, 2017. www.nytimes.com/2017/05/23/magazine
/is-it-possible-to-resist-deportation-in-trumps-america.html.

Van Ness, Justin, and Erika Summers-Effler, "Emotions in Social Movements."
In *Wiley-Blackwell Companion to Social Movements*, 2nd ed., edited by
David A. Snow, Sarah A. Soule, Hanspeter Kriesi, and Holly J. McCammon,
411–28. Oxford: John Wiley & Sons, 2019.

Vargas, Jose Antonio. "Coming Out Adds a Voice to the Chorus." *New York
Times*, September 5, 2012. www.nytimes.com/roomfordebate/2012/08/01
/is-getting-on-the-undocubus-a-good-idea/coming-out-adds-a-voice-to-the
-chorus.

Venkatesh, Vasanthi. "Mobilizing under 'Illegality': The Arizona Immigrant
Rights Movement's Engagement with the Law." *Harvard Latino Law
Review* 19 (2017): 165–201.

Villazor, Rose Cuison, and Elizabeth Glazer. "A First Step to Understanding
the Challenges of Illegal Immigrants." *New York Times*, September 5, 2012.
www.nytimes.com/roomfordebate/2012/08/01/is-getting-on-the-undocubus-a
-good-idea/a-first-step-to-understanding-the-challenges-of-illegal-immigrants.

Voss, Kim, and Irene Bloemraad, eds. *Rallying for Immigrant Rights: The Fight
for Inclusion in 21st Century America*. Berkeley: University of California
Press, 2011.

Wang, Cecilia. "What's Next for Arizona's SB 1070 and Other Copycat Laws?"
Speak Freely (blog), June 28, 2012. www.aclu.org/blog/immigrants-rights
/state-and-local-immigration-laws/whats-next-arizonas-sb-1070-and-other.

Ware, Robert. "Acts and Action." *Journal of Philosophy* 70, no. 13 (1973):
403–18.

Warner, Michael. *Publics and Counterpublics*. Princeton, NJ: Princeton University Press, 2005.

———. *The Trouble with Normal*. Washington, DC: Free Press, 1999.

White, Hayden. *The Content of the Form: Narrative Discourse and Historical
Representation*. Baltimore, MD: Johns Hopkins University Press, 1987.

Williams, Patricia. *The Alchemy of Race and Rights: Diary of a Law Professor*.
Cambridge, MA: Harvard University Press, 1992.

Wong, Kent, and Carolina Bank Munoz. "Don't Miss the Bus: The Immigrant
Workers Freedom Ride." *New Labor Forum* 13, no. 2 (2004): 61–66.

Zepeda-Millan, Chris. *Latino Mass Mobilization: Immigration, Racialization,
and Activism*. Cambridge: Cambridge University Press, 2017.

———. "Weapons of the (Not So) Weak: Immigrant Mass Mobilization in the U.S. South." *Critical Sociology* 42, no. 2 (2016): 269–87.

Zimmerman, Arely. "Transmedia Testimonio: Examining Undocumented Youth's Political Activism in the Digital Age." *International Journal of Communication* 10 (2016): 1886–1906.

Index

deportation protection and, 134, 148–49; direct action events and, 110–11; insider identity and, 137, 243n37; long campaign for, 98, 101–11, 119, 237n3; narratives of accomplishment, 113, 240n59; neighborhood canvassing and, 235n34; Obama administration and, 91, 98, 110, 127–28, 147, 155, 159; performative strategies and, 119; pressure to cover all adults, 133, 148; social belonging and, 178; in-state tuition and, 155, 190, 245n92; Supreme Court upholding of, 250n31; Trump efforts to rescind, 162–63, 182, 189, 250n31; undocumented and unafraid tactic, 101–2; undocumented organizations and, 10–11; UWD and, 237n4; work permits and, 60, 98; youth activism and, 16, 18, 91, 98, 100–101, 110–11, 128

Deferred Action for Parents of Americans (DAPA), 148, 150–51, 153, 167, 245n90

de la Vara, Leticia, 32–33

Democratic National Convention (DNC), 18, 98, 106, 112, 114, 121, 135

Department of Homeland Security (DHS), 108, 117, 129, 132, 148, 243n30

deportation: border fence reunion and, 129; campaigns against, 133–35; direct action events and, 126; DREAMers and, 108; executive discretion in, 147–48, 184–85; families not felons approach, 151, 153, 184; family separation and, 52, 123, 129–30, 132, 136–42, 148, 184; family separation videos, 129, 132, 140; immigration court hearings and, 186; Obama administration and, 91, 109, 127, 136, 147, 155, 186; Obama review of policy, 148; opportunities for leverage, 184–85; presidential administrations and, 244n46; private suffering and, 128, 133, 140, 142–43, 152; resistance to, 129; risks of, 25; self-deportation and, 1, 5, 68, 178, 231n39; state and federal custody, 185; state power and, 42, 148–50; storytelling and, 59; systematicity of, 147; trauma and, 12, 162, 230n34; Trump administration and, 182, 184–86; undocumented immigrants and, 2, 7, 25, 136, 244n46; youth activism and, 108

detention: abolitionist goals and, 150, 194; executive discretion in, 142–43; family separation and, 150; Florence, Arizona,

130, 152–53, 242n9; healing from experiences of, 61, 230n34; hunger strikes and, 142; inhumane conditions in, 130, 149–50, 152–53; mass incarceration patterns and, 147; profitability of, 147; public awareness and, 167; raid-based, 30; state threat of, 42; storytelling and, 59; trauma and, 12, 162; undocumented immigrants and, 2, 7, 25; vigil to end, 242n9

DHS. *See* Department of Homeland Security (DHS)

DNC. *See* Democratic National Convention (DNC)

Double Coming Out, 107

DREAM 5 activists, 104, 123, 125, 238n20

DREAM 9 activists, 129–30, 150, 154

DREAM Act: civil disobedience and, 104; failure to pass Congress, 104–5, 108, 134, 238n23; frustration with citizenship failures, 102–3; hunger strike and, 238n19; naturalization and, 34, 60, 237n3, 238n8; UWD and, 237n4; youth activists and, 81, 98, 100–106, 119, 189, 238n7

DREAMers: activism and, 11, 30, 34–35; border fence reunion and, 70; Chicano movement legacy and, 28; conservative castigation of, 154; deportation proceedings and, 108; direct action events and, 110; DREAM 9 challenge, 129–30; educational and cultural events, 224n34; experiential storytelling and, 53–54, 60, 167; family separation and, 137–38; immigration law expertise and, 111, 239n44; narratives of accomplishment, 102, 105–6, 113, 138–39, 240n59; performative citizenship and, 196; public awareness and, 103–4; State House vigil and, 38; undocumented and unafraid tactic, 240n59; voter engagement and, 82

Dreamers Adrift, 106, 109, 113, 115, 138, 239n28

DREAM Guardians, 108

Echoing Green Foundation, 252n53

Education Not Deportation, 108

Edwards, Bob, 26, 246n17

emotion cultures: (pro)immigrant marchers and, 3–4; activist socialization and, 63, 69, 72–73, 231n39; anti-immigrant protestors and, 3; civil rights movement and, 4, 63; community-based

strikes and, 142; immigrant activism and, 161–62; leadership and, 208; MEChA and, 28; nationwide economic boycott and, 36, 227n47; organizing approach, 66–68, 231n39; organizing practices and, 112, 184; Puente and, 7, 11, 25, 30, 64; SB 1070 resistance and, 11; on state and local allies, 187; undocumented activists and, 30–31; work with author, 215–16

Garcia, James, 37, 224n34

Garcia Aguilar, Guadalupe, 184

Gomez, Alejandra, 128, 193

Gomez, Veronica, 110

Gonzales, Roberto, 34, 41, 137, 231n50, 243n37

"good" immigrant narrative, 102, 115, 138–39, 201, 238n14

governmental actors: accountability and, 90–91, 111, 119–21, 172–73, 176; activist frustration with, 19, 102–3, 108–9, 135–36; adversarial relationship with activists, 127–31, 134–35, 161–62; alliances in, 187; anger at failures by, 104–5; criminalization of undocumented immigrants, 128, 182; cultural expression aimed at, 109; defining, 244n57; deportation power and, 148–50; failure to pass DREAM Act, 104–5, 134, 238n23; federal preemption and, 134, 242n26; litigation and, 176–77, 248n62; lobbying of, 128–30; local law enforcement collaboration, 112, 116, 135, 185–86, 243n30; oppositional tactics and, 99–101, 110–11, 116–19, 145–50; pro-immigrant advocacy, 187; skepticism of, 119–20, 127, 130, 135–36; systematicity of deportations, 147; trauma and, 162

grassroots citizenship, 228n69, 242n103

Grijalva, Raul, 36, 227n47

Gutierrez, Alfredo, 24, 32–33

Guzman, Lydia, 29–32, 205, 226n25

HB 2281 (Arizona), 222n14

HERE (Hotel Employees and Restaurant Employees International Union), 240n63

#heretostay, 160, 169

Hernandez, Javier, 110

Hildebrant, Paula, 234n11

Horne, Tom, 190

I Am a DREAM Voter campaign, 75, 233n2

ICE Removal and Detention Facility, 126

iDREAM, 107

immigrant activism: abeyance in, 182, 194; adaptability in practices, 167–68, 179–80, 183; adversarial relationship with state actors, 99–100, 127–31, 134–35; agency and, 6, 151; anger and, 104–6; antideportation projects, 129–31; asset maps and, 164–70; attrition through enforcement resistance, 21–22, 224n1; broadening vistas, 193–94; building for future work, 187, 191–96; cell phone recording of law enforcement, 32; community-based resources, 26–28, 39, 205, 253n73; community service and, 38, 112; convergence of youth and adult, 101, 127, 134; coordinating defense of undocumented, 183–86; de facto membership, 169, 247n25; direct action events and, 128–29; educational and cultural events, 28, 224n34; experience and, 164–65, 196; failure to pass DREAM Act and, 104–5; indigenous leadership and, 39; KYR instruction and, 93, 176, 248n52; la lucha sigue, 249n; legitimacy and, 170; mentoring alliances and, 195, 251n52; mobilization of, 2, 15, 22, 24–28, 34–36; national alliances and, 37; open hand, closed fist strategy, 162; oppositional consciousness and, 18, 100–101; oppositional tactics and, 100, 110–12, 124, 245n90; organizational practices and, 17–18, 20, 183, 191–94; organizing skills and, 9, 163; outreach to undocumented communities, 30; performative citizenship and, 93, 169, 196–97; performativity and, 17, 160–61, 195–203; political consciousness and, 19, 22, 164–65, 170, 233n3; political membership and, 170–73; professionalization of, 194–95; resistance and, 18, 99; resourced, 165, 246n16; resource mobilization, 166, 246n17; rights-based membership and, 173–74; role of threat in, 24; self-producing resources, 28–33; sense of belonging, 169–70; sense of capacity, 165–69; social media use, 106, 129, 132; state and local political processes, 186–91; training participants and leaders, 191–93; Trump administration strategies, 181, 187, 190; T-shirts as political symbolism, 8; volunteer canvassers, 79–85, 235n34; voting rights and, 92, 236n67; withstanding fear and, 165, 246n15. See also undocumented organizations

Founded in 1893,
UNIVERSITY OF CALIFORNIA PRESS
publishes bold, progressive books and journals
on topics in the arts, humanities, social sciences,
and natural sciences—with a focus on social
justice issues—that inspire thought and action
among readers worldwide.

The UC PRESS FOUNDATION
raises funds to uphold the press's vital role
as an independent, nonprofit publisher, and
receives philanthropic support from a wide
range of individuals and institutions—and from
committed readers like you. To learn more, visit
ucpress.edu/supportus.

9 780520 384422